Ben Nimmo

was born in Kendal in 1972 and grew up in Wolverhampton. After reading English and medieval literature at Gonville and Caius College, Cambridge, he fled academia to become a scuba-diving instructor. He has lived in such glamorous places as Egypt, Belize, Southern France and Hackney. His hobbies include learning languages, playing the trombone and tenor recorder, and going for *long* walks. His first book was *Pilgrim Snail*, this is his second.

Praise for *Pilgrim Snail*:

'This book restores your faith in human nature. It is a book of discovery – new places, new people and a new way of life ... An excellent read.'   *Sunday Business Post*

'Inspired by the murder of the girl he loved, Ben Nimmo set out to pay tribute to her memory by walking from Canterbury to Santiago de Compostela – with a trombone. The result is a often hilarious, frequently touching account of a 2000 mile odyssey across Europe. Weighed down by personal tragedy and a mammoth rucksack, Ben's personal quest is never without hope and humour. Sleeping rough, in the open or in caves and ruined castles, jamming in smoke-filled French bars, Ben battles with injuries, storms and a phantom bear, but he is helped along the way by a varied cast of saints and sinner, from jazz-loving farmers to a neo-nazi anti-bloodsports activist (who makes him a sandwich). Wonderful.'   *Yorkshire Post*

'Lively, colourful, picaresque and entertaining.'   *Scotland on Sunday*

'Nimmo is delightful and engaging company. His prose is polished, the narrative taut, funny and cleverly paced. Reminding us of the dazzling cultural diversity in Europe, Nimmo's book is the perfect antidote to all little Englanders abroad.'   *Guardian*

ALSO BY BEN NIMMO

Pilgrim Snail

In Forkbeard's Wake

Coasting in Scandinavia

Ben Nimmo

Flamingo

An Imprint of HarperCollinsPublishers

f l a m i n g o **O**RIGINAL	**The term 'Original' signifies publication direct into paperback with no preceding British hardback edition.** **The Flamingo Original series publishes fine writing at an affordable price at the point of first publication.**

Flamingo
An Imprint of HarperCollins*Publishers*
77–85 Fulham Palace Road,
Hammersmith, London W6 8JB

www.**fire**and**water**.com

Flamingo is a registered trademark
of HarperCollins*Publishers* Limited

Published by Flamingo 2003
1 3 5 7 9 8 6 4 2

A catalogue record for this book
is available from the British Library

ISBN 0 00 712334 5

Typeset in Palatino by
Rowland Phototypesetting Ltd, Bury St Edmunds, Suffolk

Printed and bound in Great Britain by
Clays Ltd, St Ives plc

For Rachel,
world's finest twin
& for Francis
who works on Mars.

CONTENTS

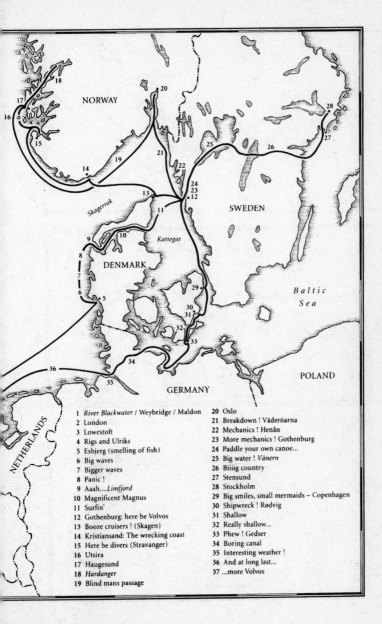

1 River Blackwater / Weybridge / Maldon
2 London
3 Lowestoft
4 Rigs and Ulriks
5 Esbjerg (smelling of fish)
6 Big waves
7 Bigger waves
8 Panic !
9 Aaah....Limfjord
10 Magnificent Magnus
11 Surfin'
12 Gothenburg: here be Volvos
13 Booze cruisers ! (Skagen)
14 Kristiansand: The wrecking coast
15 Here be divers (Stravanger)
16 Utsira
17 Haugesund
18 Hardanger
19 Blind mans passage
20 Oslo
21 Breakdown ! Väderöarna
22 Mechanics ! Henån
23 More mechanics ! Gothenburg
24 Paddle your own canoe...
25 Big water ! Vänern
26 Biiiig country
27 Stensund
28 Stockholm
29 Big smiles, small mermaids – Copenhagen
30 Shipwreck ! Rødvig
31 Shallow
32 Really shallow...
33 Phew ! Gedser
34 Boring canal
35 Interesting weather !
36 And at long last...
37 ...more Volvos

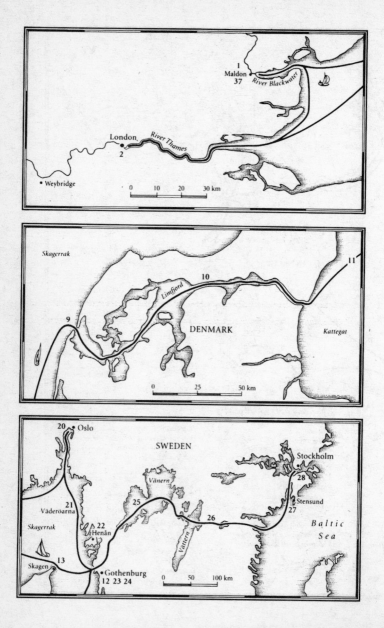

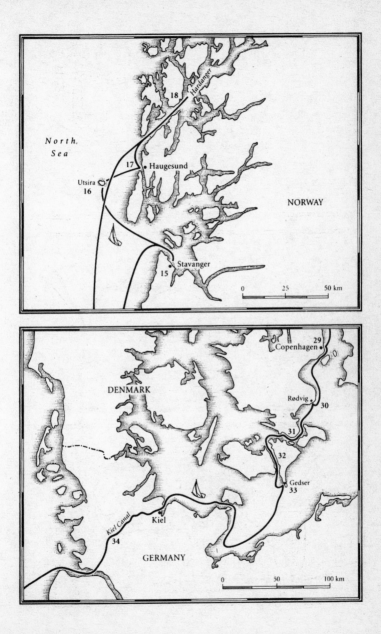

ACKNOWLEDGEMENTS

Thanks

For the boat: to Dave Pilkinton, Colin Edwards, Stewart Tollfrey, Ian Collett and all at Heybridge Basin and at Ward & McKenzie: gentlemen all. (Apart from Liz, who's a lady.)

For help with the book: to my Five Muses, Lucinda, Tamsin, Cecilia, Helen and Georgina.

For hospitality: to all those who put me up and who put up with me during the cruise and while I was writing.

And special thanks to Clan Asplund, Apes & Babes, Evelyne and the Herzberg family, Jaeren Dive Centre, and Shanel the Australian Angel, who saved my sanity and somebody else's life in Stockholm Station. The Nobel Prize is on the way.

'And yet the thoughts of my heart are now urging me to test the high streams, the tumbling of the salt waves, myself; at all times my mind's desire urges me to set forth that I may visit the lands of strangers far hence . . .'

The Seafarer, anon. Anglo-Saxon

INTRODUCTION

The problem with Sweden is Volvos.

Now the Volvo is a wonderful car. It's solid, reliable, efficient, safe. It brings to driving the peace of mind normally associated with yogic meditation. It represents everything that's best and most efficient in Swedish life. But it's not exactly sexy. Think glamour. Think speed. Think excitement, danger, thrills. I guarantee that Volvo won't spring to mind.

Think James Bond. Would James Bond drive a Volvo?

I rest my case.

Unfortunately, Sweden has become associated with its most celebrated export. Just as Ferrari has given a whole new meaning to the phrase 'Italian sex drive', so the solid, stolid Volvo has come to represent its country. It's not an image to seduce the millions.

This is a shame, because the truth is somewhat different.

As I set my foot on the topmost stair, a mad Swede opened the door.

They were wooden stairs, of course, leading up to a wooden balcony projecting from the side of a white-painted wooden house. In the garden the Swedish flag flew from a freshly painted flagpole, and below us the land sloped away to the rock-studded fishing harbour where my boat lay. So far, it was all very Scandinavian. That just left Jan, mine host.

He was tall, and balding, and sun-burned. He wore a loose

Hawaiian beach shirt and a pair of bright yellow trousers which made my sleep-deprived head spin. In his left hand he brandished a glass of akvavit, in his right a crayfish. As he waltzed towards my guide and planted a smacking kiss on her cheek I saw that his feet were hidden in King-Kong slippers. Then he saw me and flung his arms wide in a shower of industrial ethanol.

'Aha! You're the one who plays the trombone underwater!'

He gave me the crayfish, shook my other hand, took the crayfish back, spun on his hairy heels and salsa'd back into the kitchen, where his offspring were greeting the guests. I followed like a lamb to the daughter. She had a delightful smile and I should have been charmed, but all I had eyes for were the prawns. They were *everywhere*, piled high on the table, scattered in slippery heaps on the work-surfaces, overflowing from a glass bowl in the sink, a pink and smelly landslip. It was July, and Scandinavia was in shellfish frenzy. Crustacea filled my vision. It was not a scene for the faint-hearted.

Jan's wife Anita rescued me with a warm smile and steered me to a seat. I'd had twenty hours' sleep in the last five days, crossing the North Sea in a small boat, and it was starting to show. Jan himself shimmied to the bar, poured me an unhealthy measure of raw alcohol, waltzed towards me (a neat trick in those slippers), handed me the glass with the ceremonious pride of an officiating priest, let out a cry of 'Aha!' and waltzed back to the door to greet the next set of guests. It's not what I would have expected from the sixty-year-old manager of a prosperous orthodontic practice, but there you go.

My crewman Fred the Blond and his mother Barbro were already installed among the prawns. One by one the other guests arrived: two marketing executives from the coast south of Gothenburg, a shapely Finn from a neighbouring island, two old friends from the other side of the harbour. They kissed Anita and her daughter Anna ceremoniously, bear-hugged Jan, received brimming glasses of Swedish paint-stripper, shook my hand and took their places around the groaning board, looking down on crayfish and crispbread. For a while decorous conversation ruled. Then our host rejoined us.

Jan knows lots of drinking songs. He's got happy ones: 'hip hip hurray, I'm going to get drunk!' He's got sad ones: 'I'm really unhappy, let's all get drunk!' He's even got tragic ones: 'I'm so sorry for this glass of akvavit which is about to get drunk!' Each song was celebrated by drinking the stuff, and putting the glass down half-empty was *not* allowed. As I looked from face to laughing face, a gentle mist crept through my mind.

Fortunately, eating brought a respite. There's nothing like a handful of cold dead arthropod for dispelling the vapours, especially if, like me, you've never cracked a crayfish before. Anita sat beside me and instructed me in a maternal undertone as I wrestled with my monster of the deep. Gradually my mind began to clear, and I was just feeling that I was getting a grip on things when Jan spoiled it all by jumping to his feet and waving his glass in the air.

'I've got another song!' Then he threw me an expectant smile, took a deep breath and began in a rapid baritone:

'Oh, we're off to see the Wild West Show . . .'

I'm dreaming, I thought.

'The elephant and the kangaroo . . .'

I've been in this country for sixteen hours and I'm listening to a sixty-year-old dentist singing one of the songs I learned in choir when the teachers weren't around. I pinched myself. It hurt.

'Never mind the weather, as long as we're together . . .'

Oh well. When in Rome . . . I took a deep breath and joined in:

'We're off to see the Wild West Shooow!'

Barbro and Anita still talk about the performance that followed.

Afterwards, Jan sat down and wiped his eyes. I'd recalled a couple of verses that were new to him, and he seemed to approve. It took him a while to get his breath back.

'Aah, wonderful! I learned that from some English Scouts on an expedition to the Arctic. Do you know any others?' he added hopefully.

With lightning speed, Anita and Barbro jumped up and lunged for the empty dishes. 'Coffee, my sweet?' asked Anita brightly, but it was too late.

'Come on, you can teach me while they wash up.'

Sitting on the balcony overlooking the lights of Hönö harbour, I introduced Jan to the jewels of my grammar-school upbringing. God knows what the neighbours thought as we gave our best to 'Oh, Sir Jasper'. We thought we were marvellous.

Then Jan had an inspiration.

'I've got a trombone inside,' he told me. 'Want to play?'

Of *course* he had a trombone. Who wouldn't? 'Love to,' I said as if this happened all the time, stood up, and almost fell over. Akvavit's powerful stuff. We piloted one another back into the house.

The ladies were still washing up, having flatly refused our offers of assistance on the grounds that we'd need some intact plates in the morning. We lurched into the sitting-room. There on a stand stood a tenor trombone. I tacked towards it, made a grab and managed to pick it up without sending anything flying. As Anita and Barbro peered curiously round the door, I swung into my old favourite, 'Danny Boy'.

Jan patted me on the shoulder and hurried into the next room.

I shut my eyes, causing interesting red patterns to spin towards me, staggered, and found myself playing 'Basin Street Blues'. As a solo this leaves a certain amount to be desired, like a ten-piece backing band. The soloist plays the first phrase, everyone else answers it. I'd just got to the end of the solo and was wondering what the hell to do next when the strangest sound I've ever heard penetrated the room. It was like a kazoo on helium, buzzing and squeaking all at once. If you listened hard, it might have been 'Basin Street'.

Jan came back into the room, wiggling like a hula-hula girl. A *lei* of fake flowers hung round his neck, and a bizarre piece of plastic like a deformed resuscitation tube covered his nose and mouth. His eyes were narrow with concentration and his cheeks red with exertion. I stared, almost forgetting to play. Just when you thought it couldn't possibly get weirder ... *Don't tell me that's a nose-flute.*

It was a nose-flute.

Seventeen hours after steaming into Gothenburg I was playing duets for trombone and nose-flute with a dentist who knew English rugby songs.

Forget Volvos. *That's* Sweden.

1

ANGLIA

'At that time King Ethelred, the son of Edgar, ruled England ... the language in England was then the same as the language in Norway and in Denmark.'
Saga of Gunnlaug Serpent's-Tongue

There are two questions that every traveller faces: 'Why do you do what you're doing?', and 'Why are you doing it *here*?' Personally, I travel because I love people, and I love surprises. One Swedish dentist with King-Kong slippers can make my day. As for why I ended up taking a small boat around southern Scandinavia, it was the result of falling in love five times over.

The first time was when I was nineteen, a fresh-faced undergraduate, though few people would have spotted it through my colossal beard. My passion was vast, which is just as well, because so was its object: the literature of the Heroic Age of the Germanic peoples, a corpus spanning half a dozen languages and about a thousand years. I've always loved stories of gods and heroes, and at college I came to grips with the originals. I spent five years in a bibliophiliac daze, reading volume after volume of ripping yarns and wondering when the authorities were going to work out that I was having fun and find some way of spoiling it. They never did. By the time

1

I'd finished my course, I knew far more about the ancient heroes of the North Sea rim than I did about, say, John Major, who for all his many qualities never quite wielded the charisma of Beowulf, Svein Forkbeard or the Icelandic poet Egill 'Axe-murderer' Skalla-Grimsson. For five years I was besotted with my subject. Then I decided to marry it. I applied for a PhD place.

Abruptly, the magic wore off. PhD work is all about reading other people's theses, then disagreeing with them, which is a definite handicap when the texts you're studying are a thousand years old: that's a lot of generations of opponents. When I discovered that the bibliography of articles written on *Beowulf* was more than twice as long as the poem itself, I decided that academia wasn't my horn of mead. I was still hopelessly in love with Germanic literature, but as so many Victorian novels have pointed out, love isn't everything. One day I came home, hurled a bagful of reading lists on the table and shouted at my house-mate, 'How can I write about this? It's like pissing into the Atlantic!'

The words must have lodged in my subconscious. A week later I withdrew my PhD application, packed my bags, and went down to Cornwall to become a scuba instructor, pissing in the Atlantic for real.

I'd just spent five years in the University library among dusty manuscripts and dustier academics, getting excited about things that happened a millennium ago if they happened at all. Suddenly I found myself in a draughty hut on a Cornish headland, surrounded by sun, sand, the sea, and girls in tight wetsuits. Life's a beach sometimes. I fell in love with it. Within six months I'd qualified as an instructor. To celebrate my success, I took a one-week diving holiday in the Red Sea. At the end of the week a dive-centre manager offered me a job there. I went home, sold my car, packed my bags and went back, and for the next two years my life was blue water, boats and bubbles. It's amazing where a degree in medieval literature can take you.

But it took me from Egypt to Belize, and in Belize I fell in love with Anna, an English girl – who was murdered after two months in the country. To honour her memory I walked from Canterbury to Santiago de Compostela with a trombone, raising money for her memorial charity. I've told that story already,* so I won't repeat it here. Suffice it to say that on the way I fell in love twice more, with a tall German, Helena, and a small continent. Europe fascinated me. Wherever I walked, history, art and literature came spilling out around me. I played my trombone under a triumphal arch commissioned by Emperor Augustus, slept in the ruins of a robber baron's castle, followed the footsteps of Charlemagne's soldiers across the Pyrenees to Spain. Cultures swirled across my path: a day's walk in Luxembourg took me through three separate linguistic areas. And everywhere I made friends. In the aftermath of Anna's death I'd been wary of strangers, sullen and paranoid. By the time I reached Santiago I'd discovered that hospitality is universal. No matter which country I was in, 98 per cent of the people were friendly. I left Spain with just two ambitions: to see more of Helena, and to see more of Europe. The only question was where to start.

It was then that I remembered my first love.

There was a time, a thousand years ago, when England was part of Denmark.

It's not something which is talked about much. For one thing, it didn't last long. The Danish empire lasted barely thirty

---

* *Pilgrim Snail* (HarperCollins, 2001).

years before succumbing to the slings, arrows and double-headed battle-axes of outrageous fortune. For another, it's frankly embarrassing. We were conquered by *Denmark*? That's like losing to Liechtenstein at football. For a third, it's hard to take kings seriously when they go around with names like Svein Forkbeard and Cnut. It's much easier to concentrate on their successors, like William the Conqueror. Now, that's a name you can take seriously.

Nevertheless, England was Danish. The takeover began at the end of the eighth century, when Viking raiders pillaged the monastery of Lindisfarne. At first they came to loot and burn; subsequently they came to conquer. Within a generation the kingdoms of Northumbria, East Anglia and Mercia in the Midlands had been overrun, and Alfred the Great's Wessex was crumbling beneath the onslaught. By the time the political situation had stabilized in the last years of his reign, the northern half of England – the Danelaw – was firmly in enemy hands. It took the Royal House of Wessex three generations to reconquer the lost territories and proclaim themselves Kings of All England. By then many of their subjects were more Danish than English.

Then the Vikings returned. While Alfred was fighting for his English throne, civil war had engulfed Scandinavia. In Norway, the chieftain Harald Fairhair united his kingdom by killing or exiling all rivals; Iceland was largely settled by refugees from his reign. But being a man who enjoyed rape at least as much as pillage, he left twenty-two sons battling over his inheritance, and the feuds that followed kept Norway in chaos for centuries. Simultaneously, in Denmark, Gorm the Old attempted to unite the country. Acting on the commonsense principle that there's no point crossing the North Sea to burn and slaughter if you can do it just as well at home, his forces concentrated on eliminating their domestic rivals. Alfred's descendants were able to consolidate their rule, and all might have been well if Gorm's son Harald Bluetooth had had more children. Unfortunately for the English, he only had one surviving son, possibly because blue teeth were hardly a sex symbol even in those unsophisticated times. This son rebelled and, some time around the year 985, drove his father into exile.

His timing was perfect. Norway was hostile, but weakened by civil war. The Swedes were busy with affairs in Finland and Russia. Northern Germany was in revolt against the German Emperors. Only one small nest of Viking rebels in Poland threatened his reign. They didn't last long. With their destruction, Denmark was secure. Realizing that it would be far more profitable to raid someone *else*'s kingdom, he set off for England. The saga of Svein Forkbeard had begun.

Svein was far more than a hairy Viking with a peculiar coiffure. He was a skilled diplomat, a talented organizer and a great tactician. England was a richer and more populous country than his own, with a long tradition of centralized government; but under King Ethelred it had become fragmented and factional. Svein made full use of the factions, suborning or diverting the defenders. He struck and retreated with lightning speed, ravaging the coast from Bamburgh to Bristol and sweeping far inland. The only English tactic was to pay the raiders to go away. Would anyone be surprised to know that it didn't work? Year after year the Vikings returned. Initially Svein worked in alliance with Oláf Tryggvason, one of Harald Fairhair's countless great-grandsons. In 994 Oláf returned to Norway and seized the throne. Six years later Svein allied himself with the Swedish king and killed Oláf in battle, claiming Norway for himself.

It might have satisfied him, but a scant two years later Ethelred ordered the murder of every Dane in England. Svein's sister was among the victims. He returned for vengeance.

Shaken by feuds and weakened by traitors, Ethelred was powerless against him. Time and again the raiders struck unchecked. Finally, in 1013, the English ran out of patience with their king. When Svein started yet another campaign, the whole of the north surrendered to him. Ethelred fled to his wife's kinsmen in Normandy, and Svein was proclaimed king. It was to be his last act. Less than a year later he died, the ruler of Norway, Denmark, western Sweden and England: the original Great Dane.

Cultural ties between England and Scandinavia had never been so strong. In Ethelred's reign, the people of northern England spoke a language as much Danish as it was English. (If you ever wondered why Geordie sounds so bizarre, that's the reason.) English monks produced manuscripts in Anglo-Saxon recounting the deeds of legendary Danish heroes (such as *Beowulf*), while the Icelandic poet Gunnlaug Serpent's-Tongue wrote Norse poems in praise of Ethelred. In Denmark, English bureaucrats began a complete overhaul of the royal administration, while English bankers supplied the Danish mint with equipment and expertise and English missionaries travelled throughout Svein's realm. Swedish weapons were traded in England, English pottery in Sweden. Norwegians, Swedes, Danes, Englishmen, all served the Danish king. Svein's son Cnut – Canute – carried on his father's work. For a single generation, it seemed that England and Scandinavia were growing into one country.

But Cnut died young, and the empire collapsed. In the succession disputes that followed, Edward the son of Ethelred returned from Normandy to claim the English throne, and Denmark and Norway disintegrated into civil war. By the time peace was established there the battle of Hastings had been fought and lost, and England had left the Scandinavian sphere of influence for ever. French had supplanted Norse as the language of poetry and power. International relations looked south, rather than east and northeast. The Danish conquest was forgotten under the impact of the Norman one; but the conquered remained. They were the English, a bastard mixture of Anglo-Saxon and Dane, of German and Norseman. French customs and language covered and camouflaged those Scandinavian origins, but they couldn't obliterate them. Somehow, I'd always believed that the English have much more in common with the people of Scandinavia than with our southern neighbours.

I decided to go and find out for myself.

The only way to do it was Viking style, by sea. That meant that I needed a boat, a route and a crew. By a happy coincidence, the London Boat Show began the week after my return from Spain. It seemed an appropriate place to start, so after sleeping off the strains and washing off the stains of a nine-month walk, I went into action. Perhaps it was a mistake. Walking into the biggest boat show in Britain in search of a boat isn't the most focused of plans. It's like going to the British Library and saying, 'I want a book.' At first the variety was overwhelming. Gradually I whittled down my criteria. It had to be a motorboat, since my sailing experience is practically non-existent and I fancied coming back alive. It had to have two engines, for security and because that's what I was used to from my diving days. It had to be steel, to give me that edge of moral authority which makes all the difference in right-of-way disputes. It had to be big enough to live on. And it had to fit within my slender budget. The last criterion was far and away the hardest to match. In two days I heard of precisely one boat that fitted the bill. It was in Holland. North Sea trade links again . . . Ten days later, having flown via Frankfurt to visit Helena, so was I.

I didn't waste the ten days. It was mid-January, the perfect time to hone my nautical skills in the Solent: so, having made contact with a Southampton-based sailing school at the Boat Show, I headed down to the coast and spent a frantic week reminding myself why I'd always sworn never to venture onto British waters in winter. It rained. It blew. Tide and wind started attacking each other and throwing up waves that left me, well, throwing up. The heating on the school's boat didn't work; nor did the instructor. (Harsh, but what can you say of someone who keeps to the north of a 'Dangerous-water-to-the-north-of-here' buoy?) At least we hapless students had plenty of chances to learn from his mistakes as well as our own . . . I needed every one. I'd always specialized in dive-boat hand-ling, which involves driving up to perilous reefs and then jumping overboard: not the kind of technique the thoughtful skipper should cultivate. But time and practice worked their magic. After a week I was starting to feel competent. I still had a lot to learn, but at least I knew enough to keep myself alive while I learned it. It would have to do.

The first sight of the ship which was to become *Peregrino* was a shock. The vessel I'd trained on had been a typical school cruiser, leaky, temperamental and old. The gleaming arrow-head that met my eyes in the grey of a Dutch afternoon might have come out of a Bacardi advert: white, sleek and powerful. In fact, as I now know, all boats are leaky and tem-peramental, the only difference being how long they've been like that for – but that day my innocence was still untarnished. The good ship was ten years old; her engines had run a mere four hundred hours. The hull gleamed like a mirror, the panel-work (mahogany) shone, the control panels glittered with a formidable array of instruments some of which I understood, and even the engine compartment shone like new. All thoughts of moderation vanished. I looked, and I lusted.

The salesman was an expert. He saw my resistance crumbling, and suggested that, after we'd been out for an engine test, we should crane the boat out of the water so that I could see for myself what a wonderfully solid structure I was contemplating buying; going for the keel, as it were. There was no need. When we slipped out onto the river Maas with a deep-throated roar of restrained power, my heart was caught. Imagine a newly qualified driver suddenly confronted with a Rolls and you'll get the idea. I tried my hardest to look cynical, and even managed to haggle for a few upgrades to the electronic equipment, but we both knew I was faking. The boat was everything I'd dreamed of. One week later I phoned my bank manager and a marine surveyor and set the propellers whirling. It was the beginning of February. I'd been home less than a month.

I had a boat. Admittedly it was in Holland undergoing an overhaul, but a boat it was. The next step was to construct a plan.

It was more complicated than it first appeared; most plans are. My idea was to head across the North Sea to Scandinavia and see what the people there were like. As a general concept it had much to recommend it, but I couldn't deny that it was a little short on details. There's a lot of Scandinavia. Where was I going to start? The Arctic seemed somewhat challenging for a first solo voyage, so 'the south' looked a good bet. From all I'd read and heard, Norway offered more exciting scenery than its neighbours, and it was also the northernmost of my targets, so it made sense to get there first, while the weather was good. I'd never been to Oslo, which was a more than ample reason to go there, and from Oslo it was no more than a few days' passage south to Copenhagen. Unless I decided to stop off in Gothenburg and follow the Swedish canals to Stockholm ... The more I thought of it, the more the idea of hopping from capital to capital appealed. A few more sessions with the atlas brought the plan to perfection. I'd bring the boat back to the UK to register her as a British vessel, steam up the coast to Aberdeen, turn east for Stavanger, and then port-hop south and east past Oslo to Gothenburg. From there I'd take the canal to Stockholm, head south and round the tip of Sweden, come up to Copenhagen, and make for home through the Kiel Canal. It was a fine itinerary. Don't bother to memorize it, though. Most plans last about forty-eight hours. This one didn't even get that far.

Once I'd settled my route, I had to find a crew. I wasn't optimistic enough to think that I'd be able to drive single-handed from Scotland to Norway: staying awake for forty hours at a stretch has never been my strong point. At the same time I started thinking about equipment. The voyage I'd planned would take six months at least, and I wasn't going to be able to get away until June, which meant that I probably wouldn't be home until early December: warm, waterproof gear was definitely an essential. With that in mind, I headed down to London. What I wanted was equipment. What I *got* was one of my life's better coincidences.

I was in a riverside chandlery looking at sea-boots in my best Cap'n Birdseye manner. A shop assistant came bustling over.

'I'm looking for sea-boots,' I said.

'Yes, sir,' he said as if he hadn't guessed that from the fact that I was looking *at* them. 'What kind?'

'Well, I'm going to Scandinavia ...'

'Really? One of the lads here is Swedish. Why don't you talk to him?' And before I could answer, he turned round and shouted, 'Fred!'

Fred's a Swede? I thought. You've got to be joking ... A dark-haired, swarthy lad of my own age and height ambled over, killing another preconception as he went. So much for tall blond Nordic types, I'd taken him for a Spaniard. 'Yes?'

'Gentleman's going over to Scandinavia this summer. Can you give him some advice?'

His eyes lit up. 'Excellent! Whereabouts?'

'Well, where would you recommend?'

'Western Sweden,' he said instantly. 'Bohuslän's the most beautiful place in Scandinavia. That's where I'm from,' he added, spoiling the effect. He hurried over to a rack of charts and pulled out an Admiralty North Sea overview. 'We haven't got the detailed stuff here, you have to get that in Gothenburg, but look, here ... here ... here ...' His finger stabbed down at the bewildering labyrinth of rocks and water west and north of Gothenburg, a cartographer's nightmare. 'There's a hundred different ports and natural harbours to choose from. I'm going there myself this summer. It's the best cruising in the world.'

'You sail much?' I asked thoughtfully.

'I did my National Service in the Navy, and I've got my Yachtmaster's licence,' he said simply. Not just a swarthy Swede, but a *seafaring* swarthy Swede.

My brain hiccupped. It does that sometimes. Everything shuts off for an instant, and when the system re-boots there's a whole new plan waiting to be applied. I looked back at the chart. Gothenburg? That was Scandinavia ...

'When are you going home?'

'End of June,' he said. I hesitated. Decisions like these shouldn't be taken lightly. Then I decided.

'That's when I'm going over. Fancy a lift?'

His head shot up. 'Are you serious?'

'Yep.'

'When were you planning to get there?'

The pre-hiccup answer would have been 'late August', but I can think fast when I have to. My eye traced out distances on the chart. 'Oh, early July.'

He hesitated. 'My brother and a friend wanted to come too.'

'There's room.'

'With their dive kit.'

'There's still room.'

His face split into a beaming grin. 'Excellent! Is it okay if I call you this evening?'

By the end of the evening I had new boots, new waterproofs – and a crew.

At the end of May it was time to bring the boat home. With the help of three friends from the Southampton course, I steamed up the river Maas to the Belgian border, crossed into the Belgian canals and made my leisurely way down to Antwerp and the river Scheldt. Fourteen months before, I'd passed that way on foot, and two days' walk south of the city I'd been invited to become a godfather by a family who'd started by offering me a cup of tea; they came to see me on the boat, and we spent a happy afternoon chugging up and down the canals with my goddaughter shouting 'Allo!' at every passing barge. Then it was time to go, and we set our guests ashore and rode the evening tide downriver and out into the shipping lanes. The air was warm and still. The stars rocked above us. Phosphorescence tinged our wake. The sea heaved beneath our keel. Yes, conditions were swell for a crossing. Soon after dawn we reached the Blackwater river and let the rising tide carry us up to Heybridge, where I'd arranged to moor the boat while I finished my preparations.

There was plenty to keep me occupied. For one thing, I wanted to register the boat as a British vessel, which involved about as much paperwork as you'd expect with the Department of Transport involved. They wouldn't allow me the boat's original name, *San Martin*, on the grounds that someone else had got there first. *Pilgrim* met with no more approval, so I shifted languages and suggested *Peregrino*. After a surprisingly brief delay, word filtered back down from the Ministry that yes, *Peregrino* was okay, and they even spelled it right first time. Emboldened by this unexpected success, I applied for their list of safety requirements for small commercial vessels, and received (by return of post) a book with yellow pages the size of the *Yellow Pages* (some official's subconscious at work there) detailing all the horrible things that can happen at sea if you don't have the proper equipment. It very nearly scared me off the idea entirely, but somehow I stuck to my guns, had a long chat with the foreman at Heybridge and ordered a further round of upgrades.

As he started hammering, I went shopping. It wasn't the first time I'd prepared for a long journey, so I had at least a vague idea of what was needed. Besides, I'd been a fan of the books of Arthur Ransome and Patrick O'Brian for years. Soon the cabin was littered with purchases: charts, navigation implements, guides to the rules of the inland and offshore waterways (if you thought the *Highway Code* is complicated, think again), tide tables, harbour guides, signalling flags, food. If Arthur Ransome was to be believed, I'd be needing a six-month supply of pemmican and ginger beer; Patrick O'Brian veered more towards ship's biscuit, weevils and rum. Porridge was also an essential: I still treasure the memory of the checkout girl's face when I wheeled a trolley laden with nothing but oats and brown sugar past her till.

'You like porridge, then?' she asked faintly.

'It's *oat cuisine*,' I grinned, and left her looking dazed.

In between shopping trips I took *Peregrino* out onto the river to practise manoeuvres. Soon, at the cost of no more than a few dents to the paintwork, I was starting to feel at home on my houseboat. Which was, after all, the point. It was a heady feeling to be out on that narrow, winding river among the reed-fringed islands, and not just for the pleasure of sun and wind. In 991 Oláf Tryggvason led a Viking force up the same river and made camp on Northey island, right opposite the Heybridge locks. The Anglo-Saxon poem commemorating the battle that followed was the first epic I read at college, and one of the gutsiest reads of all time. Being there on the water and seeing the battlefield, knowing that I was soon to cross the North Sea on the trail of the Vikings, filled my head with dreams. It made me itch to be gone.

One week later, on a warm, grey day at the end of June, I steamed southwest across the Thames Estuary and up the river to meet my crew in London.

2

THAMES

'In this year Oláf and Svein came to London on the Nativity of St Mary with 94 ships, and made a determined attack on the city . . . and they were paid 16,000 pounds.'

Anglo-Saxon Chronicle, entry for AD 994

After a leisurely twelve-hour passage I steamed past the Millennium Dome and picked up a little buoy under Tower Bridge; and there aren't many professions where you can get away with saying that. When the tide was right, I made for the gates of St Katharine's Docks and steered into the harbour beyond.

Harbours are very like car parks. There are only two ways in which you can arrange stationary vehicles, side by side or nose to tail, and the same applies to boats. Smaller harbours usually boast a wall or jetty alongside which boats make fast, held by ropes from bow and stern: the maritime equivalent of parallel parking, and just as prone to abuse by skippers who can't judge lengths properly. Busier harbours like St Katharine's therefore adopt the parking-space approach, dividing the water in front of the jetty into a series of long thin boxes by means of floating pontoons or massive piles rammed into the seabed. The skipper cautiously edges into a box, throws a rope from the stern over a bollard or pile, edges further forwards until the bow almost touches the jetty, throws another rope over a bollard there, tightens and loosens everything in sight until the boat lies perfectly centred in the box, and then sits back and watches the sunset with a glass of pink gin, monarch of all he surveys.

That, at least, is the theory.

The problem is that boats aren't in the least like cars. For one thing, cars have brakes. Boats don't. There are only two ways to stop a boat: run the engines in reverse for *exactly* the right length of time, or ram something. For another, roads don't move. Water does, and it practically never goes in a helpful direction, so while heading very slowly and nervously into your narrow box, you have to be aware that the water is carrying you merrily sideways. Finally, and crucially, boats don't steer like cars. Cars follow their front wheels. Boats pivot about an axis just behind the mid-point of the vessel (or in front of it if you're going in reverse). So if, having realized that the water is carrying you slowly to the right of your box, you steer sharply to the left, you'll find your bow slewing round into the current, your stern slewing a corresponding amount away from it, and two hundred assorted tourists watching in awe as you fetch up sideways across at least three boxes, crimson with embarrassment.

Take it from me.

I made it into the box on the second attempt, ignoring the comments from the jetty, and ducked into the quiet of the cabin for tea and blushes. After an hour or so the stage fright died and I felt safe to run the gauntlet of the staring eyes; fortunately mob interest is a fickle thing, and the harbour's attention was turned on a colossal white motor-cruiser flying the Jamaican flag which was drifting into the lock as though the skipper didn't have a care in the world. Eclipsed and humbled, I watched with the rest, then went to chat with the harbourmaster.

It was just as well. I hadn't refuelled on the way upriver, and I wasn't going to get very far until I did. You learn little details like this when you've been on the water a while ... I knew there was a diesel barge just downriver, so it should have been easy, but just in case, I thought I'd check its opening hours. The harbourmaster didn't know, so I phoned the barge:

'Hi, are you open on Sundays?' It was Thursday, and I'd agreed with Fred that we'd leave on Sunday.

'Which Sunday?'

Eh? 'This Sunday.'

'No, my mate's ill.'

'What about Saturday?'

'Nope, day off.'

'Bugger. What about tomorrow?'

'We can do tomorrow.'

Tomorrow it was. I went back to the harbourmaster and asked if I'd be able to make a refuelling run in the time available: the problem with the Thames is that it runs out of water at low tide, which makes getting in and out of harbour tricky. St Katharine's is only accessible an hour either side of high water, which on that Friday was just before noon. Not a problem, said the harbourmaster, he'd lock me out as soon as the tide allowed, I'd have two whole hours to do the job.

Wonderful, I thought, and went shopping for the last of my food supplies.

I was knee-deep in instant puddings when my mobile rang. It was Fred, wondering if I'd be willing to make my crew's life easier by collecting them and their gear from the Embankment the next day; anything to save them schlepping half a ton of dive kit across London on the tube.

'Well, yes, but is there anywhere I can moor?' I asked. I

knew the Embankment, and I couldn't recall any public jetties on that part of the Thames.

'There's a jetty just below the bridge,' he assured me.

'Fine. I've got to be on the river anyway.' We agreed that he'd meet me at St Katharine's the following morning and act as crewman. If we locked out of the harbour at eleven, we'd have two hours to make the round trip. More than enough time.

Hah.

First problem: Fred was delayed on the tube. We didn't leave the lock until eleven thirty.

Second problem: the diesel barge was almost out of fuel. There was still enough for us, but it trickled out of the hose. We weren't finished until twelve.

The killer punch: just as Fred was loosening the mooring lines the radio crackled. It was the harbourmaster. Two Thames barges wanted to lock out at twelve thirty, so could we be back before then, please?

It's probably not legal to pass Tower Bridge at 20 knots, but we did it. The tide had turned and was starting to ebb, piling up in heavy backwashes against the pillars, and we belted upriver on a wake of solid foam. Fred was out on the bow, clinging onto a safety railing and scouring the banks with binoculars in search of the promised landing. I clung to the wheel on the quarterdeck, swaying like Ben Hur as we slammed across the wake of a heavy tug. That stretch of the Thames is never quiet: we crashed from wave to wave in a bellow of engines, battling time and tide. The current strengthened. The bridges seemed to crawl past, spitting out the ebb in shining curls and eddies. Fred came reeling astern, grinning through a mask of spray. Another barge swept past, downstream. Our bow ploughed into the waves and lurched sideways and for a second I thought I'd lost it. Automatically my hand slammed down on the throttles. Deceleration kicked us forwards. Our own wake caught us and pushed us upriver. Hungerford Bridge was dead ahead.

'There!' Fred yelled, pointing.

'Got it!' A long, narrow tour-boat jetty jutting out into the stream.

'Shit!'

'What?'

'It's closed!'

'No!' I yanked the throttles all the way back, and we rocked to a halt on the waves. There was the landing-stage, there were three sweaty Swedes jumping up and down by a pile of dive gear, there was the burglar-proof gate on the bank. Locked.

'Further down!' Fred shouted.

I looked where he was pointing.

'You're nuts!'

He was already pulling out his mobile phone to give instructions to his friends. Nuts or not, my hands were moving, shoving the throttles forwards again, jerking the wheel over, kicking us sideways across the ebb, while my conscious mind pressed itself back against the back of my skull and gibbered.

The Thames offers a thousand and one moorings for boats of all sizes, but believe me, Cleopatra's Needle really isn't one of them. Right below the Needle the Embankment wall falls sheer into the Thames. No jetties, no bollards, no convenient railings to tie to, just a wall. Upstream and downstream, it's hemmed in by socking great restaurant boats. Directly beneath it the brown water washes over a rock-studded mudbank. There's a reason for the complete lack of mooring apparatus. Nobody's stupid enough to stop there.

You can't be doing this . . . I kicked the bow upriver, let the current push us sideways towards the gap. *You really can't be doing this* . . . Fred was hurrying along the side, throwing fenders into position. *I don't believe you're doing this* . . . The depth-sounder was ticking away the metres under the keel, one and a half, one, a half. If it got any shallower I could kiss my propellers goodbye. *Adieu*, screw . . . I tried not to think about it. It didn't work. Wheel throttles depth-gauge, wheel throttles depth-gauge, flushed panting faces appearing over the wall, Fred in the bows with a rope, my stern-line coiled and ready, wheel throttles depth-gauge, forty centimetres depth, still forty centimetres, edging closer, edging closer . . .

'Catch!' Fred hurled a rope at the wall. As a hand snatched it from the air I wrenched the engines out of gear and turned to fling my own line ashore. With the faintest of squelches the fenders touched the wall and bounced us back into the river.

'Catch!' and, as I turned, a flying dive tank nearly brained me. A grinning face changed to a look of consternation with the heavy thud of metal hitting the deck, and then it was raining kitbags. Catch and drop, catch and drop, thud crash rattle bang panic, and then Fred was scrambling ashore and kicking the bows clear of the wall and the stern-line slapped on the deck and somehow I was back at the wheel and nudging out into the current with Swedish yells ringing in my ears, *I don't believe you did that*, and then I looked at my watch.

Twelve twenty-two.

But now the tide was with me: I rammed the throttles up to full power and took off downstream like a scalded catfish. The world turned to sound and speed and spray, the bridges rolled overhead like motorway flyovers, and then I was throttling back again and turning upstream by St Katharine's lock. It was twelve thirty-two.

'St Katharine's, *Peregrino*, bang on time, over,' I called in modest triumph.

'*Peregrino*, St Katharine's, can you wait half an hour? We're locking the barges through now, there'll be plenty of time for you afterwards.'

Some days I wonder why I bother.

I spent the afternoon sitting on the waterfront staring down at the tide and dreaming of distant times. Before the Norman Conquest London was one of the great cities of Scandinavia: at one time or another all the great figures in Norse politics passed its gates. Hákon the Good and Saint Oláf, both future kings of Norway, lived there, Hákon as King Athelstan's foster-son, Oláf as Ethelred's chief henchman. Thorkell the Tall, chief of the Vikings of Jómsborg, first attacked, then later defended the city; Jarl Eirík of Norway ravaged the outskirts. Even Gunnlaug Serpent's-Tongue, the Icelandic poet, visited London in Ethelred's reign. By the time Svein came to power a Norse enclave had grown up there. It's no wonder that one of Saint Oláf's first recorded miracles was performed in London. The church dedicated to him still stands, less than a mile from Tower Bridge, though the crippled Frenchman he healed doesn't.

But the most important meeting in London was in 994. In that year Svein and Oláf Tryggvason carried out their great raid up the Thames and across the Home Counties. The two men whose trail I was to follow for the next seven months stood side by side just across the river from where I was berthed, directing the assault on the walls of London. Two more dissimilar allies would be hard to imagine. Svein was a politician, a strategist, calculating and pragmatic, merciful or cruel as occasion demanded: all accounts agree that his sole aim throughout his life was the expansion of his power base which he achieved with cold-blooded thoroughness. Oláf was a very different proposition. According to the Icelandic saga which bears his name he was 'the most cheerful of men, very playful, mild and humble, exceedingly impetuous in all matters ... the cruellest of men when angry, he tormented his enemies greatly.' As soon as the Danegeld was paid for that year, Oláf set off on a wild scheme to conquer Norway and Christianize it with just a handful of followers. Svein pocketed the money, went home, and planned the next assault. Then as now, nothing in politics ever had a simple cause; but much of the drama that kept the North Sea cauldron bubbling over the following six years arose from the differences between the two heroes.

That evening the descendants of the Vikings descended on *Peregrino*. I'd invited them to eat on board, and they'd reciprocated by inviting me out to the pub afterwards, a fair exchange. My invitation was for eight o'clock. Naturally, at ten past eight I was still in the cabin, juggling hot pans over my two electric hobs, the hum of the generator rattling the floorboards. Fortunately, being Swedish, they turned up sociably late. Just as I was draining a pan of rice into the sink, the boat started to rock, and heavy sea-boots clunked along the narrow gangway.

'Ben?' Fred called, looking in through the open hatchway and waving away a cloud of steam.

'Come on in,' I shouted, peering up through fogged specs at the dark shapes on the stairs: Fred, tall, dark and swarthy; his younger brother Magnus, short, dark and swarthy; and a muscular Norse god, all blue eyes and golden tan, sporting a small sophisticated moustache, Fred's best friend, Fred. Swedish names were easier than I thought.

As I waved them to their seats and turned back to the kitchen, Fred the Blond pulled a strange wooden thing from his pocket, pointing it at me like a prehistoric mugger. It was a kind of knife, about as long as my hand, faintly sweet-smelling, striped with the wood's natural colours. I took it and stood staring at it.

'It's for you,' Magnus told me helpfully. 'It's a butter-knife. Traditional Swedish present. So's this.' He held out a white-handled cheeseparer.

Solemnly, Fred the Dark put a second butter-knife on the table. I felt as if I were officiating at some religious rite.

'Thank you,' I said cautiously. Butter-knives and cheese-scrapers? Were they joking? In fact, no. Every Swede who goes abroad takes a handful of those wooden butter-knives along. Every visitor to Swedish shores receives them in bushels. I've got a drawerful at home. If anyone wants one, you only have to ask. Please. I don't even *like* butter.

'You're welcome,' Magnus told me. 'Can we help with the food?'

Recalled to my hospitable duty, I plunged back into the galley.

I had met a Swede before, but that was in New Zealand and he'd been drunk, so I didn't think he was a fair example. (With hindsight, I might perhaps want to revise that view.) I therefore had no experience of what to expect from my crew, so in the best traditions of British foreign relations, I fell back on prejudice. What's Sweden famous for? Vegetables and Volvos. Right, I thought, here comes some stolid tedium.

Wrong.

Fred the Dark was tall, tanned, and twenty-four, and as far as I could make out, he smiled all the time. He'd just graduated from the LSE with a degree in business studies, so going into business was the last thing he wanted to do. Sweden may be a peaceable country these days, but the sea-roving genes still rule the gene-pool. Fred had spent every summer holiday since he could remember on the family yacht. There was nothing snobbish about it: Swedes have boats like other people have bicycles. He'd done his National Service in the Swedish navy, navigating a fast-attack patrol boat round the rock-strewn Baltic coast scaring various lurking Russian submarines – Sweden, being both neutral and uncomfortably close to Russia, has heard of the end of the Cold War, but doesn't quite believe in it. Whenever he talked about his exploits a piratical gleam lit his eyes; it was quite obvious that whatever the government thought, he'd seen his year's subjection to the State as the chance to drive a very expensive boat very fast. He was in a hurry to get back to Sweden for one simple reason: his family were off cruising that summer and he didn't want to miss out. If ever a man was born with saltwater in his veins, he was that man.

Fred the Dark was a Viking, but didn't look it. Fred the Blond, who did look it, wasn't. I've never met anyone who so lived up to the Aryan ideal of manhood. Tall, blond and blue-eyed, with that irritating complexion that tans if you so much as shine a torch on it, he could turn up at Valhalla and be let in with no questions asked; but if he was descended from any Vikings, it was those cautious traders who went east from Stockholm into Russia and followed the rivers down to Constantinople. Where his saturnine sidekick swung into everything with a swashbuckling grin, Fred the Blond's bronzed brow was creased by an anxious frown. Mind you, it didn't seem to slow him down. He'd served with the Dark One in the navy, learnt to dive in the icy waters off the Baltic island of Gotland, and hoped to capitalize on his own LSE education by going to Thailand and becoming a diving instructor. He wore a dive-centre T-shirt, shorts that showed off his disgustingly muscular legs, and all-terrain sandals, and it was impossible to imagine him in anything else. Trying to picture either of the Freds in a business suit just didn't work.

You *could* imagine Magnus in a suit, but only if you didn't know him. He was twenty-two and already going bald, a sure sign of an enviably misspent youth. While the Freds talked boisterously about everything under the sun, he seemed content to sit back and watch the cabaret. Growing up with a brother as buoyant as his must have been a tricky proposition, and I had the feeling that he'd always been in Fred's shadow. He, too, had served in the navy, but as a cook, not a navigator; a job heavy with responsibility, but less likely to sink the ship if things went wrong. Just like the other two, he was a diver, a sailor, an adventurer, but in a different style again. Fred the Dark swashbuckled and Fred the Blond worried, but Magnus went into adventure with zen-like calm. During the passage of the Limfjord he and I took the boat (height above water four metres fifteen) under a low bridge (observed height above water four fifteen and a half). As I ran around the quarterdeck in anxious little circles, bleating and wringing my hands, Magnus steered straight for the centre of the bridge. He glanced round once to check that the radio antenna was lined up on the highest point of the arch, nodded and took us through without even bothering to look up. Or slow down. As I slumped on a deck-box, my nerves reduced to jelly, he looked back at me and shrugged.

'What's the big deal?' his shoulders seemed to say. I didn't trust myself to reply.

We sat in the cabin devouring rice and stir-fry and sipping wine, then adjourned to the harbour pub, and I found myself looking from face to face, searching for something that would tell me, 'They're Swedish.' I couldn't find it. Their English was at least as fluent as mine, they were wearing the same shorts and T-shirts as everyone else in the bar, and they chatted and laughed freely but quietly, with no sudden uproar to startle the other patrons. Even their body language seemed

British. There's a certain fluency of hand-gesture which seems common to all the lands where Romance languages are spoken. They didn't have it. The only movement which seemed to come naturally was the hand pointing at an empty pint and the waggle of the eyebrows which means 'One for the road?' They used that one a lot. Soon our coherence had declined well past the point of decadence, and still I couldn't see any foreignness.

Just when I was deciding that we were all one big happy North Sea family, Fred the Blond opened his mouth, probed with a finger behind his upper lip, and pulled out a tiny cloth parcel which he dropped into an ashtray. Wordlessly Magnus handed him what looked like a boot-polish tin, and selecting another parcel he inserted it in the vacant space, wiggling his lip back and forth a few times to settle it.

'What the hick is that?' I heccupped.

Fred grinned. '*Snus.*'

'Bless you.'

'No, it's *snus*,' Magnus told me. 'Chewing tobacco.'

I peered owlishly at the Blond One's upper lip beneath its debonair moustache. 'But he's not chewing it.'

The brothers exchanged glances. Possibly they were admiring my powers of observation. 'It's not really for chewing.'

'But *you* shaid . . .'

'It's tobacco mixed with microscopic glass crystals. The crystals irritate your gums and increase the blood flow, and the nicotine's absorbed directly into your circulation. Much better than smoking.'

Magnus grinned and rolled his lip upwards, a skill I'd thought restricted to orang-utans, and I saw the little parcel nestled above his canine. It looked frightful.

'All right, you're foreign,' I told them, and called for more beer.

Two days later, having recovered from the hangovers, we set off down the Thames towards the distant coast of Denmark.

3

NORTH SEA AND LIMFJORD

'Then we were together on the sea for the span of five nights ... the heaving sea, darkening night, and a north wind, coldest of storms, turned against us, battle-grim. Wild were the waves ...'

Beowulf, lines 544–48

The secret of Svein's success was sea power.

The reason is simple. Even under ideal conditions, medieval armies were lucky to cover twenty miles a day. A Viking longship could sail the same distance in two hours. In 1066, Harald Hardrada of Norway invaded Yorkshire. The half-Danish Harold Godwinson, king of England, defeated and killed him at Stamford Bridge, and was then forced to march south to face some invading Norman bastard at Hastings. (The Conqueror's name in the sagas is *Viljálmr inn Bastarði*, which is due to an irregularity of birth and nothing at all to do with his style of government. Honest.) It took him almost three weeks. Hardrada's Armada could have done it in forty-eight hours.

It was for this reason that the Thames Estuary and the coasts of Kent and East Anglia were so beloved of Svein's raiders. Sailing from the Limfjord just before sunset, they could reach England, three hundred miles away, by dawn of the next day but one, with a full day's light to find the best anchorage. No doubt the English had watchers posted on the headlands, looking for the first lean silhouettes against the sunrise, but once in the Estuary the Vikings could hit any point on the coast between Dover and Harwich. If the defences seemed too strong, they could swing to port, pass the Foreland and head down-Channel, leaving the defenders far behind: not even horsemen could keep up with them for long. In the years before Svein and Cnut imposed a victor's peace on the North Sea, the list of towns raided grew almost unchecked: Portland, Southampton, Thanet, Folkestone, Dover, Norwich, Sandwich, Ipswich, Rochester and London itself.

The English replied in the only way they could, by getting massacred. I've always suspected that our legendary affection for hopeless defeats stems from this time: between 991 and 1016 the English failed to win a single notable battle, so defeat was all they had to celebrate. Head and shoulders above the poetry of the day stands *The Battle of Maldon*, describing Oláf Tryggvason's raid up the Blackwater. It survives in a single manuscript of which the beginning and end have been lost, but the plot seems to be as follows:

1. the 'Danes' (Anglo-Saxon shorthand for 'Scandinavians') sail upriver and camp on Northey island, which is joined to the mainland by a narrow causeway at low tide;
2. the Essex levies occupy the bridgehead and kill every man who tries to cross;
3. the despicable Danes, realizing their predicament, demand that the noble English let them come ashore unimpeded in the interests of fair play ('then the loathsome visitors began to cheat', the poet rages. He should have written for the tabloids);
4. the English earl agrees;

5. the Danes come ashore, outflank the defenders and kill the earl;
6. the earl's bodyguard rally magnificently, make a stand but are killed to the last man.

It's impossible to read it with a steady pulse: one by one the Essex boys stand forth from the shield-wall, hurl defiance at the enemy and go down fighting. In one curt couplet the unknown poet manages to sum up a thousand years of Bulldog Britain: 'Our wills shall be tougher, our hearts braver, our spirits shall rise higher the more our strength fades!' Shakespeare might have penned those lines for Henry V at Agincourt; Churchill might have growled them over the burning wreckage of London. Stirring stuff. Pity they lost. (Again.)

A wise man once said, 'All epic is sex and violence. Germanic epic is violence with some sex, and French is sex with some violence.' Well actually, it was me, but it's true nonetheless. The famous last stand is the stock scene in Germanic legend. *Beowulf* refers to a fight at Finnsburh in the Frisian islands, in which a group of heroes are surrounded in a chieftain's hall and, presumably, massacred. (The narrative is cut off marginally before the last hero's head.) The German *Nibelungenlied* has as its key scene the last stand of the kings of Burgundy, surrounded in Attila's hall and, yes, massacred. The Icelandic *Saga of Hrólf Kráki* does the same to Hrólf, legendary king of Denmark. *Njál's Saga* does the same to both the heroic Gunnarr of Hlidarendi and the saintly Njál. Most of these were written in the thirteenth century, by which time the French creations Arthur, Lancelot and Tristan had been mounted and thrusting away for a generation. And it's not as if the northerners didn't know it. *Grettir's Saga*, which is all about how the strongest man in Iceland went around killing trolls and giants before losing his luck, becoming a murderous outlaw, and – you guessed it – dying in a famous last stand, borrows wholesale from the northern French *Romance of Tristan*, which is mostly about the clever ways in which Tristan and Iseult managed to get into bed without Iseult's husband Mark knowing. The epic writers knew about all this new-fangled fashion of fornication, they just refused to talk about it: 'no sex, please, we're Norsemen'. The main role of women in Germanic literature seems to be – a blow for feminism, this – bullying their menfolk into finishing off feuds. If anyone reading this believes that women in the Middle Ages were down-trodden, might I advise you to go and read *Njál's Saga*? The heroes' wives have an argument. Six corpses fall before a fragile peace is restored. It might be one reason the Vikings travelled so much. Anything was better than the hell they got at home.

The cult of the heroic loser isn't the only British trait to stem from those times. There's our humour, which we call 'irony' and Americans call 'What?' I'll admit that few Germanic epics are exactly rollicking rib-ticklers, but if you want grim jests, the Icelandic sagas are the place to go. One hero is stabbed in the back as he leaves his house; he looks down at the bloodstained iron jutting from his chest and remarks, 'These broad-bladed spears are all the rage, aren't they?' before expiring. Another, who bed-hops his way from Norway to Russia and back, lightens the mood with his chat-up lines: 'The iron bar between my legs needs softening, have you got somewhere I can put it?' is one you'd probably better not try out in the bars of Oslo these days. In Njál's saga, a noted murderer has his right arm cut off. He looks down at the lacerated stump and says, 'It's about time someone did that, that arm's caused a lot of damage.'

Finally, there's our 'special relationship' with the sea, which works on the basis that it messes us around because it can, and we put up with it because we're British. Generations of poets have put their love for the oceans into words, few more stirring than John Masefield's 'Sea Fever': 'I must go down to the seas again, to the lonely sea and the sky . . .' Ever since the Elizabethans realized that sea power was the source of all other power, the romantic image of the British as 'born with the sea in their blood' has grown; but nowhere in the whole span of English literature is the sailor's longing and suffering so clearly expressed as in the anonymous tenth-century Anglo-Saxon poem *The Seafarer*:

> Yet no man on earth is so proud, nor so blessed in his
> gifts,
> So active in his youth, nor so brave in his deeds,
> Nor so favoured by his master,
> That he is not always worried about what the Lord will
> send him on the sea.
> He does not think of harping, nor of receiving rings,
> Nor of the pleasures of a woman, nor of the joys of the
> world,
> Nor of anything but the surging of the waves;
> And yet he who sets out on the waters always feels
> longing.
> The groves put forth blossoms, cities grow fair,
> The fields are beautiful, the world comes to life;
> All these urge the eager-minded man's heart to a journey,
> On which he intends to travel far over the watery
> ways . . .

A thousand years later, the words still hold true. Why else were the four of us off cruising?

We left the mouth of the Thames at sunset and set off in Forkbeard's wake.

One of the key messages of *The Seafarer* is that sailing is not for the faint-hearted. Modern vessels might be a far cry from the open longships of Cnut's day, huge and powerful and equipped with every navigational device that technology can provide, but until someone comes up with a gadget that can calm the waves and control the weather, all that means is that the mariners know exactly where they are when they're suffering.

We were crossing at the beginning of July, and we still had a hard journey. Fog hit us as soon as night fell, and Magnus and I navigated through clinging wet curtains that gleamed angry red and bilious green in the light of our navigation lamps. Once the radar-alarm beeped a warning, and as I turned hard to starboard a reeling channel buoy churned past a boat's length over the side. The fog lasted until the following afternoon, and then the wind began, a cold breeze out of the northeast which tossed us around like a rubber duck in a jacuzzi. None of us slept much, and when night fell the fog returned. As I came on deck to start my watch, we were passing one of the oil-platforms that stud the coast off Holland, a web of amber lights caught in the mist. I stared at it until it was out of sight, realized that my stomach was churning, staggered to the rail and donated my dinner to the hungry waves. The Swedes call this process 'calling Ulrik'. Apparently that last agonized groan sounds like 'Ul . . .' to them. I was too busy retching to notice.

Peregrino is a state-of-the-art boat. Unfortunately, the art in question is regurgitation. She's small, and that means that the basic laws of the sea apply to her as they did to Forkbeard's fleet: waves throw her around, push her off course and soak everything in spray. In fact, the Vikings would probably have found their crossing easier than ours was, because their longships were longer and broader, and therefore more stable, than my shortship. If weather patterns no longer play much of a role in the planning of international ferry timetables, it's only because modern ships are so huge that it takes really big waves to have any effect on them. Small-boat cruising today is exactly the same as it was a thousand years ago. That Anglo-Saxon poet knew what he was writing about.

We'd started off heading roughly northeast to take us to Esbjerg, cruising at a steady eight knots. As the wind picked up, we were forced to slow down and angle north to ease the impact of the waves. They were as high as our quarterdeck, and when you run head-on into a boat-high wave which is coming the other way at the speed of the wind, the impact rattles your bones and shakes your *snus* loose. The fog made us slow down more. No matter how good your electronics, it's still terrifying to head at speed into the clinging blindness. Whatever the screens say, instinct screams that the next thing you see might be the bows of a supertanker looming overhead. Each time we slowed it put hours on the voyage. We'd left on Sunday. It wasn't until Wednesday that we reached Esbjerg to refuel.

From Esbjerg we ran north along the Jutland coast. As we did, the wind shifted into the west. Now, instead of being head-on, the waves were coming at us from the side, with the full width of the North Sea to build up speed and height, and they hit so hard that we had to strap ourselves to the quarterdeck to stay on our feet. Blunt and wide-bottomed, as so many of us are, *Peregrino* rolled like a jellyfish in the surf. We'd been planning to round the tip of Jutland and head southeast across the Kattegat to reach Gothenburg, but by the time we approached the turning-point the waves were so violent that it would have been dangerous even to try. The weather was at the very borderline of safety, and we were far gone in fatigue. It was time to change our plan. Right under our lee lay the harbour of Thybøron, and behind Thybøron the Limfjord wound its way clear through Jutland and out into the Kattegat. The decision was made with the speed that comes from desperation: 'Quiet water? I'll do anything!' We clawed our way round until the wind was right behind us, and rode the breakers between rock-strewn headlands into the narrow inlet of Thybøron. It was the first time in my life that I realized you really *can* surf a twelve-ton boat: all you need is a big enough wave. Sixteen hours after leaving Esbjerg we tied up in the fish-smelling concrete harbour for two hours' collapse. Then, buffeted by bitter wind, we steamed out onto the steel-grey water and wound our way past short-cropped green banks, studded with sheep and stunted trees, heading for Sweden.

It was here, in the Limfjord, that the Danish empire began. In Harald Bluetooth's day everyone knew its significance as the most sheltered body of water in the North Sea, the strategic link between that sea and the Baltic. Early in his reign Harald had a colossal fortress built at Aggersborg on the very shores of the fjord to defend its eastern entry. His power thus consolidated, he invited the then king of Norway, Harald Grey-cloak, to a parley. The Norwegian – who, having come to power over the backs of his dead rivals, including our hero Oláf's father Tryggvi, should have known better – accepted. Anchored in the fjord, he was ambushed and killed by Blue-tooth's nephew, yet another Harald, Gold-Harald. (The fabulous Viking nicknames – Sigurd Snake-in-the-Eye and Ragnar Hairy-Breeks are my favourites – are no mere affectation. It's the only way to tell the beggars apart.) As payment for his action, Gold-Harald demanded a share of Harald Bluetooth's power. Bluetooth promptly had him killed by the exiled

Norwegian Jarl Hákon, who had been feuding with Grey-cloak for thirty years. Freed of their rivals, Hákon and Harald joined forces and invaded Norway. Without Greycloak's leadership the opposition crumbled. Soon Hákon was installed as Harald's regent in Norway and the Danish dream of empire was born.

It proved short-lived. Around 985 Harald and his son Svein came to blows over a division of power, and son drove father into exile in Poland, where the Danes had extensive settlements. Taking advantage of the civil war, Hákon rebelled, declaring Norwegian independence. Thus when Svein took the crown, he faced two immediate challenges: the destruction of his father's supporters in Poland, and the restoration of Danish power in Norway. Contemporary accounts are silent on the way he dealt with the crisis. It wasn't until the middle of the thirteenth century that Icelandic historians told the 'full' story of his early victories.

By then, they'd had time to jazz things up a bit.

The story is worth recording for three reasons. Firstly, it gives a fine insight into Svein's Machiavellian mind. Secondly, it chronicles the first major engagement in which Svein, Thork-ell the Tall and Eirík of Norway, the conquerors of England, took part. Thirdly, and by far the most important point, it's a great story. If more history were like this, there would be more historians.

To the tale. Chief of the Danish settlements in Poland was the mighty fortress of Jómsborg, the original land of the free and home of the brave, which had been founded in Bluetooth's reign. The saga's account of its laws reads like a blueprint for heroic brotherhoods down the ages:

No man shall run from any opponent who is his equal in courage and equipment.

36

Each must avenge the others as his own brothers.
None shall speak fearful words in any situation, no
    matter how hopeless it looks.
Anything captured on raids shall be taken to the banner
    for fair distribution, both greater and lesser treasures,
and anyone failing to do this shall be driven away.
None shall start spreading slanders . . .

The chapter of the saga which deals with their laws finishes, 'They were thought to be great warriors. Few were their equals at that time; and they were called the Jómsvikings.' Cue fanfare.

One by one the other characters are introduced. Most are historical: Svein, Thorkell, Jarl Hákon and his bastard son Eirík, Bolesław I of Poland. Fictional, or at least historically unknown characters join them: Thorkell's elder brother Sigvaldi, the Viking Vagn of Bornholm, and Vagn's faithful sidekick Bjørn the Welshman, whom I include here because I love the idea of a Welshman called Bjørn. Bolesław, like Hákon, is paying tribute to Svein. Like Hákon, he resents it. All it needs is a spark to ignite the Baltic powder-keg.

Naturally, it starts with a woman. Sigvaldi is in love with Bolesław's daughter. In order to win the father's favour he and his Jómsvikings kidnap Svein and bring him to Poland. It does the trick. Sigvaldi marries his beloved. The hapless Svein is forced to annul the tribute and marry Bolesław's younger daughter. (The youngest had already married Oláf Tryggvason, who fled to Poland when Harald Greycloak murdered his father.) To add insult to injury, Svein realizes at the marriage feast that Sigvaldi's wife is more beautiful than his, and thus the necessary feud is born. All sagas are about feuds. Like I said, Germanic epic is mainly violence.

Soon Sigvaldi and Thorkell's father dies in Denmark. Svein

invites the Jómsvikings to the funeral feast. In case any reader should be daft enough to think that this is a friendly manoeuvre, the saga adds drily, 'Most men thought it inadvisable for them to go, and suspected that the friendship between Svein and Sigvaldi had been strained by what had happened before. But they would not hear of refusing.' Suitably prepared for skulduggery, the reader is in no way surprised when Svein gets the Viking leaders drunk – which must have presented a challenge – and suggests that they play a game: each in turn is to promise to do something to make his name famous. In case the Vikings miss the kamikaze hint, Svein himself opens the bidding, swearing that 'before three years are out I will drive Ethelred King of England from his realm'.

The scene which follows is described in stately, measured prose. This is all wrong. It wasn't a committee meeting, it was a feast. In the interests of verisimilitude, I've therefore decided to update the narrative. Think of the Jómsvikings as a rugby club at a victory dinner, all alcohol and testosterone, and you'll get the picture. Just to help, I'll provide the background noise.

Sigvaldi: 'I swear that before three years are past I will ravage Norway and kill Hákon, or die trying!'

Vikings: 'Hurrah! Wa-*heyyy*! Get in there, Siggi!'

Svein (in the style of a gameshow host, *à la* Davina McCall): 'Good one! Good luck to you and do it well. Now it's your turn, Thorkell. Do it like a man!' (That, incidentally, is a quote.)

Thorkell: 'I've ... *hic* ... I've decided to follow my brother Sigvaldi, and not to flee before I see his ship's stern.'

Vikings: 'Hurrah! Yip yip! Stern, hahaha! Thor-*kell*! Thor-*kell*!'

Svein: 'Well said! I'm sure you'll do it. Now, Búi the Fat, over to you! Let it be something *really special*!'

By the end of the evening, Búi had sworn to follow Sigvaldi, Vagn had sworn to follow the others to battle, kill Hákon's chief henchman Thorkell Leira and ravish his daughter, which must have got a great reception from the floor, and Bjørn the Welshman had sworn to go along with Vagn. Then, as the saga helpfully informs us, they all went to bed.

Next morning, as so often seems to happen, the Jómsvikings had forgotten all about it. Svein gleefully jogged their memories. The scene shouldn't require too much imagination. That sick feeling of 'I didn't, did I?. . . I couldn't have . . . Tell me I didn't . . . I *did*?. . . Oh God,' is not confined to the tenth century. Sick at heart as well as stomach, the Jómsvikings decided that the only course of action was go through with their oath. They gathered their forces and sailed north to the Limfjord, then crossed to the Oslofjord, sacking everything in their path. Unfortunately for them, a messenger escaped and brought word of the invasion to Hákon and Eirík, who promptly summoned their forces. By the time the Jómsvikings had pillaged their way round the coast, always a slow process, the Norwegians were waiting.

Naval warfare in those days was simple. The opposing fleets lined up and rowed at one another, attempting to break each other's line, grapple and board. The tactic was only practicable in calm conditions, which is why so many Viking fights took place in sheltered bays: hence the battle of the Haralds in the Limfjord. What followed was later called 'one of the two hardest battles ever fought in the Northlands'. It raged all day and into the late evening, with savage casualties on both sides. Not even a blinding sleet storm slowed the fighting. But the Jómsvikings were outnumbered, far from home and tricked into a battle they didn't want. Eventually they cracked. Sigvaldi was the first to flee. Thorkell followed. Few others escaped. The Norwegians were in no mood for mercy.

So Norway remained in Hákon's hands, but the battle was still a triumph for Svein. The Jómsviking host which had defied him was reduced to a handful of prisoners. Never again would they threaten the Baltic power balance. The few survivors were brought ashore, bound hand and foot, and the scene describing their fate is perhaps the most famous in Norse literature. Thorkell Leira, the executioner, walked along the line of captives and asked each one in turn what he thought of death, then killed him. The replies make a compendium of Viking defiance. One answered, 'I'm glad I'll be sharing my father's fate'; when asked what happened to his father, he answered with true Norse pith (or at least taking the pith), 'He died.' Another said, 'I've always wondered, will my body realize I'm dead if you behead me *really fast*? Tell you what, I'll hold up my dagger if it doesn't.' He didn't. A third said, 'I want to piss first.' (There's always one.) He then looked down at his penis, shook his head regretfully and said, 'Ah well, I'd been saving this for the Jarl's wife. Funny how things turn out.' Needless to say, his captors were not amused.

The next victim was Vagn. Thorkell asked the standard question. The reply was, 'I don't mind dying as long as I fulfil my vow.'

'And that was?'

'To kill you and **** your daughter.'

Thorkell, enraged, hacked at Vagn. 'But Bjørn the Welshman kicked Vagn's leg so that he fell over. Thorkell missed Vagn, tripped, and lost his grip on the sword, which fell and cut Vagn free. He jumped up, seized the sword and gave Thorkell his death-blow. Then Vagn said, "At least I've kept half my oath. I feel much better."' Eirík the Jarl was so impressed that he gave Vagn and Bjørn places in his household, married Vagn off to Thorkell's daughter, and spared the remaining survivors.

Now *that's* History.

As night fell on Thursday we followed a fat-arsed German tanker out of the fjord and turned north for Sweden. No other word describes tankers adequately; they may look long and elegant in profile, but seen from the stern they bulge. It was a long night, and we surfed our way through it, bleary-eyed, tight-lipped and unshaven. Just before Friday's dawn we crossed from Danish territorial waters to Swedish ones, steered past the Troubadour light marking the entrance to the Gothenburg archipelago, and picked up the first of the channel buoys. All night it had been blowing hard from the west, but now we were in behind the bulwark of the islands; after the permanent challenge of negotiating the waves it was an effort just to stay awake. Gradually the night was lifting. Slowly the shapes of islands came into view on either hand, low, smooth, rounded like arching porpoises. The sky grew brighter. The lights of the channel buoys faded. Ahead the dark coastline opened into the mouth of the Göta Älv river. Car headlights like jewels traced along the banks and poured in a steady procession across the river-bridge. Everywhere lights shone, orange floodlights on the oil refinery, rippling flashes of amber on the great Gothenburg radio mast, aching white spotlights on the container docks, winking yellow pinpoints where some roadmen had made an early start. Beyond the bridge the great white Stena ferries blazed like the Wembley floodlights. Orange streetlamps glowed, quick-changing traffic lights, strip-lights in office windows. Slowly they faded. Dawn came, grey and warm. Dead ahead was a tower-block with a sloping roof, streaked with red and white glass, a multi-use office-block known to Gothenburgers as *Lipstiftet*, the Lipstick. To port a giant drydock loomed; on its side was printed 'Welcome' in half a dozen languages. Beyond it to starboard was a cluster of old steamers, hung with lights and bunting, restaurant ships, a museum and a youth hostel. Beyond them an

41

old Second World War frigate sheltered a cluster of ancient warships. Beyond them, yachts, a stone quay, a narrow harbour mouth and at the base of the Lipstick, a colossal four-masted square-rigger, her spars thick and yellow against the dawn.

'Anywhere in there,' said Fred the Dark softly, pointing. Between the quay and the square-rigger a little square pool was crammed to bursting with pleasure boats. 'That's Lilla Bommen harbour. That's the Opera House behind it,' indicating a sharp-edged confection of steel and glass. 'It's a good place.'

I looked at it without enthusiasm. There was so little free space I could have walked from one side of the harbour to the other over the boats.

'It's very popular,' he added.

'So I see.'

I picked up the VHF and called the harbourmaster. Early though it was, he was on the job.

'Lilla Bommen, *Peregrino*, have you got space, over?'

'*Peregrino*, Lilla Bommen, how long are you?'

'Eleven metres.'

There was a short pause. 'What's that in feet?' asked the harbourmaster. Sweden's only been metric for a couple of centuries, so they're not quite used to it yet.

'Thirty-seven foot.'

'Okay . . . How wide are you?'

I calculated frantically. I hadn't expected to go imperial. 'Eleven foot.'

Another pause. 'What's that in metres?' came the question. Whatever happened to international standards?

'Three metres, sixty.'

'Sorry, no room. Can you tie up outside?'

I looked at the outer quay. Right by the harbour two

42

Norwegian-flagged boats were moored side by side. Behind them, a well-worn yacht with a Russian tricolour. Behind him, a Swede. Behind him, space.

'Fenders out,' I said. The two Freds hurried along the deck, dropping the fenders over the side, getting the ropes ready. I concentrated on the wind and the current and bringing her in without a bump.

Just before six a.m. we tied up outside Gothenburg Opera House and went into town for a coffee. The Freds knew an all-night café in the student quarter, famous for its cakes and pies. We staggered in, salt-stained, unshaven and clad in full-body waterproofs and sea-boots, made for the counter, peered, pondered.

'Well, order then,' said Magnus with a grin. 'In Swedish.'

I drew a deep breath, smiled at the waitress and embarked on my very first Swedish conversation:

'*Hej. Jag skulle vilja ha en bit av den där rabarbertårtan, takk!*'

'Sure. How do you say *rabarber* in English?'

Welcome to Scandinavia.

4

GOTHENBURG ARCHIPELAGO

'And when Hákon made landfall off the Göta skerries
in the east, he came ashore and made a great sacrifice.'
Saga of Oláf Tryggvason

My first impression of Gothenburg was not favourable. I've always admired spontaneity, but that Friday morning was an antidote to every spontaneous bit of enthusiasm I've ever felt. I haven't seen so many hostile aliens since *Independence Day* hit the big screen. The esplanade in front of the Opera House was swarming with them, suited businessmen on the way to work and early-morning yacht fanciers come to admire the boats in the harbour. Dozens of spectators stopped to watch as we worked on deck repairing the ravages of the voyage, and every time I looked up to say hello they flinched and hurried away. And I'd even shaved. My main technique for meeting interesting strangers has always been to make eye contact, grin and see what happens. After three hours in Lilla Bommen I was ready to admit defeat. Not one passerby had met my gaze. There's not a town or port in Britain where that's happened to me. Despite the example of the Freds and Magnus, I was beginning to believe that Sweden had absorbed the Volvo philosophy right into its soul.

Then Fate, fed up of waiting for others to smile on me, decided to do so herself.

She took the form of Fred the Blond's mother Barbro, who met us at the harbour just after nine o'clock: a slim, straight-backed woman with chestnut hair, ironic eyes, and an elegance of movement and expression that I had thought reserved for the French. She threw herself into her son's arms, emerged to welcome me to Sweden in fabulous English, and invited us all to brunch. Fred the Dark and Magnus declined, saying they had to get the train to Stockholm to meet their parents' yacht; Fred and I accepted.

Four hours after docking we were in a smart restaurant by the Göta Älv, sipping vile Swedish coffee. Only a truly rough crossing could have made me appreciate reaching those solid grounds. I was just wondering whether Swedes mixed glass into their coffee the same way they did with *snus* when Barbro turned to me and said, 'I've been invited to a party in the archipelago this afternoon.' (Yes, she used the word 'archipelago'. See what I mean about her English?) 'I told Jan you're here and he'd love to meet you. You're invited too.'

Four hours after docking I'd accepted the *second* invitation of the voyage. Things were starting well.

I tried to sleep that afternoon, but it didn't work. What Swedish coffee lacks in bouquet it makes up for in authority. When Fred and Barbro came to pick me up at five I was washed, shaven, smartly dressed and buzzing like a radio with a loose connection. Which is a pretty apt description. They poured me into the back seat and took off for the ferry terminal, chatting happily in Swedish. We drove past ranks of industrial estates: through a long tunnel; into a wasteland of grey-green bushes and shivering birch trees; past a colossal Volvo factory which might have explained the atmosphere prevailing in the city; and swung down towards a shining sea inset with low, smooth, dark islands.

It's a ten-minute ride from the mainland to the Hönö terminal, on a yellow rust-streaked slab-sided monster of a ferry, open to the sky. Fred and I scrambled out of the car as soon as we'd boarded, and climbed to a minuscule viewing platform, letting the wind blow the cobwebs from our minds and staring out over the bare, rocky skerries, white-sailed yachts tacking between them. The sea was flat, stitched with ripples. It was a different world from the surging dance outside the islands. From the terminal we drove past wooden houses painted white, red or yellow, over a narrow causeway, through snug streets lined with white fences, and finally drew up outside a tall house perched on a slanting plane of bedrock. Two small cars and a large motorboat on a trailer were parked outside.

'We're here,' said Barbro, and led us round the house and up a flight of steps to the balcony. As I set my foot on the topmost stair, a mad Swede in King-Kong slippers opened the door.

I spent the week following Jan's party in Gothenburg. I hadn't planned it that way – in fact I'd been hoping to take off for Norway as soon as I'd caught up on sleep. Midsummer was already past, and I wanted to see the north before the seasons turned. But July in Sweden is holiday time, and holiday time is social time. Whatever their attitude towards complete strangers, Swedes love welcoming friends of friends of friends.

Barbro started it. Two days after Jan's epochal party on Hönö she invited me to her house on the mainland for some akvavit and prawns. The day after that I returned to Hönö to meet some more of Jan's friends at a prawns-and-akvavit party; the day after *that* Barbro invited me to an akvavit-and-prawns party at a friend's place on the mainland. One of the guests was a girl of my age called René, a marine biologist who'd just done her Master's at the University of Hawaii. She happened to live just down the road; we agreed to meet for a pizza (prawn) the following evening, and ended up chatting until midnight. Jan had also been at that party; by popular request we reprised our legendary 'Wild West Show' duet. Swedish culture will never be the same again.

The next day there weren't any parties planned. I slept late, then walked to the harbour chandlery to pretend to look at spare parts for my generator (which had broken down during the North Sea crossing), and actually to chat with the red-headed shop-keeper, Mia. (Actually she's blonde, but there's a strong trend for blondes in Sweden to dye their hair red, which says something about the high incidence of blondeness in the population.) I was halfway round the harbour basin when two middle-aged men sitting on a bench with a four-pack of lager shouted at me.

I turned round. '*Förlåt?*' I asked politely.

'Oh, you're *English!*' the neater-looking one exclaimed: a man of about forty in battered denims with a short, energetic haircut and very level blue eyes. He was the first stranger to make eye contact all week.

'*Scottish*,' I growled, which is about 60 per cent true. He grinned and threw his arms wide.

'That's even better! Sit down and have a drink!'

To his surprise, I did.

His name was Tommy. This is another common Scandinavian name. His friend, tall, unshaven and lugubrious, was Bengt. They were construction workers, they told me; in fact Tommy owned the company, as I discovered when he gave me his business card. They often came down to the harbour on sunny days 'to watch the pretty ladies and try and get a fuck', as Bengt said, then turned away to call 'Hello, pretty lady!' to a passing woman. She smiled and walked on, uncon-cerned. In Sweden you can get away with anything if you're drunk. They were supposed to be at work, but they'd been at a party until dawn, exchanging naked massages with a couple of nurses, and decided to take the day off. It's easy when you're the boss.

'Have another drink,' Tommy urged me, pulling another four-pack from under the bench.

'I can't,' I said regretfully. 'I've got to get to the shop.'

He nodded sagely. 'There's a sexy girl in there,' he said as if that explained it, which of course it did.

'I'd noticed.'

'What are you doing later?'

I thought fast. Did I want to spend a drunken evening with a couple of lecherous locals? Well, was there a better way of seeing the country?

'Nothing much.'

'Good!' Quickly we set a date: seven o'clock at my boat, and I hurried off to look at – boating equipment.

At quarter to seven I was on my knees in the cabin, surrounded by twisted wires. The mended generator was purring away, but no power was getting through, and I had no idea why. I was about to start in on some hammer therapy when Tommy and Bengt swung aboard. They didn't need to swing, but they'd been drinking all afternoon, so I guess it was appropriate.

'What's the problem?' asked Tommy as they came into the cabin.

'No idea,' I said bitterly.

'Bengt,' he called sharply; and to me, 'He's my best electrician.'

'What? But . . .' I was going to say something about taking an evening off, but Bengt had pushed me gently aside and was already peering into the fuse-box.

'Has he got a multi-meter?' he asked Tommy, in English. Possibly he thought he was using Swedish. Tommy relayed the message.

'No,' I said.

'No,' said Tommy.

'Oh,' said Bengt. 'Has Torsten?'

'Has Torsten?' Tommy asked me.

'Who's Torsten?' I asked.

'Oh.' A light flickered back on in his head. He pulled out his mobile phone. As I watched in bewilderment, he made a call in rapid Swedish, hung up, and told me, 'Torsten's my other electrician. He's coming out with a multi-meter.'

'But . . .' It was gone seven o'clock. I couldn't afford the call-out charges for an emergency electrician. Tommy understood my distress.

'Buy him a beer and he'll do it for free.' Then, as if to a toddler, 'I told him you're a friend of mine. We don't take money from friends. Now,' he added, rubbing his hands and looking around the cabin, 'how about a drink?'

We were sipping Scotch and gossiping in English when Torsten came in: a bulky, taciturn man with a large toolbag. Tommy fired a volley of instructions at him, turned to me and said, 'He'll fix it for you. I've got a digital video camera in the car; can I film your boat?'

'Er . . . yes.'

So while Torsten grunted and probed in the fuse-box, Tommy sat in the doorway filming everything that moved, and Bengt leaned close to me and told me in a tearful undertone that his girlfriend had left him three years before, 'But I still love her, I still want to fuck her senseless, I do.' You couldn't fault his command of idiom.

After a few minutes Saint Torsten started doing things with a screwdriver. Shortly after that there was a crackle of sparks, a gasp, a curse and then a triumphant 'Ha!'

'Try the power,' said Tommy, eye still glued to the viewfinder. I flicked on the hob, and a cheerful halogen glow winked.

'Told you he'd fix it. Now, what about a beer?'

We adjourned to the *Viking*, the four-master just upstream, once a grain ship, now one of Gothenburg's more popular hostelries. Two of the bars were closed and a third was hosting a private function, but the fourth, on deck and right in the bows, was doing a brisk trade in hideously costly alcohol. Forget all the stories you ever heard about overpriced drink in Scandinavia – the truth is worse. Two girls in low-cut tops were behind the bar; a dozen drinkers leant on the bar itself, or on high tables around it. Tommy and Bengt oozed up to the bar between two unattached women of their own age.

'Hello, pretty ladies,' said Bengt, a silly smile dripping down his face. They smiled tolerantly and carried on their conversation over his head. When I turned back to Tommy I almost rammed into a spreading expanse of trouser-seat; cheek to cheek, as it were. He'd hauled himself right up onto the bar and was busy videoing the barmaid's cleavage on maximum zoom. She didn't seem to mind. I looked around hastily for avenging bouncers of a rather different sort, but they were conspicuously absent. When I said Swedes can get away with anything if they're drunk, I meant it.

'Come on, have a drink!' Tommy told me, sliding back down to ground level. 'We are!' And, leaning in close, he added in a confidential whisper that probably reached to the Opera House, 'I want to kiss her nipples.'

There wasn't much I could say.

Sweden has what you might call a special relationship with alcohol. It's a mildly social-democratic country in the way that ant colonies are mildly collectivized. National welfare is an overwhelming priority. In the mid-1970s the trend had become so extreme that the Ministry of Health ran a poster campaign advising everyone to eat at least six slices of wholemeal bread a day. And, from motives of pure altruism and a sincere desire to help their fellow-men, they declared alcohol a state monopoly and organized a system of state liquor stores, the *Systembolaget*, where fine wines, spirits and the stronger beers are sold with the sort of tax mark-up that the British government reserves for its petrol. All, of course, to spare its citizens the pains of alcoholism. Oddly, it doesn't seem to have worked. Every day I crossed from the harbour to a neighbouring shopping centre via a pedestrian walkway which smelt as you'd expect in an area where the public toilets shut at sunset. Every day I passed a small community of unwashed, unshaven, inebriated types clinging onto cans of beer, watching life roar by on the six-lane highway.

On my last day in Gothenburg I paid a visit to the main Systembolaget myself. I was heading out to Hönö that afternoon, and I wanted to bring Jan and Anita a present. It was an experience. Two mall security guards loomed outside a wide glass sliding door. Inside a red sign invited visitors to take a ticket; below it was the kind of ticket-machine normally seen in travel agents'. Beyond that the shop opened up into a vast semicircular bay. The floor was of polished pine, the walls gleaming white, illuminated by recessed spotlights: it might have been a designer furniture store. Free-standing display cases held individual bottles, like museum exhibits. Around the walls glittering cabinets held further samples, each with its own label, giving origin, year, price and stock number. Right ahead, in the belly of the semicircle, was a huge wooden counter with a dozen checkouts. Further screens above allocated successive queue numbers to free tills. Forget anything democratic like picking out the bottle you want. Take a ticket, pick a stock number, wait for your turn, and then ask the young lady to fetch it for you. Nicely. There are always security guards in earshot, and traditional Swedish tolerance is *not* in their ethos. I had seen a system like that before, but only in the tax-free tourist shops in Egypt. Finding Islamic control in the EU was, to put it mildly, surprising.

Between traditional Lutheranism and current controls, you might be forgiven for thinking that Swedes disapprove of heavy drinking. But as I'd already seen, nothing could be further from the truth. Ex-pats living in Sweden normally claim that the locals only have two levels of sobriety: dead sober and dead drunk. If so, it might explain the government's desire to cut down on alcoholism. However, it seems unlikely, because the central tenet of Swedish life is the mysterious and all-pervading *lagom*.

There's no adequate English equivalent for *lagom*, which is a shame, because I seriously doubt whether you can go to Sweden without hearing all about it. Dictionaries usually define it as 'just right', a fair approximation of the original meaning: 'the amount of mead you should swig from the horn before passing it on so that everyone at the camp-fire gets an equal share and there's none left over at the end'. Honest. But the word has now taken on a far wider significance. It must be something to do with the social-justice thing. *Everything* in life should be *lagom*, moderate, neither too little nor too much; Goldilocks' Smallest Bear was undoubtedly Swedish. Looking poor is a definite no-no, but so is looking too rich. Some friends of mine went so far as to say that Swedes actively resent those who make a fortune. Others argued that it's okay to be filthy rich, as long as you don't show it. Whatever the rights of the matter, both camps agree that *lagom* is critical. Perhaps Tommy and Bengt were so tolerated because their binge was, indeed, only moderate by Swedish standards. In that case, God help their livers if they ever drink seriously.

After a week in Gothenburg I moved downriver to Hönö. Jan had spent most of the week bombarding me with invitations, and I liked him far too much to refuse. Having signally failed to catch up on sleep, I headed out into the teeth of a westerly gale. The blessed islands intercepted the worst of the weather, but the eight-mile stretch of open river provided more than enough space for the waves to build up again, so I spent a merry hour or so slamming from crest to crest in a perpetual shower of spray. It was frightening for the first few minutes. Rough weather always is. You can't help thinking, 'What if this gets worse?' Gradually I accepted that there weren't any hurricanes in the immediate vicinity, and started to enjoy myself. Power-boating in calm seas is even more boring than motorway driving. Wave-dodging adds a certain zest to life. It was a skill I'd practised many times in Belize, but that had been in a fibreglass skiff. Making the step up to a twelve-ton cruiser kept me fully occupied.

The three main islands of the Gothenburg archipelago lie a mile and a half offshore, so close together that you could chuck a stone from one to the next. The southernmost and smallest is Fotö, a cluster of steep outcrops tiered with houses. Its harbour is a tiny affair, a stony gut winding into the island, so short of flat land that the fishermen's huts project out from the rocks on stilts. With their weathered timbers and the jumble of nets and lobster-pots, they give the place a Caribbean look. From Fotö a high single-span concrete bridge leads to Hönö, its larger neighbour, over a narrow strait studded with skerries and underwater forests of kelp. Hönö might be a flattened version of Fotö, lower and less rugged, but with the same bald granite heads scoured by the wind, the same rambling wooden houses. Every one flies the Swedish flag. To the north again is Öckerö, the chief island in the chain, site of the ferry terminal. Like Hönö, it's become a suburb of Gothenburg, every inch of flat land crammed with houses, old plots of land being subdivided and re-divided to satisfy the growing demand. Until 1961 the islands were a separate world, a slowly dying cluster of fishing harbours battling rising costs and dwindling catches. Then the government opened the ferry. Now barely one per cent of the islanders still work in the fisheries. The rest commute to the mainland.

Late on that windy afternoon I turned into Hönö Klåva (pronounced 'clover') port for the first time and tied up to the long stone quay. It's an artificial harbour, built around a mile-wide bay behind the island of Långholm. The outer basin is little more than an approach channel; giant marker posts to starboard delineate the entry, and behind them broad-backed rocks stud the bay. You don't sail there unless you want to lose a keel. Round a sharp corner to port is the sport harbour, its stone jetties divided into numerous boxes; to starboard is the working harbour, concrete quays, tarred sheds, bullet-browed trawlers and an eternal reek of nets. Along the quay in the outer basin, the fishing boats come to unload their catch and take on ice. In the autumn it's piled high with lobster-pots. On the long summer evenings the fishermen stretch out their nets to mend them. The island's two pubs stand side by side at one end, in converted fishermen's workshops. Next to them is the island's Fisheries Museum; in front of it a replica longship rocks at the quayside. Behind that, three narrow streets hold all the island's shops: bakery, grocery, super-market, fishmonger, hairdresser, florist, jeweller and diving and adventure shop. Something for everyone. Behind them the rocks rise in grey-green tiers, westwards, towards the sunset.

I felt at home the second I'd tied up. Gothenburg had been full of noises, but here it was almost silent. The odd car roared past the harbour, a few boats thudded out to sea, the wind rattled the yachts' metal shrouds against the masts, gulls called and circled, but somehow as I looked across to Långholm and the bulk of Fotö beyond, the scene reminded me of the tarns below Scafell Pike: the same stubborn stone, the same clusters of sour green grass, the same smooth, gleaming islets lapped by endless ripples. Ducks and divers ducked and dived around them. The gale whistled through the broken windows of an abandoned shed. Once a trawler pulled out of the main harbour and swept majestically past me, a sole crewman coiling a hawser as thick as his arm. He looked at me, at the Red Ensign I was flying, and at the last moment gave me a friendly wave. Seconds later they forged out past the breakwater and were lurching out to sea. *Sooner you than me*, I thought, and waved back.

I rang Jan to let him know I'd arrived. 'Good,' he said, 'come on up,' and how could I refuse? I found him and Anita sitting on their balcony sunning themselves, while their backpacker son honed his juggling skills on the grass below. A cup of tea steamed in front of an empty chair; Jan waved me to it, grinned, and started asking about the journey. They wouldn't hear of me going back to the boat that evening; I stayed for tea, then for a drink, then to listen to Jan's jazz collection, and ended up stumbling back to the harbour long after midnight. I was just surfacing at ten the next morning when Jan knocked on the window.

'I was just fetching the bread. Come and have breakfast,' he told me. 'Anita's put the kettle on.'

Adoption is as simple as that.

5

ROGALAND

'The Jómsvikings kept straight on to the Limfjord, and
from there sailed out to sea . . . sighting land at Agdir
and heading north to Rogaland.'

Saga of Oláf Tryggvason

I lingered for five days on Hönö. It ruined my plans, but the
whole point of travelling is to meet people, and with Jan and
Anita I'd found a home from home. Every morning Jan
dropped round to fetch me for breakfast. Every evening we
ate together in their house or on my boat. Twice I took them
cruising round the Öckerö archipelago, dodging between the
hump-backed rocks to watch seals sunning themselves. Three
times Jan took me on car- and ferry-tours of the islands, showing me churches and bays and sun-drenched hidden dells. I
would have happily stayed a month; but the seasons were
rolling on and I wanted to see Norway before the autumn
storms started. I left with promises to return, and steamed
across a bright-blue sea to Skagen in Denmark, where hordes
of Norwegians and Swedes treated the place pretty much as
the Brits treat Calais, a cheap place to stock up on booze. From
there I cut across the main shipping lane to Kristiansand in
Norway, and followed the appalling wrecking coast west and
north to the green, rock-studded fields of Rogaland.

Every mile of the way was hero territory. Most of Scandinavia's history was decided in the Skagerrak and Kattegat. Hönö itself lies off the coast of Götaland (pronounced 'yurtaland'), not to be confused with Jutland ('yutland' or 'yulland') or the Baltic island of Gotland. The tribe who gave their name to the region were the Götar, Gautar or Geats (pronounced 'yats'), who are not to be confused with Jutes, Goths or any other Germanic marauders; their greatest king was Beowulf, hero of the Anglo-Saxon poem. His story criss-crossed the Kattegat: he sailed from the Göta Älv ('river of the Geats') to Sjaelland to aid Hrothgar, king of the Danes. He came home in time to intervene in the wars of the Swedes, a small tribe from the Stockholm area. (In those days 'Denmark' covered the whole of western Sweden south of the Göta Älv.) He became king when his lord died raiding the Frisian islands. The sundering seas are simply the conduit by which invading forces pass. It's no wonder the coastguard was one of the highest Danish officers after the king.

By the time *Beowulf* was written, Norway had arrived on the international scene. Harald Fairhair united the kingdom at the battle of Hafrsfjord, southwest of Stavanger, and turned his eyes abroad. From then on until Norway's union with Denmark in the late fourteenth century, the main activity recorded in the kings' sagas is 'harrying' in the Kattegat, the Oslofjord and the Baltic. Every chieftain in the Northlands seems to have done it, Norwegians, Danes and Swedes mingling in a wild whirl of alliances and attacks. Gradually the world of the sagas widens to take in Iceland, the British Isles, even America and the eastern Mediterranean, but the right-angled neck of sea between Lindesnes, Skagen and the Göta Älv is always the key.

Nothing changes. The same stretch of water saw the passage of the heavy traders of the Hanseatic League, the fishing fleets which were Northern Europe's most important resource, diplomats shuttling back and forth at the behest of the four-teenth-century Queen Margaret, who quite without authority bound Norway, Sweden and Denmark together in a union that lasted a hundred and twenty-six years, more diplomats hurrying to Sweden when that kingdom finally achieved Great Power status at the end of the Thirty Years' War, Nelson's dreadnaughts, Dönitz' invasion fleet, the pocket battleships *Scharnhorst* and *Gneisenau*, and a thousand admirers of Danny Kaye's Hans Christian Andersen. Keels leave no mark on the water and shipwrecks crumble away, but still, for me, the ironbound coasts and grey sea lanes between Norway, Sweden and Denmark hold a special magic. Three miles off-shore the mountains heave into view, stark and forbidding, reaching up to forested heights. At that distance, buildings are invisible: Svein and Oláf must have seen the same view.

Four days after leaving Hönö, I steamed past the Hafrsfjord, rounded a low headland, and ran down between wooded isles towards the lights of Stavanger.

It was the worst arrival of the voyage. Stavanger's best-known harbour is right at the head of its fjord, a narrow U of land closed off by two pontoons forming an awkward dogleg. Note the emphasis in that sentence: *awkward*. The entry channel can't be more than ten metres wide, which is a real sod when you're in an eleven-metre boat, especially when some clown has parked halfway down it.

I shouldn't have tried. I should have ducked out and made for an alternative harbour, of which God knows there are enough in Stavanger, a city which spreads across two head-lands and numerous islands. But I'd been driving for twelve hours already, and it was enough. I turned into the dogleg. I dodged the inconvenient boat. I misjudged the turn and scraped my port side along two other yachts. Someone yelled at me from the jetty. A furious boat-owner appeared on deck, hurled abuse and jabbed at my hull with a broom. A gust of wind caught me and I struck again. Puce with embarrassment, I pushed off, turned round and fled.

I was well out into the fjord on the way to another harbour when I heard someone shouting 'Come back!'

I turned back. There didn't seem a lot of point running. A young lady in a Red Cross jumpsuit was standing on the outermost pontoon. It wasn't easy pulling alongside: wind and current were both against me and I was shaking like a leaf. I managed with gritted teeth and looked down. She was standing by the back end of my boat, ready to deliver a stern reprimand.

'I'm in charge here,' she said angrily. The Red Cross runs most Norwegian harbours; it's a neat way of collecting funds. 'I want you to leave.'

I gaped at her.

'People have complained,' she said. 'I want you to leave.'

'I already was,' I said coldly.

'What?'

'What?'

We exchanged a glare that would have melted tarmac.

'I want you to leave,' she repeated. She could do that bit.

'Right. Do I have to pay anyone?'

'What?'

Glare. Glare.

I put on my sweetest, most venomous tones and repeated the question in French. Then, just to really annoy her, went on in every other irrelevant language I could think of. Which added absolutely nothing to the amount of information conveyed, but made me feel better. Finally she got the message.

'No. Just go.'

I turned my back on her, pulled in my mooring line, swung the bow round and blasted out to sea. My wake set the pontoon rocking and washed all over her nice clean shoes. When I looked back a few minutes later she was still staring. I just hope I annoyed her as much as she annoyed me.

I finally stopped in a harbour on one of the city's islands. It wasn't easy: there were free berths aplenty, but could I find a harbourmaster? I traipsed twice round the harbour, was directed to his house by a kindly stranger, thumped on his door, and then was told by another passerby that he was on holiday. Well, what else would the master of a tourist harbour do in the holiday season?

'Has he left a replacement?'

'No.'

So I sorted out my own mooring, plugged into a spare power-point, and went for a walk to calm down. Two minutes later it started to rain. Some places captivate me the first time I see them. Stavanger wasn't one of them.

It rained for three days, by the end of which I was so gloomy I was considering jumping ship and scuttling home, or rather, the other way round. The locals were just as unforthcoming as the people of Gothenburg, my ego was lacerated by my incompetent arrival, and a leaking hatch which I'd instructed the Dutch boatyard to mend and which they'd assured me was watertight had started dripping all over again. To add insult to injury, the generator, which I'd had repaired in Gothenburg, broke down yet again, and when I checked the manual I discovered that the nearest service station was back in Sweden. For three days I moped, sitting in my millionaire's pleasure yacht cooking on a small and smoky camping stove. Then I took action.

Across the water from my harbour, by a jetty lined with a thousand used truck tyres, was a diving store. I'd noticed it on my first day. It's hard to miss a nine-foot Day-Glo model frogman. Shortly after nine o'clock on a cool grey dripping morning I walked in, hoping for a friendly chat with a fellow-professional. I had no intention of diving in Norway's biggest oil-port, but it would be a nice way to spend a morning.

Not quite all Scandinavians are called Fred or Tommy, but you might be excused for thinking so. The instructor who welcomed me was Fred Anton, a short, stocky lad with a Number Two haircut and a size-sixteen grin. His colleagues were Tommy and Tom Willy, taller, but with the same coiffures and general demeanour. They all spoke beautiful English, though for reasons best known to himself Fred Anton affected a Scottish lilt. They'd done most of their diving in Norway. I hadn't, so for a happy hour we swapped anecdotes of warm- and cold-water exploration, wrecks, reefs and sharks. After a while we turned to discussing students, and then the group they were currently training. For a month they'd been teaching them in the local swimming pool. The following weekend they were going to take them into open water for the first time.

'What are they like?' I asked. My depression had melted away: after so long feeling incompetent on the boat, I was back in a world I understood.

'Good,' Tommy said. 'They breathe too fast and they forget about buoyancy, but they don't panic. They'll be fine.'

'How was Tine?' asked Tom Willy, and I sensed a certain *frisson* in the air. Fred Anton rolled his eyes.

'In that wetsuit? Oh, laddie!'

'Pretty girl?' I asked innocently.

'Oh wow.' Tommy grinned. Tom Willy rolled his eyes. 'She smiled at me. I tell you, laddie, the water boiled!'

I laughed. 'I wish I'd been there!'

There was a sudden, ringing silence.

'Excuse us,' said Tom Willy, and they went into a huddle. Fred Anton's head popped up.

'You've done drysuit diving before?'

I had.

Tom Willy surfaced. 'How many students have you taught?'

'About a hundred and forty.'

They looked at one another, then started to grin. I knew what was coming. I grinned too.

'Look, Tommy's wife's pregnant. She's got to go into hospital on Saturday and he really wants to go with her, but we'll have to find a replacement instructor. How about it?' Fred Anton asked me.

'Sounds good,' I replied, and that was that.

The dive site was off the island of Mosterøya, a few miles to the north of Stavanger. Once it had a ferry terminal and a little fishing port, but they'd closed down when the economic might of the area shifted into oil; now the island was a green haven of fields and woods, scattered with holiday homes. That same day I left the still-masterless harbour and moved up to Askje, the harbour on Mosterøya, where yet another tyre-lined quay stood empty. The dive centre had bought the terminal and was busily converting it into a school, complete with kit stores, classrooms, accommodation and air-compressors: pine-wood boards were stacked under the eaves and the whole harbour smelt of resin. Behind it the island rose, greener and gentler than Hönö. All around, narrow webs of sea separated other islands, some smoothly sloping, others plummeting sheer into the water. Behind them in the cloud-checked distance, the saw-backed highlands of Norway rose. A few yachts cruised lazily down the channels; a long procession of ferries circled the townships on the fjord. Prepubescent boys on mountain bikes sped around the deserted car park, shouting and spraying gravel; a couple came to introduce themselves, stare at the boat and hurry off. Next day they made a point of waving and shouting 'Hei Ben!' whenever their friends were there to admire; I made a point of replying. By the end of the week I had a regular fan-club. The horrors of my arrival were quite forgotten. I spent my days sunning myself, reading, writing, chatting with Fred Anton and his girlfriend Anne Gro, who popped by whenever they got the chance, and drinking strange herbal liqueurs with German tourists.

On Saturday the students arrived.

We'd been ready for them since dawn. Being an instructor is about 20 per cent diving; the rest is a combination of mob psychology and odd-jobbing. No dive centre in history ever employed a specialist to do a job which an instructor could botch: in my time I've been boat-handler, engine repairman, equipment servicer, tea-wallah, painter, plumber, porter and translator, and I've got off lightly. We started the day by filling two dozen dive tanks; a slow and noisy job, but it allowed us to wake up and start discussing Monty Python, Fred Anton's other passion. I was really cramming in the new experiences, I've never serenaded the sunrise with the 'Philosophers' Song' before ... One of the students' drysuits had a leaky valve which needed replacing; while I fixed it Tom Willy sorted through piles of one- and two-kilo lead weights, making up a series of weight-belts. Fred Anton, in charge of life support and first aid, was making the coffee, the most important job on site. Then came the inevitable hunt for the talcum powder – vital for getting into a latex-sealed suit without flesh wounds – and the struggle into our 'woolly bears', thermal jumpsuits worn under the drysuit. After that we shambled around in slippers, checking that every equipment box held a buoyancy jacket, mask, fins, snorkel and regulators.

By the time the students turned up the whole forecourt was littered with gear. They stood in a little nervous cluster on one side, as students always do, then slowly moved towards us. Tom Willy made the introductions: 'This is Ben. He's helping us instruct today.' He neglected to tell me who they were so, as they spread out and started putting their gear together, I went to mingle.

One, at least, was easy to spot: a tall girl with flowing blonde hair and green eyes, wearing a black T-shirt with 'National Springboard Championships' printed in white. She smiled at me as I bent over her air tank.

'Hi, I'm Tine,' she said unnecessarily. 'Is this right?'

It was right. She smiled again. I felt slightly dazed.

'Okay, Ben?' Fred Anton called. I could *feel* his grin through the back of my neck.

'Fine,' I answered, and moved swiftly onwards. The next client was a middle-aged oil executive with a paunch and disconcertingly hard eyes. He'd put his gear together perfectly and was already starting to advise his neighbour. Unlike most macho students with that irritating habit, he was doing it right. By the time I'd checked him Tom Willy had done the rest. The sun was already high and strong, and we were starting to sweat. We clustered into the shade of the building, and Tom Willy gave the briefing.

To keep things simple, we'd decided to split the group into two for the underwater work, but let Tom Willy handle the briefings, since my Norwegian wasn't what you'd call fluent. Or even existent. The first dive was an orientation session, getting the victims used to the fact that the sea is not a swimming pool, so the briefing took some time. I leant against a wall and watched my students watch the briefing. You can learn a lot about a diver from their behaviour up above. It saves unpleasant surprises later.

Being a diving instructor has to rate pretty high on the list
of World's Coolest Professions. No job involving sun, sea, sand
and Beautiful People in tight suits is ever going to lose you
street-cred. Add exotic locations and ever-present danger, and
the combination is pure magic. Admittedly, the first time I
told a girl in a bar that I was a diving instructor, she stared
at me in undisguised admiration and then burst out, 'But aren't
you afraid they'll crash?', but once I'd sorted out my speech
impediment I was onto a winner.

So much for glamorous dreams.

Diving is an unrivalled opportunity to explore the wonders
of the natural world. *Instructing*, on the other hand, is all about
ignoring them completely while you watch your students do
what you told them not to. Good instructors have the reflexes
of a mamba, the slit-eyed intensity of a wolverine on a diet,
and a stress level that leaves Wall Street traders looking very
laid-back indeed. It's a survival thing. Any instructor who acts
cool and sophisticated underwater hasn't been doing it long
enough.

Drysuit diving in particular is not a glamour activity. Glamour and seven-millimetre neoprene just don't mix. Even Tine,
who makes tracksuits and smelly trainers look like Gucci,
walked like a penguin in her drysuit, and we mortals were
beyond description. Tom Willy had given me four students:
the hard-eyed Ørjan, his girlfriend Inge, a red-faced front-row
forward of an oil executive called Øystein, and a smiling young
man named, inevitably, Tommy. We struggled into our drysuits and zipped one another up: a great way of building trust,
if you get it wrong you'll find the North Sea pouring into your
boots, and it won't stop until it reaches your neckline. They
helped one another into their equipment, groaning under the
weight of a twelve-kilo dive tank and buoyancy jacket, and
went into their safety checks: Inge hesitant, Ørjan confident,

prompting her, Tommy and Øystein cheerful right up until the moment I pointed out that they'd forgotten to turn their air on. I made my own check – jacket inflator and deflator, suit ditto, weights, jacket releases, air supply, fins and mask – and led them to the jetty.

'Don't jump on any jellyfish!' Fred Anton called cheerily. I laughed, shuffled to the edge of the jetty, and looked down onto a nightmare. There were jellyfish everywhere. It looked like the world's nastiest school dinner. There was no way I could send my students into that.

At times like this an instructor's duty is clear: tell your assistant to clear the things away. Failing that, there's only one option.

'It is a far, far better thing I do . . .' I muttered, and jumped.

My fins slammed into the water. My jacket kicked my shoulders. Delicious cold spray spattered my face. Then I was splashing in a circle pushing amoebae away with my fins, a human Moulinex. When the soup dissipated, I called my students in, splash-flop. They hit the water, lurched towards me, realized they weren't sinking and began to relax.

'Everybody ready?' Automatically my hand-signals echoed the words: ringed thumb and forefinger sweeping round the circle, *All OK*? They nodded, nervous or impatient.

'Let's go.' Thumbs down: *Dive*.

One instructor and four students. According to the manuals, it's a good ratio. The visibility in Askje harbour was relatively good, six metres at least, and my foursome were nervous enough to stick close to my fins. Losing sight of them wasn't going to be a problem. Losing my grip on them might be. Whatever the manuals say, any instructor who goes diving with more students than he has hands is going to have his work cut out. One look at them underwater told me that it was going to be one of those days.

The whole secret of diving lies in buoyancy control. Any object placed in a philosopher's bath will, to quote that famous phrase, 'experience upthrust equal to the weight of fluid displaced'. If the object is denser than water, it'll sink. If it's less dense, it'll float. And if it's the same density, it'll remain at whatever depth you place it, happily breathing bubbles and admiring the wonders of nature. The whole point of diving is to pump just enough air into your buoyancy jacket or drysuit to create that neutrally buoyant effect. Unfortunately, most divers have to breathe. Breathing in adds air to the body, which starts floating up. Breathing out dumps it and makes you sink. Under control, this phenomenon is a pleasure: you can cruise above and around cliffs and coral heads without ever touching your jacket inflator. Out of control, it can take you on a fast trip to the surface.

And air density varies with depth. A balloon containing one litre of air at the surface will be compressed to half a litre ten metres under. A buoyancy jacket perfectly adjusted to hold steady ten metres underwater will take off like a rocket from five metres, or sink like a rock at fifteen. It takes practice to control it. This is why students have instructors. Going up and down too fast underwater is bad for the health. It's also why instructors find it hard to relax.

I can't tell you much about the underwater marvels of Mosterøya. My memory holds a vague imprint of pale, quivering mudflats, spreading meadows of sea-grass and algae, half-sunken wrecks of shopping trolleys and milk-bottles, a dogfish rocketing away in a muddy cloud. Mainly, I remember flailing limbs, flashing fins, erupting mud-clouds and chaos. Tommy was one of those divers whose bones are made of lead. His finning style involved crawling along the bottom in a cloud of silt. When I signalled him to come up a bit, Inge thought I was talking to her, blasted air into her jacket and took off like a Polaris missile. I twisted, lunged, caught her in mid-water, dumped all my air, started to sink; then saw Øystein go up head-downwards with a bewildered look on his face, caught him with the other hand; felt myself rise, saw Inge dump her air; let her go, shoved Øystein's flailing fins back downwards, turned him upright; saw him pressing the inflate button on his jacket, hit the deflate, tried to pin his still-kicking feet, felt my head break the surface; swore, kicked upwards, let momentum carry me down; saw Tommy going past on the way up like a flying starfish with Ørjan the Blessed clinging onto his fins and slowing his ascent; grabbed *him*, thought weighty thoughts, and touched down in the clinging silt. My two protégés then drifted gently downwards and kicked my mask off.

Like I said, it's a glamorous job.

They got the hang of it in time. The point of the first dive is to let the students make their mistakes while hoping the instructor doesn't make his, and they obliged. Anyone watching would have thought I was practising to be an international goalkeeper, if they could have seen through the clouds. But they persevered. I stayed in front of them, finning backwards (one of my cooler tricks), getting them to breathe slowly, use their inflators sparingly, watch their depth, check their partners. One by one they started to relax and enjoy the scenery. By the time we came back in and surfaced through the curtain of jellyfish, they were looking almost competent. I was frazzled.

Fred Anton knew I'd had a hard time. Possibly the sight of flailing fins breaking the surface had given him a clue. After the second dive, which was like the first but with emergency drills thrown in, he took me to one side.

'Hey laddie, I'm going for a fun dive with Anne Gro. Want to come along?'

'Cool!' Fatigue dropped away in an instant. 'Where to?'

He pointed across the fjord to the island cliff-face opposite. Stunted trees clung to the vertical slope like a patch of ancestral jungle.

'Cliff dive. It goes down seventy metres. Nice rock formations.'

'Rock'n'roll!'

As the last student drove away, we filled three more tanks, piled our gear into the centre's inflatable, and roared across the still waters to the cliff-face.

There was no obvious anchorage, so we tied the painter to a handy tree and wriggled into our gear, no easy task in a swaying inflatable when two of the crew seem hell-bent on throwing one another overboard. Fred Anton and Anne Gro have a wonderful healthy relationship based on tripping, splashing and tickling one another whenever possible. After the tension of having students, it was a delight to behold.

'Safety check?'

'That works, that works, that works, see you in there!'

I rolled backwards, splashed, surfaced, and watched Anne Gro pour a bailerful of water over her beloved's head. He laughed and rocked the boat until she screamed.

'Any time today, children,' I called with heavy sarcasm.

They gave one another a meaningful look, winked, and hurled themselves overboard. Twin tidal waves engulfed me. Luckily, there were no jellyfish.

'See you down there,' Fred Anton said, and dumped his air.

Instructors without students are the same the world over. Whether they're divers, skiers, parachutists, or mountaineers, the policy is always the same: get rid of the clients, then do all the things you told them not to. We emptied our jackets, duck-dived, let our own weight pull us down, went into a modified sky-dive position and swept down a vertical rock-face in a cloud of bubbles. Twenty metres down I hit my suit's inflator to brake, feeling the blasting air like ice on my chest. Fred Anton and Anne Gro plummeted down. Ten metres below me in the green twilight they levelled off on the lip of a dizzying drop. I drifted above them, watching my reflection swell and split and shiver upwards in their bubbles. Then I barrel-rolled and went down to join them. It's dangerous to follow a shallow dive with a deep one; but sometimes it's worth the risk.

To go underwater is to enter a different reality. Every sense changes. Touch brings the chill thickness of the water, the tightness of the suit. Taste brings dry air, salt, a rubber mouth-piece (Fred Anton's was strawberry flavoured). Hearing, unnaturally acute, brings the click and rasp of the breathing gear (think Darth Vader), the rumble of bubbles, boat noises from far away. Breathing slows, deep and measured to maximize efficiency. It feels like yoga, relaxing, distorting the sense of time. Even sight betrays you. Everything you see is magnified and blue-shaded by the water, even your hands. They look swollen, pale, like somebody else's. They move fluidly, languidly; you can't help it, the water gets in the way. On land, you stand upright, battling your own weight. Down below, you lie down and fly.

We drifted along the cliff-face, three slow-moving figures cruising the clouds. To the right, empty waters yawned greeny-blue. Far above the waves gleamed like pewter, scattering the evening sunshine: ridges of silver, ebony troughs, endless star-edged patterns spreading round our bubbles. Fred Anton rolled on his back, pulled out his mouthpiece, blew an air-ring that rose and grew, spinning slowly like a film of a car wheel. I popped up over it and dived through, feeling the air tug at my fringe, then pulled out my own mouthpiece and sent a copy spinning after its shards. It was good to be flying again . . . I rolled all the way over, bent at the waist and went back into freefall, dropping down towards a ledge. A metre above it I stopped and hovered, watching a spider-crab with legs like Michael Jordan's and a nut-like body scuttle into a crevice. Then I coasted onwards, forgetting time and gravity.

It was late when we got back to Askje.

I spent another four days there. Yet again, that hadn't been the plan, but Tom Willy had told me that Tine needed one more dive to finish off the course, and she was only free on Wednesday, so would I mind awfully taking her out and finishing her off? No, I said, I had no objections to going diving alone with a stunning international gymnast (that T-shirt was hers by right); just to please him, of course. In the meantime I spent most of my time with Fred Anton, learning about Norway.

I couldn't have had a better teacher. For one thing, his English was perfect. For another, so was his sense of humour. He was the first foreigner I'd ever met who really *understood* Monty Python's humour, as opposed to laughing nervously at it. Again, he was a natural storyteller. Most of all, he really *loved* his country.

It's not something I've met very often. Nationalism these days is suspect, the preserve of soccer thugs and neo-extremists, the public face of racism. Any feeling of pride in one's own land has to be carefully balanced by admiration of everyone else's, an intellectual juggling-match leaching the colour out of the base emotion. In eighteen months' voyaging I hadn't met a single person who could put their hand on their heart and say, 'I'm proud of my country.' Americans do things like that. Most Europeans I know find it embarrassing.

But Fred Anton really believes in Norway. He holds a commission in the Territorial Army, and his pride and joy is recounting victory stories: victories against the Germans in the Second World War, victories over American élite troops on NATO exercises in his own time, victories over the Swedes whenever and wherever he could think of them. (Sweden has been Norway's chief enemy and oppressor for the last five hundred years or so, and the grudge between the two is as sharp as the Anglo–Scottish one.) But his proudest moment came when he spoke of the Norwegian space research centre. In the 1990s that noble body launched a space probe without, unfortunately, remembering to warn the Russians first. Moscow thought it was a nuclear strike. President Yeltsin later claimed that his counterattack was already warming up when the frantic explanations came down the hotline. Fred Anton sports a proud T-shirt, 'We almost started World War Three!'

I thought he was a one-off. Well, he is. How many other Norwegians would give a guest a sombrero as a going-away present on the grounds that it's a local tradition? But his outright affection for his country is shared by many of his compatriots. Perhaps it's the natural result of their history and position: a small country on the European rim, eternally the junior partner in union with one or other of its southern neighbours. It's certainly connected with the North Sea oil phenomenon, the biggest influence on Norwegian history since the longship. The Norwegian Museum of North Sea Oil is in Stavanger. Its proudest exhibit, the centrepiece of its advertising campaigns, is the drill bit which struck oil on Christmas Day 1969. Nowadays only Saudi Arabia exports more oil to Europe. Norway's oil income runs into billions – this in a country with half the population of London. Of course, politics being what it is these days, the government doesn't dare to spend any of it, as nobody can agree on the best way to use the windfall. But hand-to-mouth poverty is definitely not a feature of Norwegian life. In all my time in the country, I was only to meet one person who felt uncomfortable there. She'd just come back from four months' voluntary work in Africa. Everyone else I met, without exception, revelled in the country's wealth. Time and again I heard the comment, 'It's nice to go travelling, but I'd never want to live anywhere else.'

Astonishingly, Fred Anton and many of his compatriots admire Britain; and they know lots about it. Norwegian TV is heavily biased towards British and American programmes. The national news routinely reports details of English and Scottish football matches and the state of David Beckham's hair. Øystein, whose Aberdeen accent came from the Scottish quarter of Stavanger (he grew up among oil workers), used to follow the fortunes of Scotland's rugby team with a passion that until then I'd only ever seen at Murrayfield. Stena ferries were even advertising a special offer while I was in Stavanger: a weekend shopping trip to Newcastle. I'd never have thought of Newcastle as a glamorous centre of international consumerism; shows how little I know. Fred Anton laughs at the Brits. It's not personal, he laughs at everyone; but other Norwegians I met later were a little wounded by the fact that their regard for us was so seldom reciprocated. 'We know that Britain's a great power,' they said, 'but it's sad that you don't know more about us. We're cousins, after all.' Having seen what I have of Norway, it's our loss.

6

UTSIRA

'North Utsire, South Utsire, south to southeast five,
thundery rain, moderate with fog patches, becoming
good.'

Radio 4 Shipping Forecast

On the following Thursday I left my mooring at last and pulled
away into the fjord, followed by shouts and waves from my
juvenile fans (including Fred Anton). The sun was shining and
the wind blew cool from the hills as I made for the open sea.

I was heading for a literary encounter of a different sort.
It's one of the peculiar facts of history that many of the world's
most moving poems aren't actually poems at all. The King
James version of I Corinthians 13 (faith, hope and charity) and
the Third Collect in the Anglican Evensong are hymns without
tunes; the closing paragraphs of *The Lord of the Rings* are the
final chords of a symphony. James Thurber's playful description of a journey in *The Thirteen Clocks* dances like jazz on the
page, and for graver matters, Sir Thomas Malory's epitaph on
Sir Launcelot at the end of the *Morte d'Arthur* peals like a
funeral bell.* As far as I'm concerned, though, the most

---

* See the Bibliography.

bewitching use of words ever penned comes in the Radio 4 shipping forecast.

It reads like an incantation. No matter that it's a simple and practical way of identifying sea areas by their outstanding geological feature. No matter that every word of the forecast has a precise and numerically defined meaning: the mysterious rune 'Dogger, Fisher, German Bight: southwest four, a thousand and two, rising more slowly, fair, moderate to poor,' simply means that the wind over the central North Sea and the Danish and German North Sea coasts is blowing from the southwest at between eleven and sixteen knots, atmospheric pressure stands at 1002 millibars and has risen by between 0.1 and 1.5 millibars in the preceding three hours, and that it's not raining but that surface visibility is fluctuating between five nautical miles and a thousand metres. The shipping forecast is music in words.

Viking. The Viking banks, northeast of Shetland. *Dogger.* The Dogger bank, so overfished that it's the only British bank worth less than Barings. *German Bight*, the German bay. *Rockall* and *Malin, Trafalgar* (early mornings only) and *Finisterre*, Portland* and *Dover*, the cliffs and capes. *Humber, Thames, Forth, Tyne*, the rivers. *Biscay* and *Irish Sea*, the bays. *Faeroes* and *Southeast Iceland, Fastnet* and *Scillies*, the islands.

North Utsire and *South Utsire*.

Norwegians call it Utsira, with the stress on the first syllable: *Ut*-sira. It's an island. Just one island, a lumpy rock a mile and a half long and two miles wide, nine miles off the Rogaland coast, surrounded by long chains of spray-washed skerries.

---

* In February 2002, the Finisterre shipping area was renamed 'FitzRoy' to avoid confusion with the French area of the same name. Robert FitzRoy was captain of Charles Darwin's famous ship, the Beagle, and founder of the Meteorological Office.

In, as it were, skerried ranks. Its eastern and western flanks build up into brooding granite howes like the Lakeland peaks, frowning across the water. Between them a broad green valley runs north to south, plunging at each extremity into a rock-edged channel where the breakers burst in foam. The prevailing winds here are northwest and southwest. To the southwest, the next land is Shetland, over two hundred miles away. To the northwest, it's the Arctic. When the north-westerly gales drive the waves onto the rocks, the whole island seems to shudder.

It's that weather pattern which led the *sirabu* – the natives of Utsira – to build a harbour at each end of the island. It's the only solution which makes sense. When the northwesters blow, roaring breakers smash clear over the rocks sheltering the northern harbour and fill the channel with surf. Fishermen and ferries divert to the southern harbour in the lee of the eighty-metre hills. When the wind shifts into the southwest the southern channel becomes a hell of tossing water. Anyone still at sea makes for the north side. Contrary to popular belief, and whatever the Met Office may say, the two harbours don't have different weather patterns. They're a mile and a half apart in the middle of the North Sea. What do you expect?

There was a fresh westerly breeze blowing the day I went there. Either harbour was an option, but I was approaching from the southeast, so South Utsira made more sense. The channel marker buoys were hard to find – one skerry looks very like another to my eyes, and the buoys were tucked in behind them – but, after a few minutes' bewildered cruising among the rocks, I found the first beacon and worked my way into the channel. Like so many Scandinavian harbours, it was an alliance of nature and artifice. The rocky inlet bent sharply to port, then opened out in a shallow bay. Just before the bend a massive concrete sea wall jutted into the water, halving the width of the channel and sheltering the basin behind. A fish-processing warehouse had been built on it, a white-painted concrete hangar. Behind it, inside the harbour, were a ferry landing, a water-supply shack, a tiny shower-block for leisure-boat visitors, fishermen's work-huts, a sweep of sour green tussock-grass, and a final concrete quay lined, as always, with tyres. There aren't enough trucks in the whole country to supply that many tyres: they must import the things specially. Perhaps twenty boats could have squeezed into the little harbour; there were barely half a dozen there. All around the hillside, a scattering of wooden houses looked down on the harbour. Just above the water's edge a low, modern-looking general store represented the throbbing mercantile heart of South Utsira: grocery, hardware store, liquor shop, post office and gossip centre combined.

I moored alongside the paint-splashed quay, well away from the commercial wharf and therefore out of everyone's way, and went harbourmaster hunting. There was no information on the jetty, nor, when I checked there, on the shower-block, so I made for the general store to see what I could find. As I walked up the road towards it, my deck-boots crunching on the gravel, two women came out. As they passed me I heard the elder say in English, 'And that's the only shop we've got.'

I dithered for a second, then turned to follow them. I didn't know if it was a guided tour or a friendly visit, but either way, I might end up learning something.

The main road – a single-track tarmac ribbon – led steeply uphill between tall white wooden houses with wide lawns and wire fences, levelled out, and then began the slow descent towards North Harbour. To the right, a handful of houses sheltered behind a dark stand of pines. Behind them a sudden outcrop heaved up forty metres above the fields, all rugged granite boulders and thin, wind-blown grass. To the left, the flat green bottom of the valley was divided into fields of sheep. Half a mile away more granite bluffs rose towards the skyline. On the highest summit, the lens of a lighthouse caught the westering sunlight.

I followed my Anglophones at a discreet distance. A month in Scandinavia had made me wary of barging in on strangers. They stopped at the last house beneath the pines, consulted for a moment, then went in. Ambling up behind them, I saw that it was a gift shop. What better place to meet strangers? I tapped on the door and walked in.

I found myself in a small, sunlit parlour with bright floral curtains. Once it must have been homely; I could imagine a grandmaternal parlour full of china dogs, faded armchairs and pot-pourri. Now the floor was bare, and here and there stood shelves of tourist knick-knacks ranging from 'Presents from Utsira' modelled in driftwood and shells, to stone and wooden carvings of human forms. The women I'd been following were standing in front of a cash desk covered in dismembered dolls and the paraphernalia of stuffed-toy surgery; behind the desk a woman in her early thirties with mouse-brown hair and calm eyes was watching them.

'I like this one,' said the younger visitor in a rich American accent. 'How much is it?'

The cashier looked at it. 'Sree hundred crowns,' she said hesitantly, then added something in Norwegian. The older woman translated.

'She made it herself.'

I watched the triangular conversation curiously. La Americana seemed intent on admiring everything in the shop. The elder woman, known as 'Mom', translated in good-natured English as the shopkeeper explained exactly how her various wares were made. My admiration for Scandinavian linguistic skills ratcheted up another notch as she explained the intricacies of double cross-stitch without breaking into a sweat. Now and then the conversation was interrupted as a four-year-old with a runny nose and scabbed knees charged in on a plastic tractor, hurtled around the shop, pinched a biscuit from the desk and vanished again. The second time he did it he nearly took my feet out from under me. I somehow managed to stop both of us going headlong into a display of local china, and looked up in time to meet the impresaria's gaze. She gave me the friendliest grin I'd seen since Hönö.

Five minutes later the visitors left. She looked at me quizzically, waved me to a chair and said, 'Want you a coffee?'

'*Ja, takk,*' I answered, not to be outdone in the broken linguistics field. She smiled and poured some roofing tar into a polystyrene cup.

It was the perfect place to spend a sunny afternoon. One of the many charms of Utsira is that it's not exactly on the tourist trail: Tove's job in the gift shop seemed to consist of brewing coffee and hosting impromptu Women's Institute meetings. Island life is based on the difficulty of a daily commute to the mainland, and the fact that fishing doesn't really pay any more. Anywhere else in the world, the society would have collapsed a generation ago, but this is Norway, and Utsira lies on the tanker route between Stavanger and the offshore oilfield. Most of the men on the island work in the oil industry, on the rigs themselves, the supply ships or the tankers. They spend two weeks away on the job, working twelve-hour shifts and earning princely wages, then go home for a fortnight to spend it. As a result, Utsira is among the richest communities in the country, and gives more to charity each year than Oslo. Despite extensive government propaganda, few island women work on the rigs. Somebody has to stay home and look after the children, but since the island boasts a school, gym, library, community centre and party house, and since the island's kids, being kids, would do *anything* rather than hang around with their mothers, they tend to have time on their hands. Initial observations indicated that they spent most of it drinking coffee with Tove.

In quick succession I was introduced to two neighbours with assorted small children, a visitor from South Harbour and a friend who'd cycled up from the North Harbour for a chat. (Until the road was built there was fierce rivalry between the two metropoles. Nowadays the situation is peaceful, though Southerners still claim that theirs is the happening, swinging side of the island, while the North is populated exclusively by old fogeys – this despite the fact that the island's only bar is on the North Harbour waterfront.) The South Harbour visitor greeted me with the words, 'Are you the English-man from the boat?', which says something about the efficiency of the gossip network. In between visits, Tove asked me about my travels, and I asked her about her life. She was a genuine *sirabu*, with generations of ancestors buried in the churchyard; her partner, however, was an outsider from the South. He was the island's resident environmental officer, responsible for planning permission, wildlife protection and education; he was also a fanatical bird-watcher, fond of getting up before dawn in midwinter (i.e. about lunchtime) to immerse himself waist-deep in the North Sea and watch migrating geese. Wondering how insular the Utsira community might be, I asked if he'd been accepted by the locals; yes, she said, but it had taken years. Other newcomers had been less lucky. One family had moved to the island a few years before. Their children had been born there, went to the local school, and had made every effort to integrate. If they were very lucky, *their* children might be regarded as proper *sirabu*. They weren't disliked, far from it; but they were still *utlenninger*, foreigners.

'How long are you stay here?' Tove asked after a while. I shrugged. I'd been there for an hour and a half and two cars had driven past in that time. I like places like that.

'Maybe a week.'

She looked surprised. I had the feeling it was unusual to spend half a day there.

'Have you been to Haugesund?' she asked. I didn't even know where it was.

'There is jazz festival there next week.' It was Friday. 'You should go. *Sildajazz*, herring jazz festival. Ask about it in café.'

'Where's the café?' I asked.

'North Harbour,' she said. I waited for more details, but none were forthcoming. It's not that big a place.

'I live in the house there,' she added as I took my leave. 'Come in some time.'

I liked Utsira.

I went to the café that afternoon. It was in an old fishermen's hall right on the North Harbour jetty, a beautiful wooden building whose interior gleamed brown and gold and smelt faintly of pine. But it was closed until eight o'clock, so I strolled back up the road, enjoying the sunlight and the scent of grass and sheep, bought a couple of tins of beans and sausages in the general store, heated them up on my camping stove and sat out on the quarterdeck to drink in the sights of the quiet harbour: gulls swooping, the shadow of the hills slowly lengthening, and a solitary fisherman mending his nets on the commercial wharf opposite. As the sun sank behind the hills I lifted my mountain bike off the stern railings where it had stood ever since London, and pedalled back towards the café through the gloaming.

The climb up to Tove's house was the hardest exercise I'd

had in weeks, but as I panted my way past her gate she looked out of a window and waved. I waved back, almost came off the bike, and heard her friendly laughter trailing in my wake as I pushed on over the top and into the long descent. I was whizzing over the gravel without a care in the world when I glanced over my shoulder and almost swallowed my tongue. An arm's length behind me, another bike was racing in ghostly silence, its rider a Viking made almost entirely of red cheeks and a grin.

'Hi!' he shouted as soon as I saw him. 'Are you the Englishman?'

I could hardly deny it.

'Are you going to the café?'

Was there anywhere else?

'Good! I'm Martin! Come and have a drink!' He started pedalling furiously, shot past me, whizzed round a corner and vanished in a cloud of dust.

I caught up with him at the café. Martin was a *sirabu* who'd moved away to Stavanger, where he had his own sailing boat, but whenever the wind was in the right direction he came back to his roots to drink and chat up the local girls. He certainly seemed on familiar terms with everyone there. We spent a happy hour swigging beer with his various friends, and I grew used to the question, 'Are you the Englishman from the boat?' Sitting in a corner overlooking the room, table by table Martin pointed out the locals and the visitors (half a dozen yachts from Trondheim and Bergen had come into the North Harbour that afternoon), told me about their jobs, their names and their disreputable pasts. The air grew thick with cigarette smoke, loud with conversation and music. One of the visitors had brought a guitar with him; soon the sailors had pushed four tables together to accommodate the whole party, and were singing with great gusto. I remember 'We Are

Sailing', 'Amazing Grace' and 'The Wild Rover' being among their favourite hits; I don't recall any Norwegian songs. The locals ignored them and huddled over their own conversations. It was a peculiar evening.

After an hour Martin stood up with a crash. 'This is boring,' he said. 'Let's go to the party.'

'Party?' Nobody had mentioned a party.

'Sure! It's someone's eighteenth.'

I looked hard at him. Unless I was completely wrong, his eighteenth had been about the time the current celebrant was born. I wasn't used to the Utsira phenomenon.

'Come on,' and it was back onto the bikes and away uphill again.

We turned left just before Tove's house, ground our way up a minor precipice, topped the rise and heard music thumping. Just ahead, proudly perched on a rocky outcrop, was a building which looked for all the world like a schoolhouse: huge windows, imposing front door and playground. Disco lights flashed from the windows, blending with the regular sweep of the lighthouse behind us.

As we pedalled towards it, dark figures materialized on the path: two revellers, harbour-bound. Martin gave a joyous shout and shuddered to a halt. After a rapid flood of excited Norwegian he dismounted and gave his bike to the girl. The boy turned to me.

'Are you the Englishman from the boat?'

Yes, nothing had changed in the last half-hour.

'Can I borrow your bike?'

I hesitated, but only from surprise. Nobody was going to try and pinch the only English bike on the island . . . I handed the rust-bucket over and the pair wobbled off. Martin and I stood looking up at the party.

'Looks like a school!' I shouted over the din.

'It is!' he replied. 'Old schoolhouse! Come on!'

He led the way up a gravel path and into the ringing hall. Trestle tables laden with assorted alcoholic beverages lined one wall. Around them gaggles of awkward-looking youths stood and sat on tiny school chairs, shouting intimate gossip above the bellowing music. The rest of the hall was taken up with gyrating figures lit by a single cluster of lights. One gangling young man stood swaying on the edge of the stage, waving a bottle. As we walked in he threw himself headlong into the crowd. Laughs and delighted squeals erupted. The revels were in full swing. While Martin launched himself onto the dance-floor, I made for the bar, and was promptly intercepted by a shouted, 'Are you the Englishman from the boat?'

'That's me!'

'Have a drink!' And he thrust a bottle of beer into my hand. I found a convenient seat among the revellers, sat back and enjoyed the show.

I could have watched for hours. Most of Utsira's population under thirty was there – thirty people at least – and the drinking had been going on since teatime. Dance styles ranged from a fine display of body-popping through some spirited jive to the Drunken Lurch. The Birthday Girl herself had passed through the lurching stage some time ago, and was reeling from guest to guest, grabbing whatever extremities she could to maintain her balance and claiming a tithe from every cup she passed. When she got to me she snatched at my shoulder, missed, staggered, and only a swift lunge on my part kept her on her feet. She smiled up at me, dewy-eyed.

'Zhzhzh Englishman zhzhzhzhz?' she asked. I was impressed.

'Zhzhzh yes,' I replied, and steered her gently on her way.

I don't know if some kind of bizarre etiquette was at work, but once recognized by the hostess, I found myself in demand.

Britain has never struck me as the world's most exotic location, but just being from there guaranteed me popular appeal. Teenager after teenager – the loose term including everyone up to a couple of thirty-somethings – came up to ask me about London culture, London clubs, London music and Manchester United, which says something about where all the marketing experts are working these days. In return, I found out that they were all *sirabu* who lived and studied on the mainland, in Haugesund or Stavanger, but came home for the weekends to enjoy the social life. That was something I'd never even heard of before: teenagers leaving the bright lights and the biggish city to return to the comforts of home. Island solidarity in action. They brushed off my surprise by saying that they had unrivalled facilities on the island – well, a party room and free access to alcohol, which is what counts – but only one girl really explained the situation.

'We grow up here, we go to school together, we never see any other children. When we go to senior school in Haugesund we have to live there during the week, it's too far to go every day. So our parents club together and we live in flats. We've been together every day since we were born.'

No wonder it's a hard community to join.

My bike hadn't reappeared by the time the party broke up some time in the small hours. Martin suggested coming back to a friend's house and watching a porn movie – the friend in question was not quite seventeen – but I could hear my sleeping-bag calling. I walked back down the winding lanes to the harbour and oblivion.

I awoke next morning to a thumping noise and a sudden jolt, never a good sign on a boat. I shot out of my cabin in time to see a mud-bespattered urchin wriggle through the forward escape hatch and drop onto a seat. An inverted head followed, grinning. As I turned round I saw another small form clambering on a deck-box to inspect my flag. Utsira's youth had discovered me.

'*Hei!*' I said to the world in general, decided that there wasn't anything breakable in reach and that I needed caffeine, stepped into the galley and lit my camping stove. With a whoomph and a roar, a tongue of white flame shot halfway to the ceiling. In the sudden silence I turned and saw six pairs of eyes staring at me, enthralled.

'Morning,' I said, and got on with making tea.

Peregrino became a playground. I brewed up to the thunder of small feet on deck, shrill cries of infantile delight and the appalling swearing of their favourite game, 'Let's beat up Harald'. Most of the curses came from Harald himself, a waiflike figure with red hair, appealing eyes and an unerring ability to punch attackers in the groin. He confined himself to Norwegian, but his contemporaries were not so restrained. On the third morning of my annexation I awoke to the sounds of Homeric conflict on the quarterdeck, right above my bunk. D.H. Lawrence would have approved of the vocabulary deployed.

'Where did you learn your English?' I asked one ten-year-old blasphemer.

'*South Park*,' he said, and added, 'Fuckity fuckity fuck,' to confirm it.

It's not that Battling Harald was ignorant of gutter English, he just seemed shy of using it in front of his more fluent playmates. Removed from their inhibiting company, it was a different story. After a day or so of merry bloodshed he took me back to his house to meet his mother, having failed to notice that she'd been watching us from the quay for most of the day. She had a visitor that day, yet another *sirabu*, an extremely attractive girl of my age who'd moved to Stavanger to work. Never have I found it so hard to carry on a conversation. She was intelligent, charming, articulate and well-informed. Who knows what beautiful friendship might not have arisen had Harald been elsewhere? Sadly, the little treasure had secreted himself behind the sofa where I was sitting. I spent an hour trying to chat with a pretty girl while a subterranean treble murmured, 'Look at her. She wants your penis. She wants to take it right now and . . .' Nightmares are made of moments like this. I couldn't ignore him. I couldn't reach back and give him a clip on the ear. There was nothing I could do but sit there with my eyes growing wilder and my answers more random. The ladies must have wondered about my sanity. The visitor left hurriedly after an hour, drawing her skirts aside to avoid contamination: one travelling acquaintance I won't be staying in touch with.

Being the owner-occupier of a fast boat made me an instant hit. When the news leaked out that I had diving equipment on board as well, my popularity knew no bounds. The kids took the news that I wasn't going to let them use it for real surprisingly well; instead we spent a happy afternoon playing with every bit of gear I had. Happy, that is, from their point of view. I was too busy stopping four-year-old Jonathan jumping overboard, keeping Arve the Blasphemous away from the boat controls, and removing assorted knives from tender hands before Harald could try to redress the island power balance, to have much fun. After a few hours, however, the novelty wore off. Not entirely to my surprise, I found myself besieged with requests to let them have a go in the water.

'Tomorrow,' I promised them. I'd already consulted their mothers.

On the morrow we piled into a maternal Volvo, drove up the hill to the community centre, and watched as a whooping horde carried my dive gear into the island's swimming pool.

It wasn't easy. I had two wetsuits, one buoyancy jacket,

three masks and one pair of fins, which wasn't much to share out between four excitable boys. The only way I managed to avoid serious feuding was by setting my stop-watch and making sure that every one of them had *exactly* the same time to play as the rest. Even then, complaints like 'He had five more seconds than me!' weren't uncommon. I cruised the pool between splashing forms, occasionally stopping to reinflate a deflated jacket or pull a couple of howling figures off Harald's head. Now and then, just for variety, they decided to stop picking on him and ganged up on me instead, which I took as a compliment. Harald's mother watched from the poolside, laughing, but I noticed she was careful to keep well out of splashing range.

The time was coming to leave the island. I'd decided to head over to Haugesund, two hours away, in time for the jazz festival on Wednesday, and the day we spent at the pool was Monday. The only problem was my mountain bike. If Sweden is a social democracy, Utsira moves close to perfect communism, at least where velocipedes are concerned. Friday's borrower had thoughtfully left it at the old school after the party, but some other, later reveller, nipping home to find fresh supplies of booze, had seized both opportunity and bike, wobbled home, and collapsed in front of a forthright late-night movie. Despite my best efforts, I'm still hazy as to all its moves over the weekend. Everyone knew it was Ben's bike (I'd graduated from being 'the Englishman' to 'Ben' in the aftermath of the party) and that I wasn't planning to leave just yet: they all meant to drop it back by my boat the next time they were passing, it just never quite worked out. 'Well, I was taking it down to the harbour, but then Jørgen asked to borrow it,' was the classic comment. I suppose I should be flattered. I might not have been accepted as a *sirabu*, but at least my bike had.

It gave me plenty of exercise. I must have circumnavigated the whole island three times on the trail of the elusive machine, from the lighthouse on the highest western cliff to the environmental education shelter nestled above an eastern beach, and from the fish-smelling rope-stacks of South Harbour to the low, sloping rocks of the north. Everyone was friendly, everyone was helpful, nobody knew exactly where it had got to, 'But I think Jan had it last.' After two days' search I went to consult Tove. She'd gone over to the mainland for a day, but her partner Atle was in, and we spent a happy afternoon sitting in the sunshine watching his offspring tear paths of destruction through the shrubbery and having a kids-who'd-have-'em conversation.

'When are you leaving?' he asked.

'Tomorrow morning.'

'Don't worry, it'll be there.'

Sure enough, when I awoke the next morning, my prodigal Dunlop was leaning against the harbour shower-block, fit and happy and looking as if it had enjoyed its holiday. Some kind soul had even oiled the chain for me, as I discovered when I heaved the thing aboard and looked down to see sprocket-shaped oil-marks all over my trousers. I manoeuvred it back into position between the deck-boxes and the after rail, tied it in place, and got on with the process of making ready for sea. As always, it took an hour or so to convert houseboat into sea boat. Everything that I'd left lying around in the cabins had to be packed away in lockers and under-bunk storage spaces, the dining table transformed back into a chart table, the charts themselves marked and the GPS programmed, the water tanks filled, the VHF radio checked, the deck cleared, and the emergency equipment laid out ready to hand; all this done in my normal inimitable style of forgetting things, stopping halfway through one job to finish off another, and tripping over ropes, fenders and my own feet.

When it was done, I went ashore for the last time to say goodbye to my friends. As I reached the foot of the hill a garden gate crashed open and Jonathan, the youngest of my infant friends, came hurtling out, waving a toy aeroplane and making buzzing noises. He whizzed straight by me without even a glance. That hurt. *So much for being welcome*, I thought, and carried on up the hill.

Twenty metres further on, I heard running footsteps pattering on the gravel behind me. A small figure rocketed to a stop beside me and a hand was thrust into mine. Jonathan smiled up at me. My answering grin must have split my head in half. We walked on hand in hand. Then he started tugging my arm and pointing at my shoulders. 'Up! Up!' he said. I picked him up and swung him onto my back. He squealed with delight. We careered up the hill together. Jonathan made Spitfire noises and steered us by twisting my ears. At the summit his mother smiled and led us inside for a cup of hot chocolate and a mountain of cakes. Welcome? Believe it.

Late that afternoon – six hours later than I'd planned – I steamed reluctantly back down the rocky channel and blasted off across the water for a date with jazz and herrings.

7

HAUGESUND

'In Haugesund there stands a church, and hard by the churchyard, to the northwest, lies the grave-mound of King Harald Fairhair . . .'

Saga of Harald Fairhair

It may be possible to visit Scandinavia without eating herring, but I seriously doubt it. *Sill* to the Swedes, *sild* to the Norwegians, its effect on the peninsula's history and culture has been indelible, if not quite inedible. Delicatessen shelves offer a dozen different styles, sour pickled, sweet pickled, curried and marinaded. Prawns may dominate the summer months, but for the rest of the year, herring is king. The whole economic history of the North Sea coast is tied up with the enigmatic *sillperjöder*, the herring times when the fish population boomed and entire communities grew up dedicated to catching and salting the harvest. A dozen skerries in the Öckerö archipelago bear the crumbling ruins of wooden salteries, memorial to the last herring boom. They're abandoned now. Not even the tourists go there.

It's hard being a herring these days, but even harder being a herring fisherman. Their boats still scour the coasts, great bullet-prowed slabs of steel built to withstand hurricanes. On sunny evenings you can see them spread their great green nets out for mending in the little harbours; in the dark before dawn you can watch them go out, their lights vivid jewels in the blackness. But they're fighting for survival. In medieval times, they were the kings of the coast. Then the herring stocks collapsed, fished to oblivion. Barely one per cent of the coastal population still works in fishing. It's no wonder Norwegians hunt whale. There's nothing else left to catch.

Haugesund – home of the Sildajazz jazz festival, a fishy concept if ever I heard one, though at least it promises some interesting scales – is a typical Norwegian small town. In fact any small town is typically Norwegian; the whole country's a small town, except perhaps Oslo. Bustling, metropolitan, cosmopolitan or, d), none of the above? It's d). Reading Norwegian newspapers is like tapping into a village gossip network. International affairs do not feature strongly. Nor do international visitors. As far as Norway's concerned, foreigners are something you get in other countries. You can't fault their logic.

Haugesund, astonishingly, lies along the Haugesund, a hundred-metre-wide channel between the rocky mainland and an equally rocky island. Sheltered from all directions but the south, the channel forms a superb natural port, and the town grew up to take advantage of the fact. The jetties and wharves there stretch for a mile along both sides of the sound, a solid red-brick procession of old warehouses and factories, some still in use, some derelict, some converted into chandleries and souvenir shops. Behind the quays the town rises steeply in nondescript layers; unusually for Norway, most of the buildings are concrete rather than wooden. The main shopping streets of the town run parallel to the quay, along the hillside: pleasant, broad streets faced with plate glass, neither spectacularly beautiful nor abominably ugly. Fashion boutiques and sports shops predominate. Music stores outnumber bookshops, burger bars outnumber restaurants (there's only so much you can do with herring), locals outnumber visitors. Little clusters of youths (another wild northern tribe, not to be confused with Jutes, Goths or Geats) hang around in the streets waiting for something to happen. Drink is expensive, the cinema opens late, drugs are frowned upon and whatever else they might want to do together, they don't do it on the street. Or in groups. When they knew that I'd left London to come there, they were amazed. Nightclubs, cinemas and cheap beer? It's their idea of Heaven. Small-town life is never easy for teenagers. And what do you do when the whole country lives that way?

At least, when I arrived, they had something to gape at. Sildajazz is a jazz-and-boats festival, and the harbour was in chaos. One long stretch of quay was taken up with ranks of traditional wooden boats, four or five per berth. South of them, a hundred-metre gap was marked with a colossal 'No moor-ing. Working boats only' sign; a Swedish cruiser had tied up to it. Beyond that, under the slender arch of a single-span concrete bridge between mainland and island, were the yachts. Lots of yachts, or should that be lachts of yots? Rows of them, nose-to-tail along the quay, five or six or even seven side by side on each berth, with a tangle of ropes swooping out from them at all angles. Parties had already formed, figures in shirt-sleeves sitting in the sunshine with glasses of wine and cans of beer, stereos were playing, generators humming, and a great babble of music and conversation echoed off the island ware-houses. Steeply packed on the hill, the concrete town stared down in wide-windowed astonishment. I did the same. I'd never seen so many boats together. Self-consciousness cut in as I swung back upwind towards the mooring, but Fate was with me for once. I drifted in alongside a gleaming ocean racer, felt the lightest jolt as our combined fenders took the shock, and found two crewmen already taking my bow- and stern-lines.

'Hei!' called one of them, then saw my flag and shifted languages. 'Welcome in! How was the crossing?'

'Interesting,' I said wrily, remembering the North Sea.

'Are you on your own?'

'Yes,' I said. His eyes widened.

'Come and have a drink, then!'

It was a good arrival.

Haugesund is not the crown jewel of Norway's coastline. Concrete may be the material of which architects' dreams are made – which says something about architects – but it should never be allowed in a country famous for rain, snow and *long* winter nights. The name Haugesund means 'sound of the grave-mound' (how do grave-mounds sound? Sepulchral, presumably), and nothing the architects have done to the waterfront since Fairhair's death has animated it. It does, however, have the distinct advantage of providing an expansive and well-drained open space conveniently near the city centre, ideal for all kinds of public events. (I should be writing brochures.) And whatever you may say about the traditional reserve of Norwegians in public, when they party, they do it in style. By six o'clock that afternoon, the first of the festival, most of western Norway had turned up to celebrate. I stood on the town bridge to watch the party, and it was like looking down on a Cuban fiesta. The long, broad quay was jammed with brightly dressed revellers, many of them in towering velvet jester's hats. This was no village fête, all sobriety and soggy bunting. Beercans glinted, plastic beermugs sloshed, laughing locals *got* sloshed, children ran around garrotting each other with the strings of helium balloons, fishmongers shouted their wares, and as the bars flung their windows wide the squeaks and doodles of warming-up musicians turned to a full-throated 'When the Saints'. There are other Dixieland tunes, but none are memorable.

It was a bad year for herring. Normally this means that the fishermen haven't caught many, but in this case it was the fish themselves which had suffered. Whole sections of quay were draped with dried, smoked, peppered and freshly caught fish, the ground littered with buckets and crates of shellfish. I spent a happy ten minutes watching a fishmonger fighting a running battle with a platoon of jail-breaking crabs. To my delight, one crab tipped over onto the tarmac, bolted for the water, sidestepped the fishmonger's desperate lunge (not that crabs can do much else) and hurtled back into the safety of the briny. It was nice to see him back in his own plaice. It certainly left the fishmonger floundering.

Normally, when there's jazz on in town, I'm the first one to slide in with my trombone and make a nuisance of myself. The problem was that Sildajazz is a festival for professionals. Musicians come there from all over the world: for unlikely as it may seem, Haugesund is firmly established on the international jazz circuit. Amateurs need not apply. When I went trawling through the town saying 'Hi, I'm a trombonist,' the answer I received most often was a cold, 'So am I.'

However, this turned out to be an advantage, since it meant I got to sit back and watch the fun. I like Norwegians, so I'm allowed to laugh at them. I like jazz musicians, so I can laugh at them too. The combination of the two was almost bound to offer some amusement. The key to jazz behaviour is showing off. The key to Norwegian drinking etiquette is a certain boisterous heartiness, a red-faced slap-on-the-back mentality which hasn't changed much since the Stone Age; then as now, Norwegians had a lot to put up with in terms of climate and environment, and the best way to do it was to be drunk and noisy. Thus when jazz performers meet Norwegian audiences, it is a clash of the Titans. The players are trying to show off to listeners whose main trait is showing off, and since there's not much else to do in Haugesund, the listeners are absolutely everybody in the town.

I spent one happy evening watching a British salsa band strut their stuff in front of a home crowd – salsa because the Sildajazz organizers realized very early on that a four-day diet of nothing but Dixieland jazz is the sort of thing that drives strong men to violence. They were a fine professional outfit, and since they spoke not a word of Norwegian their leader had come up with the bright idea of making a joke of it. He'd brought a huge yellow cue-card on stage, and at appropriate moments he read from it in a stilted BBC accent, pausing in all the wrong places and occasionally stopping to confer with the rest of the band as to how you pronounce 'øl'. (Which means beer, unlike the German *Öl*, which means oil. *Never* confuse the two. It's not pretty.) The audience loved it, and decided to join in.

Conductor: '*Hei!* And welcome to . . . er . . . Howge . . . no, that's not right . . . Horege . . . no . . .'

Voice from the audience: 'Haugesund!'

'Aha! Thank *you*, sir! Haugesund. Are you having a nice virgin?'

Whoops and cheers as the band's Norwegian host hurries on stage. Swift confabulation.

Conductor, in English: 'Right. If anyone sees a guy called Tommy here, kill him for me, that was his translation . . .' In Norwegian, 'Are you having a nice *festival*?'

More cheers from the crowd.

'Good! Now we're going to start playing. If anyone has any requests, please bring them here with a bottle of oil . . . er, beer!'

And they did.

I'm pretty sure the band weren't expecting it. They were halfway through their theme-tune when a tall Norwegian elbowed his way to the stage, grabbed the conductor by the ankle and deposited a tray full of pints between the amplifiers. The conductor looked down and almost dropped his baton. The band jerked like a skipping CD, then swung on with the tune, their eyes glued to the tray. By the time they'd finished the piece another friendly local had brought another round. There were so many glasses on stage that the only way for the band to move was to drink themselves out of it. Which they did.

Conductor – without prompt card – in English, 'I can do this bit. *Skål!*'

'*Skål!*' from the floor.

Relative decorum returned for the next couple of numbers. The audience were bright enough to realize that if they kept the beers coming at that rate they might well kill the band, so they concentrated on their own drinking. Unfortunately for me, I was standing at the back of the hall to watch the show, and that put me directly on the flight-path for the toilets. Norwegians may be a peace-loving and organized people these days, but they're useless when it comes to queueing. The national tactic seems to be to walk over anyone smaller than you and elbow your way past anyone larger. Amazingly, it doesn't lead to many fights, which is just as well since if it did it might depopulate the country, and there aren't that many Norwegians left. In fact, perhaps that's why . . . It rather spoiled my appreciation of the concert. I'd just be getting comfortable when some burly Norseman with his mind fixed on his digestive tract would push me to the ground and trample along my spine. It doesn't take many such moments to ruin a festive occasion. At length I revealed a Napoleonic grasp of strategy and retreated to the other side of the bar. There all I had to worry about was being flattened by late arrivals. Of whom there were thousands. It wasn't much of an improvement.

Then the band decided to do a walkabout. They were playing 'The Peanut Vendor', which is so repetitive that players have been known to fall asleep halfway through, wake up ten minutes later and still be playing the right bit, and they decided to enliven the show by going down among the audience. It was like the Charge of the Light Brigade without the horses. One by one they hopped off the stage, still playing, and pushed into the Valley of Deaf. The audience loved it. In the best back-slapping manner. By slapping them on the back. I was watching their trombonist when it happened. One moment, there he was, happily twiddling away with the tedious 'Da-DUM! Da-DOM! Da-DUM! Da-DOM!', and the next a jovial Titan smote him between the shoulderblades. He almost swallowed his tongue. His eyes bulged, his face turned scarlet, and the only reason his slide didn't fly off the end of the instrument and impale someone in the crowd is that a second Viking turned round just in time to catch it in the ribs. Meanwhile the tuba player was desperately fighting off a determined attempt to pour beer down his bell, and the alto saxophonist, oblivious to the carnage, was leading a conga-line in the direction of the bar. Suddenly his instrument shot up an octave in an astonished squeak. The conga dancer behind him had leaned forward and blown gently in his ear.

On the whole, I was glad I wasn't playing.

Haugesund may not be a multicultural metropolis for most of the year, but it makes up for it during the festival. Not only were there bands from all over the world, but they were playing all kinds of music. There was Dixieland, swing, blues, modern jazz. There were soul guitarists and singers, a steel band, a Bavarian oompah band, an Irish folk singer looking very lost. There was even a pop band. What they were doing there I'm not quite sure but the audience liked them.

It's a sad truth that few jazz greats are exactly a feast for the eye. Unlike certain pop stars (insert names as it suits you), the legendary figures of the jazz world seldom achieve public acclaim for the way they look. Go round any jazz festival. Look at the top performers. Imagine them cavorting around in lycra and sequins. Believe me, your eyes *will* water. The ingredients that turn a little-known jazz performer into a household name are a mystery to me. Suffice to say that beauty is not part of the package. Most of today's big names have been doing what they do since the 1960s: drinking beer, smoking too much, staying up late and living in cheap hotels. Chippendales they ain't.

This pop band were different. For one thing, they were young; the oldest was twenty-six, the youngest twenty-three, and the youngest-*looking* might have been fourteen. There's no justice. For another, they really believed in image manipulation. They were an octet, four guys, four girls, but you wouldn't guess it to watch them. Their organization ran thus: four girls in bright, eye-catching, figure-hugging costumes at the front of the stage, and four guys in khaki and grey as far back as they could get without falling into the lighting ducts. Pop marketing at its best. I was lucky enough to catch their first show, on a run-down stage on the waterfront. They were talented musicians, but to be frank, it wouldn't have mattered if they'd been tone-deaf. They must have lowered the average age of performers at the festival by about twenty years, and doubled the number of women. The all-male audience was broadminded and vocal in its appreciation. When they announced that they'd be doing a show in the musicians' pub that evening, I decided that I *had* to be there. I'd never seen the jazz and pop worlds meet face to face before. Something told me it would be worth watching.

The musicians' pub was a converted warehouse at one end of the docks, conveniently close to my mooring. Thick, square wooden pillars draped with nets and old glass floats supported a warped, resin-stained ceiling; long heavy tables and benches lined the floor. It wouldn't have been surprising to see Captains Haddock and Birdseye sitting at a table smoking their pipes, or heavy-set fishermen in sea-boots, thick jerseys and tattoos spitting tobacco over the floor. The laid-back collection of dinner-jacketed jazzmen inhabiting the bar seemed about as appropriate as penguins in a lumber camp. At least, being musicians, they had the right mannerisms. Some were leaning heavily on the bar. Others stood in little clusters, talking loudly and turning the air blue with cigarette smoke and anecdotes which would not have gone down well at a feminist symposium. If I shut my eyes and listened to the boisterous voices, smelt the smoke and the alcohol, I could imagine myself among the rugged chevaliers of the waves. Only the occasional sentences such as 'And then you go through A flat seven and end up in C *minor* . . .' betrayed the secret.

Imagine, if you will, a bar full of professional jazz musicians. Most over fifty, white-haired or balding, sagging around the middle (they call it 'diaphragm support'), resting pint mugs against their stomachs, dress-shirts hanging out. Imagine the younger ones, clutching beers and savouring cigars, playing darts or watching the football (there's always football) or ogling the dancers on MTV. The few single women either sit and drink with the men, dressed in dinner-jackets and treated as honorary males, or wander in sequinned dresses between tables of younger players, basking in their admiration. Assorted female concubines, attached and therefore officially sexless, orbit the groups, chatting with old friends. Got the picture? Now imagine four fresh, dewy, clean-cut, beautiful Norwegian students clambering on stage to sing 'Eye of the Tiger'. Oh, and four guys.

You could have heard the eyes popping in Oslo.

Hormones hit Haugesund. The older musicians, most of whom hadn't moved fast since about 1971, erupted. The first phalanx made it to the tables by the stage with a speed that would have scared the half-life out of a subatomic particle; the second wave, blocked by their peers, developed a Michael Owen-like ability to find the strategic gaps. The younger generation, turning in a blasé fashion to see what was bothering their elders, straightened with a sort of collective jolt and surreptitiously started adjusting their cravats. A quite astonishing number suddenly remembered things they'd left lying about beside the stage and had to hurry over to, yes, have a closer look. By the time the band's hour-long set was done every jazz player in Haugesund was crowding into the bar to see what was going on.

Then came the jam session. Jam sessions are the unorthodox bits of a jazz festival, the musical equivalent of what diving instructors do when they haven't got students to worry about. Normally it's the older players who join in, the ones who are well enough established that they don't worry about playing in front of the real experts; the younger set prefer the bar and the TV. Besides, it's *so* uncool to be enthusiastic about anything these days ... I doubt anyone's ever seen a free-for-all like Sildajazz before. The table next to the pop band's was suddenly piled high with instrument cases. Eager performers clustered around it, waiting to get on stage and show off and not lurking around the girls at all, Your Honour. Up on stage, solos passed from player to player with a quite amazing number of unexpected quotes, practically all of them drawn from the pop band's repertoire. The girls sat chatting with their attendant gentlemen, smiling benevolently on the chaos. Imitation is the sincerest form of flattery. By the look of things, the trad-jazz festival had just been hijacked.

I propped myself up at the bar and watched the mêlée. Old jazzers chasing new pop was incongruity raised to art. Next to me swayed a tall, heavy-set man in his late forties, a legend of British jazz, quietly building a rampart of shot-glasses across the stained wooden top. His eyes, red and swimming, were fixed on the pop idols, and as he turned to me I saw a tear distilled of Scotch and sorrow run down his cheek. He heaved a heavy sigh.

'I'm in the wrong job,' he said, and crumpled gently down the bar.

I rounded off the evening by carrying him back to his hotel.

The pop band came from Trondheim. I'd been hoping to get that far north myself, and not just because I met them. The Trondheim district is the most historically important part of Norway. Forget Oslo. In the Viking Age the Oslofjord was a permanent battlefield. Trondheim was the power in the land, maker, breaker and killer of kings.

It was there that Harald Fairhair established his residence, in Lade, just east of the modern town of Trondheim. His chief supporter was his father-in-law, or at least one of his fathers-in-law, Hákon, Jarl of Lade, who acted as regent whenever the king was off raping and pillaging, i.e. most of the time. When Hákon died his son, Sigurd, succeeded him, and became the most powerful man in Norway after the king. When Fairhair died, war broke out between his sons Eirík Bloodaxe and Hákon the Good. Sigurd backed Hákon, and his support proved decisive. Eirík fled to York to die in exile, and Hákon became king.

The years passed and Eirík's sons grew up. Egged on by their mother in traditional Viking style, and led by Harald Greycloak, the eldest surviving brother, they returned to Norway, killed King Hákon, claimed the throne, and bribed Jarl Sigurd's brother to kill him. The rolling feud of Norwegian politics surged on. Sigurd's son, another Hákon, seized power in the Trondheim district and declared war on his father's killers. The eastern counties rebelled in favour of Tryggvi Oláfsson, yet another descendant of Harald Fairhair. For the next thirty years Norway was bathed in blood and fire. Eventually Tryggvi was killed, his son, our hero Oláf driven into exile. Hákon was forced to flee to Denmark, where he found shelter with Harald Bluetooth. Together they plotted and contrived Greycloak's death. Hákon returned to Norway as Bluetooth's regent. And when civil war broke out between Bluetooth and Forkbeard, he took the power for himself, and neither Svein nor the Jómsvikings could dislodge him.

All this while Oláf Tryggvason was growing up in exile. As soon as he was old enough he took to the Viking life, raiding the Frisian and Flemish coasts. His success as a pirate and his generosity as a leader swiftly became legendary: by 991 he was captain of a mercenary army drawn from all over Scandinavia. He was also a Christian, having, most improbably, been baptized on his travels. It was then that he launched his great attack up the Blackwater river. For the next three years, until Ethelred bought him off, he was the scourge of the Channel coast and the most feared man in England.

But Ethelred's gold and diplomacy gave Oláf a new dream: the seizure of power in Norway and the Christianization of the kingdom. He moved with astonishing speed. Scant months after he and his partner Svein were paid off in London, he landed in Norway. There he learnt that civil war had broken out between Hákon and the men of Trondheim. The Jarl was in the Medal valley south of Trondheim, with few supporters. Oláf allied with the Tronders and marched. But Hákon, cunning to the last, evaded capture. He and a single thrall, Kark, fled to the Jarl's lover's hill-farm with the pursuit hot on their heels.

As Oláf's men climbed towards the farm, the fugitives took shelter in a pigsty while the farmhands went out to challenge the attackers. Measuring his response for once, Oláf declared that his feud was with Hákon alone, and that whoever killed him would receive honour and wealth. Jarl and thrall heard it all.

The Jarl said, 'Why are you so pale, and sometimes as black as earth? Is it that you want to betray me?' In Icelandic poetry the traditional belief is that a man whose colour changes is a man about to die.

'No,' protested Kark.

'We were born on the same night,' the Jarl warned him, 'and brief will be the time between our deaths.' Foresight is the gift of the doomed.

His words bought him an hour as the searchers looked and failed to find them. Night came, and Kark fell into an uneasy sleep. When he awoke Hákon asked him what he had dreamed.

'I dreamed that Oláf Tryggvason placed a ring of gold about my neck.'

'Then Oláf will put a blood-red ring about your neck, if you go to him. So guard yourself, and I will reward you well, as I always have done before. Do not betray me!'

The tone must have been desperate. He knew, and the reader knows, what was to come.

And then Hákon in his turn fell asleep and dreamed, and

the visions he saw made him cry out in terror. He was dreaming his own death; and as he writhed and shouted, Kark panicked, and in dread of discovery pulled out a knife and cut his lord's throat. The ruler of Norway bled to death in the mud of the sty, and even Oláf's saga declares, 'It was the greatest misfortune that such a chieftain should have died in that way.'

The thrall took the Jarl's body to Oláf to claim the promised reward, but he should have heeded Hákon's words. Oláf took one look at his burden, and had him beheaded.

Thus Oláf became king of Norway, usurping Svein's claims. Hákon's son Eirík fled into exile in Denmark. There he met Svein and his erstwhile opponent, Thorkell the Tall, who now served Svein. In the face of the new northern threat, the three men agreed to overlook their differences. It was their alliance which was to break the power of Oláf – and of England.

I spent a couple of days in Haugesund, flitting from concert to concert and enjoying the people-watching. All the while the town and the moorings were filling up. By Friday evening the waterfront was swarming with visitors who'd decided to make a long weekend of it. The fish-market and assorted jazz vocalists were in full swing. I sat on the quarterdeck nursing a mug of tea and stared southwards down the channel, where a couple of racing yachts were tacking up towards us, shaving the quays with each evolution, then walked up to the road-bridge to look down on the sea of white decks. Over two hundred boats were now moored along the waterfront. The Red Cross functionaries had long since given up trying to collect mooring fees. Perhaps they'd fulfilled their quota for annoying people.

'When the Saints' assailed my ears for the seventy-eighth

time. By then I'd heard the tune so often that it no longer even registered, much as dwellers on the Heathrow flightpath get used to passing Jumbos, but this time was different. For one thing, it was being played by a solo sax. For another, it was coming out *Andante funeroso*, dirge tempo, and whilst there's a great New Orleans tradition of street funerals, something about this performance didn't fit. It took a little while to cross the flood of passersby – two elbows in the ribs and a kick in the shins were all it cost me, so I was doing well – and then I saw her: a girl in a long raincoat, fishnet tights, knitting-needle heels, a tulle wedding veil and a crown of orange blossoms, the ensemble completed by a battered tenor sax and a sign hung around her neck, 'Last chance today – kiss me while you can!'

A giggling girl with a video camera enlightened me. She was getting married in the morning, and she was selling kisses to sponsor her hen night. I'm not going to comment on how business went, but when I staggered back to the boat next morning I saw her party reeling in the opposite direction, still swigging from bottles of champagne. 'Hot lips' normally refers to trumpet players. Someone else had just earned the accolade.

(Incidentally, I learnt later that this is a local tradition. Some may find it in dubious taste, but it strikes me as rather more harmless than the German hen-night tradition of getting together to smash crockery. On the other hand, perhaps both are good practice for married life.)

After a while I moved on. 'When the Saints' was the only tune she knew, and besides, I'd left my money on board. The sun was low, and already the waterfront was brightly lit with trails of Christmas lights. Half a dozen restaurant boats were moored to the quayside, each with its own band, and the air was full of clashing chords and the smells of burgers, hot dogs, frying onions and pickled herring. The waterfront was a solid mass of people, moving at snail speeds in both directions. Occasionally a car inched past, and I noticed that whatever Norwegian pedestrians' faults might be, their drivers were models of politeness: apart from a very occasional genteel toot, they proceeded in patient silence. Perhaps the fact that they were all driving Volvos helped. The solid worthiness of those cars would tranquillize a drug-crazed crocodile.

It was sunset by the time I got back to the moorings. It seemed a good moment to sit and watch the sun go down. Sunset usually is. I sat back with my feet propped on a pile of diving equipment, cracking hazelnuts with a convenient monkey-wrench and tossing the shells overboard. A small swarm of seagulls swooped and hovered over the drifting remnants, stabbing, veering, squabbling, and building themselves into a squawking fury without spotting the joke. The water of the sound was black, streaked with crimson in the dying light, gently lapping against countless hulls, and the sky above was a palette of reds and golds.

I threw the last nutshell into the water. A hovering gull swept down on the big prize, snapped it up with eager beak, spat it out and swam off in disgust, and I stood up and stretched. The salsa band were on again that evening and I was looking forward to it. I was turning to cross the rafted yachts to the shore, when a dolphin surfaced right behind my boat, rolled over lazily and blew out a cloud of fish-smelling breath.

I froze. The great barrel body drifted up under my stern-ladder and scratched luxuriously against the bottom rung. A sudden babble of voices rose from the surrounding yachts; footsteps thudded along decks and the water broke into crazy ripples. Flash-guns flickered in the reflections like a breaking storm. Two small children ran down the quayside steps and started slapping the water. Lordly, the dolphin drifted towards them. They lunged. It ducked. They drew back; it surfaced again. The blaze of flash-guns was a rolling barrage. I scrambled up onto the railing just as the dolphin surfaced at last, rubbing along the children's hands. Their eyes were as bright as the besieging flashes. What a lone dolphin was doing in a crowded harbour during the busiest week of the season, I had no idea. I wasn't even sure that dolphins were supposed to live in these northern seas. Who cared? It was worth sailing a thousand miles to see it. Which was just as well, given that I just had.

Inevitably, the festival ended with a parade. Organizers love parades because they're a chance to take over the town. Audiences love them because, well, it's a parade. A certain anarchic type of musician loves them because they're an unrivalled opportunity for fooling around. I love them because they're easy to gatecrash. With a massed band of four hundred musicians drawn from a dozen different genres, one unauthorized trombonist is just lost in the crowd.

We assembled at the crack of jazz dawn – just before noon. The event was scheduled to start at twelve thirty, so naturally, at twenty to one we were all standing around, tuning up and cooling down and waiting in clueless anticipation for someone to tell us what to do. I revelled in the view. On one side was a German sousaphone player in lederhosen and a felt cap, on the other a slender French Arab in Dior shirtsleeves, a roll-up drooping from his supercilious lip, idly spinning his clarinet. Two Brits whom I recognized from the salsa band were conversing in low tones – one on the trombone, the other on the tuba, I mean *low* tones – and behind them another well-known pillar of British jazz was dressed up as Wonder Woman, complete with sable wig. He made a fine figure of a woman. Of *two* women. Eyewatering stuff.

Then a small sweating American in a waistcoat and baton started jumping up and down and blowing a whistle, and we decided that he was trying to attract our attention. We talked about this for a few minutes, then decided to see what he wanted.

'All right!' he rasped. 'Is everyone ready at last! Right then! Trombones over there, trumpets behind them, then winds, percussion in the middle, hurry please! We're late.'

We looked at one another. Gradually, with the caution of a chess grandmaster advancing a pawn, a lean Norwegian saxophonist sidled towards the indicated position. After a moment two clarinettists slunk after him. We stood watching them for a while, but they weren't particularly interesting. Just as we were about to carry on our conversations again, the drum sergeant-major blew his whistle again and shouted with false cheer just short of genocide, 'Okay, folks, a little quicker, *if you don't mind.*' The last phrase came out through gritted teeth.

'Is it us he means?' asked an Australian trombonist in a fetching bonnet, and led a general shamble in completely the wrong direction.

'No!' yelled the sergeant-major in anguish, and dispatched a faithful servitor to fetch us back.

'Right,' called the servitor, a burly Norwegian with scars showing where his sense of humour had been surgically removed. 'Two groups, we're splitting into two groups. Trombones, trumpets, woodwind, percussion, woodwind, trumpets, trombones, please!'

In the past generals were shot for giving orders like that. Musicians are simple souls, or like to pretend that they are, and giving orders as confusing as 'split into two groups' was simply begging for trouble. There seemed to be a certain hint of impatience in the air, so in double-quick time we'd split into five groups of trombonists sandwiched in between three woodwind sections, four lots of trumpets and one very lost-looking steel drum player. In a corner the scarred minion was quietly sobbing to himself.

'Ready ... and ... *march*!' yelled the sergeant-major. A whistle blew, a drum pounded, and we were off.

Now the problem with the sergeant-major was that he was a Dixieland professional. This meant that he not only knew what he was doing, he'd done it so often that the training had settled into his bones. Thanks to Sildajazz's eclectic management, most of the rest of us were Dixie virgins. This led to a slight conflict. *He* was used to signalling the next piece by blowing a particular pattern on his whistle. Most of *us* had only heard those combinations at Wembley. The few players who knew the trick did their best, but most Dixie pieces sound so similar anyway that, frankly, they didn't have a chance.

So we progressed into the crowded town, the sergeant-major leaping and twirling with all the passion of his native New Orleans, the rest of us shambling along any old how. I found myself caught between the bonneted Australian and the trombonist from the salsa band. The Antipodean was blowing away with ferocious majesty, cheeks puffed out like Louis Armstrong; the Brit indulging in wild arpeggios.

He turned to me.

'What the fuck are we playing?' he asked.

'Buggered if I know,' I replied.

We swung up our slides and started tootling anyway. Everybody else was, and with four hundred musicians going at once, nobody would be able to tell the difference.

Then we came into the town square. It's actually a steep rectangle tilted down the hillside, with a long central green flanked by shallow steps which lead down to the quay. The drum-major swung an imperious arm and hurtled off to the right. Since we were coming in on the left-hand side of the square, half of us decided that that was far too energetic and kept on going down the left-hand stairs. The massed onlookers on the green watched in bewilderment as the parade split into two utterly unequal halves and came streaming and squeaking down both sets of stairs. Of course, since we were all watching the sergeant-major's furious baton, we were all playing in time, but since a good fifty metres now separated the halves our revered conductor thought that the left-hand side was a beat behind. He turned with a furious grimace, waving at us to speed up. We obliged – anything to be helpful – with the net result that by the time we crashed back together at the bottom of the stairs, we were at least a beat ahead of the Other Side. They promptly speeded up as we slowed down, leaving the conductor waving his baton in a pattern which had nothing to do with anything any of the rest of us were playing.

As we swung onto the quay, the music changed again. Suddenly I realized that, against all probability, *I recognized the tune*.

I turned to my neighbour in delight. 'I know this one! It's "Didn't He Ramble"!'

He glowered. 'You bastard! I thought you were on my side!'

'It's easy. It goes like this!' I blared the tune towards him. He was a real musician, he picked it up at once. Having been utterly lost for the last fifteen minutes, we launched into it with all the zeal and zing we had. Our teachers would have been proud of us.

Just as we swept into the rousing finale the Australian turned with a look of venom and screamed, 'Will you bastards play "Down by the Riverside" like the rest of us?'

Dixie all sounds the same to me.

We finished off, of course, with 'When the Saints'. Everyone knows 'When the Saints'. We'd poured down onto the quay by then and were standing five deep across the waterfront, serenading the town and shaking the windows across the sound. Behind us the docks and walkways were a solid mass of aficionados; rows of heads as small as beads lay silhouetted along the road-bridge rampart. The sergeant-major, grinning, swung his baton round to signal one last chorus. Some of us decided that he meant 'Speed up'. Others, remembering the chaos on the stairs, reckoned they were being told off again and slowed down. You couldn't create a sound effect like that with a studio full of computers. I saw the sergeant-major's neck stiffen, a strange gory blush creep across his ears. When he turned and finally brought us off his eyes were glazed.

'Thank you. Thank you,' he said quietly, just before applause engulfed us. He bowed gracefully to the adoring crowd, straightened, and shot us a look of venom. I'm told there's a video of that morning's performance. I'm sure it brings tears to his eyes.

8

EAST ABOUT

'Because the main coastline and the mountain spine
of Norway have a general northeast–southwest trend,
a ship sailing from, say, Bergen to Oslo was said to
be headed east (not south then north), one sailing in
the opposite direction, north.'

Lee M. Hollander, footnote to *Saga of Harald Fairhair*

The festival finished in the small hours of Sunday morning.
Some time after dawn the moorings grumbled back to life,
and started thinking about leaving.

Pilotage, these days, is a tricky business. According to most
modern sailing schools, *navigation* is the art of working out
where on the sea you are and how to find land again. *Pilotage*
is what you practise when you do. It could be defined as the
art of not running into things, and vast resources of time and
money have been spent over the years to make it a less dangerous business. All but the smallest creeks are strung with
channel marker buoys, red to port and green to starboard as
you head into harbour, unless you're in the Americas, in which
case it's the other way round. Safe water is marked with red-
and-white-striped buoys, isolated dangers with red-and-black.
Larger dangers are ringed with 'cardinal' buoys: two cones in
vertical line with their apices upwards, for example, mean

'keep to the north of this mark'. Major channels are marked with lights: paired leading lights à la *Swallows and Amazons*, which tell you that you're in the right channel as long as you keep one directly above the other, sector lights which change colour if you stray too far to one side. Every one of these is marked on charts, with its light pattern, sound and radar signals, and regular reports are broadcast on VHF radio warning of changes to charted buoys.

With the sea lanes so thoroughly signposted, the main danger to shipping these days is shipping. The *International Regulations for Preventing Collisions at Sea* were established in 1972 to stop idiot skippers running into each other, and go into the whole business with desperate thoroughness. Everyone knows that steam gives way to sail, but did you know that vessels engaged in fishing (two vertical cones with their apices together or red over white light) give way to vessels restricted in their ability to manoeuvre? (Vertical ball-diamond-ball or red-white-red.) It all seems a bit extreme given that the most dangerous ships in the water today are 100,000-tonne tankers. How can you *not* see a ship the size of Buckingham Palace? You'd be amazed.

Unfortunately for the maritime world, pleasure-boaters don't have to bother with all that complicated right-of-way stuff. It might get in the way of their enjoyment. The legally required knowledge for navigation of pleasure vessels on the high seas is precisely zero. Hence the situation in Haugesund that sunny Sunday morning, as 230 boats moved off southwards down a channel a hundred metres wide.

It started well. I was on the southernmost-but-one raft of boats, and chatting with my neighbours the previous afternoon, we'd worked out a rough plan of campaign. With the precision of the Red Arrows the boats of the southernmost raft cast off their lines, peeled away and steamed south. Once

114

they were gone, we moved. Those planning to stay longer untied and shifted to the empty berth, clearing the way for those departing. Having agreed to leave just after nine, by nine thirty, with no more than minimal shouting and confusion of ropes, a motley collection of sailing-yachts and motor-cruisers was heading south at eight knots, watching all hell break loose behind.

The situation on the other rafts was complicated. Firstly, not everybody wanted to leave that morning, and those who did wanted to leave at different times. On the raft immediately to the north, the outermost three were planning to stay an extra day, the next two wanted to leave at noon and the sixth at nine. Number six therefore had to wake his neighbours, untie himself from them, pass a line from number five (outer neighbour) to number seven (inner neighbour) to stop the whole raft drifting away, and reverse out of the gap without fouling any other ropes with his mast. Naturally, since the outer boats were now only held by a single loose rope, the southerly breeze swung them out into the channel, neatly blocking the fairway for the seventy-three other boats rapidly proceeding towards them. The sound rang with shouts and the roar of engines going into emergency reverse. In a panic, boat number five, who'd left his engines running just in case, cast off his own lines and roared backwards, trailing ropes like jellyfish tentacles but with rather more risk – a rope round your propeller can wrench the drive-shaft clean out of its bed. The crew of boat four suddenly found themselves adrift in the channel, rafted up to three sleeping yachts. They hurled more ropes to boat number seven. The first two attempts failed (they always do). By the time order was established and the four castaways dragged back to the raft by main force, the sound to the north was a choked mass of shipping drifting under a solid cloud of swearing.

Meanwhile, life in the southern channel was getting interesting. The breeze was from the south, which meant that sailing yachts going south had to tack against it; this in a channel a mile wide, which isn't a lot when over a hundred boats are going that way. The sailors therefore had the choice of leaving their sails furled and motoring at four or five knots, or sailing at a good eight knots, but advancing in zigzags. Some chose one option, some the other: soon the sound was a mass of white hulls and criss-crossing sails. I wasn't in a hurry, and besides, this was free entertainment, so I tucked in behind my neighbours' ocean racer, which was motoring, and we headed calmly south.

Then the first motor-cruisers broke out of the scrum behind us, saw the sound full of slow-moving sailors, decided that it would be girlish and wimpy to go slow, and opened their throttles wide.

Boat after boat roared through the mêlée, motorists waving happily to sailors in the comradeship of the sea without actually noticing the effect of a powerboat's metre-high wake on a half-metre-high yacht's deck. The sea behind them was filled with wildly rocking masts and wildly shaking fists. One group of clowns steamed past me so close that I could see their hi-aren't-we-cool grins. They waved at me and zoomed on. Five seconds later their wake hit. *Peregrino* slewed sideways. A terrible crash came from the galley as a cupboard burst open, spilling my plates all over the floor. Right ahead the ocean racer rolled so far over that I thought the helmsman was going overboard, then lashed back the other way. As *Peregrino* whipped back, the shock sent my chair careering across the deck. Before the aftershocks had died another idiot belted through. I glared in his wake, resisting the temptation to chase and ram. The ocean skipper ahead yelled a volley of imprecations, then looked back to me and raised a questioning thumb.

I'm okay, I signalled back.

Wankers, he gestured. You can say a lot with hand-signals.

I was heading south to Stavanger to meet a friend: Mark, whom I'd first met on expedition in Belize. He'd just graduated, so a fortnight's cruising in Norway seemed just what the doctor ordered. He brought two friends with him, his girl-friend Elly and another expedition veteran, Aled 'not *the* Aled?' Jones,* so for the first time since reaching Sweden I had a crew. The fortnight which followed was delightful. From Stavanger we headed north to the legendary Hardangerfjord, which was everything a fjord should be, sheer-walled, topped with forest, waterfalls trailing white mares'-tails into the void, the water still and green as a jade mirror. We anchored in bays that might never have seen another boat, walked up river-valleys so deep the sun scarcely reached them, gazed in awe at the snow-capped cliffs, steamed back out to sea under a sky full of stars. Then we returned to Stavanger, where the harbourmaster *still* hadn't come back from holiday, spent a wild day and night with Fred Anton and Anne Gro in their favourite, traditional Norwegian-Mexican restaurant, and set our bow, at last, for the south. I would have loved to stay and explore the endless convolutions of the coast, but autumn was approaching and it was time to seek safer waters.

Trouble struck on the morning we left. The starboard motor, normally a pillar of reliability, refused to start. I checked all the connections, crawled out of the way to let Mark and Aled do the same, and called for a mechanic.

After a short examination he looked up from the pit. 'It's either your starter motor or your relay,' he said.

---

* No.

'How can we work out which?'

'Hit it.'

I passed him the lump-hammer and turned the key. Buzz – whang – ROAR, and the engine shuddered to life.

'Starter motor,' he said laconically. 'Get it replaced.'

I checked the engine manual. The only repair shop for that make of engine in the country was in Oslo. That was fine by us. He offered to ring ahead and make sure they had a starter motor ready for us.

'Thanks,' I said.

'Don't mention it,' he said, and left us.

The following four days proved entertaining. The starboard starter had decided that it was going to make life difficult, and it succeeded. Every morning began with a brisk session of beat-the-hell-out-of-the-motor, all three gentlemen working in relays until the thing fired. Aled proved to have the surest touch – 'it's all in the wrist', he explained – but starting the engine became an exercise in misery. To get to the offending unit we had to remove the air filter, crawl in behind the exhaust system and then wrap ourselves horizontally around the back of the engine, swinging the lump-hammer at a target which was conveniently lodged under two fragile water pipes, over a collection of wiring and six inches from the starboard diesel tank. And then, once it had started, get out again, pressing ourselves against a couple of tons of hot and throbbing metal. There are better ways to start the day.

But it was worth it. Norway's coastline resembles the wilds of New Zealand more than any scenery you'd expect to find in Europe, and although the southern zone doesn't match the far north for sheer extravagance, it's still a wonderful cruising ground. The coast is hazed with rocks and islets, green-shadowed with trees, webbed with countless channels, and everywhere tiny hamlets and clusters of holiday homes cling to improbable landings. We saw houses on stilts projecting from the rocks, houses with garages for jet-skis, houses with diving-boards projecting from balconies, houses with navigation lights on the roof, even one glorious house with a wooden bridge running to an adjoining islet, where stood two loungers, a parasol and a wine-cooler. It gave a whole new meaning to having a drink on the rocks . . . Chief of the glories was Blindleia, the Blind Man's Passage, a twenty-kilometre channel between the islands so narrow that at times Mark and Aled, standing on opposite decks, could touch both sides without stretching, but all along the coast from Egersund, past Lindesnes (Norway's southern tip, on the same latitude as Inverness) and round to Oslo the mazes called, beguiling. The late August weather was dreamlike, day after day of gentle winds and blue, blue skies. We could have stayed there for ever – but my friends had a plane to catch.

Twelve days after they joined me, we steamed up the Oslofjord and into the bay at its end.

Kipling once called Auckland 'Last, loneliest, loveliest, exquisite, apart'. Many would agree with him, but those whose budget and timetable won't allow a visit to the Antipodes can achieve the same effect by taking the ferry to Oslo. No other European city I know comes close to the beauty of the northern City of Sails, as you see it from the head of the fjord. It sweeps round a broad bay studded with islets, a shining city backed with a great horseshoe of wooded heights. To one side the remains of Åkershus castle – one of the few castles in Scandinavia – protect the old harbour. To the other, in the Frognekilen inlet, loom two strange pagodas, the old homes of the Royal Sailing Club and the Oslo Rowing Club. It's best not to look too closely: behind them lies the concrete wilderness of the Oslo docks, all rusting rails and piled containers and skeletal, preying cranes. Above, on the wooded hillside, a colossal ski-ramp rears up, a white tick on the landscape. The town itself has none of the architectural extravagance of Florence or Berlin. At its best, it's stately, dignified, cool and comfortable. At its worst, it's a big city, although being Norwegian it scarcely plumbs the abyss of urban misery. But seen from the water, as we saw it under a golden August sunset, it's truly magnificent.

We arrived on a Friday, so there was no point looking for a mechanic. On the Saturday we walked into the city centre, where all the city's sporting associations had gathered to seek fresh converts. Norwegian society is sports-mad, and it showed: the quays fronting the Town Hall were crammed with activity, from kick-boxing to roller-hockey to ski-jumping. Ski-jumping? Yes, a scaffold had been set up at the water's edge, with a long ski-ramp projecting over the harbour, and happy Vikings in ski-boots and wetsuits were flying down the ramp to splash-land in the briny. From there we wound our way through the stately streets to one of the city's many parks, where the Oslo Philharmonic was indulging in an Outdoor Spectacular which – practically uniquely in my experience – didn't finish off with the *1812 Overture*, although Tchaikovsky did feature largely, no doubt because he writes loud pieces and is therefore audible across open spaces. Haydn's string quartets are marvellous music, but their subtle modulations tend to lose impact when you can't hear them over the noise of the crowd. After that we wandered back to the docks, where a spirited game of children's roller-hockey was in progress, and went to the tourist bureau to ask what else there was to see.

I include the following conversation as an insight into one difference between modern Brits and Norwegians.

The man behind the counter was short, balding and middle-aged, and his shirt was so covered in language-proficiency badges that it must have had reinforced seams. It was a hot day, and when I took a swig from my water bottle he smiled and said, 'That's right, have a snifter.'

'You speak wonderful English,' I told him.

'I worked there. You have to learn the language if you want to meet people, talk with people, have sex with people, eh? Eh?'

And we, all grown men, looked down and blushed.

Following our libidinous linguist's advice, we spent the Sunday museum-hopping. We'd found a berth in the Frognekilen inlet, and by great good luck some of the best museums in Norway are on the Bygdøy peninsula, just across the water. Elly, having rowed for her college, ferried us over in the fibreglass bathtub I called a dinghy. Once there, we went to ogle ships.

Contrary to popular belief, the Vikings did not make their entire living from the sea. Herring was a major feature of their diet – how times change – but the great bulk of the Norwegian population worked on and lived from the land. Landowners and farmers were the major political groups in the country. Even the kings were essentially full-time farmers and only part-time politicians; in pre-Christian times rulers were re-membered for the number of good harvests their reigns saw. For every chieftain who went off raiding overseas, two or three stayed behind to mind the farm, and the only reason that so few sagas and praise-poems deal with them is that farming is, well, boring. No poet ever made a fortune singing about crop rotation. Sex sells, but not when it's germinating beans.

This is why the Viking longships hold such fascination. They're the sexiest things that ever sailed.

There are three Viking ships on Bygdøy, housed in a glori-ous cruciform building with high, arched roofs and white walls. It's almost church-like, and the reverence is entirely justified. Forget all the technicalities of sailing ability and navigation in the days before magnetic compasses. Forget that they are ships for a second. Just go there and look at as them as works of art. It's worth it. One ship – excavated at Tune on the eastern Oslofjord in 1867 – has been left in the shattered condition in which it was found, laid open like a herring on a slab, and even its ruins are poignantly elegant. The second, found at Gokstad on the western Oslofjord, has been fully restored, and there's nothing poignant about it. If ever a boat had the soul of a super-model, this is it. And the third ship, excavated at Oseberg, half a day's sail north of Gokstad, is everything that ship ever was, with decorations. Too small and light to face the open seas, it was once a great lord's pleasure yacht. Nobody knows whose; it was buried in the mid-ninth century, the grave of two great ladies. But whoever it was had a ship that would make modern boat-builders weep. It's twelve hundred years since that ship sailed, and we still haven't made anything as beautiful.

But for hardiness, the Gokstad ship stands alone. It's not a traditional longship, but a scaled-down replica, a cutter rather than a ship of the line. To judge by the number of shields hung along its side, its crew was 'only' 64, which gives some impression of the manpower needed on the full-sized long-ships – half again as large – on their raids. Still, its seaworthi-ness is astonishing. In 1893 a Norwegian crew built a full-scale replica and sailed it across the Atlantic to the Chicago Trade Fair. A century later, a Danish team built a replica of a similar ship and sailed it round the world; on the run from Newfound-land to Iceland they sailed through a full hurricane unscathed. It's no wonder that Svein ruled the North Sea rim. With ships like this, you could do *anything*.

It's still terrifying to think of. The ship may look fluid, supple and elegant, but that's because it is: although the planks of the hull are nailed together for strength, they're only attached to the internal frames with birch-root lashings. The 1893 crew reported that in heavy weather the entire hull flexed under the impact of the waves. If that had ever happened on any boat I'd been on, I'd have jumped overboard. Added to that, the deck is open to the sky. What covered space there is was used for storage, and being a wooden boat, making a fire and preparing a hot meal were not an option for the wise. The crew must have slept, when they slept, on deck, open to the elements, without even the hope of a decent feed until they reached land. If the wind failed, they had to row, and at eighteen tons this is no skiff. And as for seaworthiness, it may be supple, but if a wave ever broke into the ship it would be bail or drown. No wonder the bow and stern are so high and backwards-curved. They were all that turned the heavy waves aside. The aesthetic effect is sheer coincidence. The thought of heading out into the North Sea in that boat – the sea as I knew it, capricious and violent – was appalling. Crossing the Atlantic? I couldn't imagine it.

The Bygdøy museums made me feel very unadventurous. Not far from the Viking ships is the *Fram* museum, detailing the adventures of Fridtjof Nansen. Convinced by the discovery of Siberian wood in Canadian ice-floes that an icy current crossed the North Pole, he commissioned a specially strengthened ship and sailed into the ice in 1893 to see what would happen. For three years the *Fram* (which means 'Forward') was frozen in, slowly drifting westwards from Siberia to emerge from the ice off Newfoundland; the twelve-man crew spent the entire time living on board* making scientific

---

* Though having run out of cigars, conversation and (presumably) patience, Nansen and a single colleague left after two years to sledge to the Pole.

observations without, apparently, going mad. Opposite that monument to human stubbornness is the *Ra* museum, home to the rafts *Ra* and *Kon-Tiki* on which yet another mad Norseman, Thor Heyerdahl, set out to prove his theories of population migrations in the Mediterranean and Pacific basins. Looking at the balsawood home in which he'd confronted the most violent ocean on earth, I could only shudder. Contemplating those three museums and the mentality which they represent, I stopped wondering how the Vikings managed to conquer half the world. I stopped wondering why Amundsen not only beat Scott to the Antarctic, but got back alive. If ever I plan a trip to the edges of human endurance and beyond, I'm taking a Norwegian with me. They've had the practice.

Next day, my friends went home, so I went out to make some new ones.

September was upon us, but the weather was unseasonably warm. Every evening Oslo's sailing community came down to the harbour to stroll among their boats. If this had been Gothenburg they would have ignored me, but Oslo's a proper city, and the people there can handle strangers. I grew used to sitting on deck enjoying the sunshine and exchanging greetings with passersby. Most visitors were businessmen, active types in their late thirties, but there were also grizzled seadogs, a couple of long-term sailors who, like me, lived aboard, the odd young couple with children – you could often see the kids tacking around the harbour in tiny sailing dinghies – and even a lone woman in her fifties, who'd sailed single-handed from Stavanger. She had arrived soaked to the skin in the middle of a gale, her hands so numb she couldn't fasten her mooring lines. Seeing that she was struggling, I lent a hand, then brought her aboard and made her tea. I've never made friends faster.

One afternoon I was sitting on deck thinking about nothing much, when a small sailing yacht cut across my vision. A man slightly older than I was at the helm, calling out instructions in the manner of yachting husbands the world over, whilst his wife crouched on the bow fiddling with ropes. It should have been a classy entry into the berth, but a sudden gust from the fickle wind caught them at the wrong moment and shoved the bow against the jetty. Without stopping to think, I leapt ashore and fended it off. The lady sprang past me like a perfumed gazelle and busied herself with ropes, and the gentleman killed the engine and stepped neatly ashore.

'*Takk*,' he said, dropping a loop of rope over a bollard. His boat was old and somewhat battered, but both rope and knot were flawless: evidently his barque was worse than his bight.

'*Takk ska du har*,' I replied, having picked up that useful phrase somewhere on the way.

'Oh, are you the guy from London?' he asked in distinctly BBC tones. I was about to hate him for his linguistic superiority when he added, 'Ta for the catch,' in English so English that I knew I'd found a compatriot.

'Cup of tea?' I asked. 'I've got a brew on.'

He looked at his watch. 'We've got time. Why not?'

Another new friend.

He was an archaeologist from Devon, she an Oslo TV producer. They'd met studying at the University of Rouen, fallen in love, and eventually moved to Oslo together and married. Being such an international couple, they attracted cosmopolitan friends. One evening they held a dinner party, at which I met two Norwegians, two Bretons from the University of Oslo, and a long-haired Californian in a beach shirt who'd decided to renounce his hippy beliefs in favour of hunting a fortune in internet share-dealing. Two days later, they invited me out for an evening's fishing. We dragged our mountain bikes onto the underground and took the train out into the suburbs. It must be the most spectacular metropolitan journey in Europe, along the back of a wooded ridge, the blue bay spread out below flecked with brilliant sails. At the last but one stop – the Norwegian equivalent of Totteridge and Whetstone – we hopped out and pedalled down a quiet road, over the edge onto a dirt track, and out into the woods. At once the city was forgotten. We bumped across stones and down rutted short-cuts, the dark pines closing in around us, the air heavy with the scent of resin, finally stopping beside a little lake. David and Arnaud broke out the rods, and for the next two hours they fly-fished with delicate casts, while I, not having fished since I was twelve, was posted a strategic distance further down the bank to play with a spinner. After a while I left them to it and strolled along paths still warm with the day's sun, watching the dusk fall and the stars pricking out through the deepening blue. Soon it grew cold; I made my way back between the trees to the bold fishermen, who hadn't had a bite all night. After another chilly hour we rode back along the stony trails and out onto the top of the ridge. The city below us was a web of lights. The track zigzagged down the flank of the ridge, and we whizzed down it laughing like maniacs and jumping potholes half-seen in the darkness. Within quarter of an hour the track turned into a suburban street, and we were back in the capital.

There aren't many places in Europe you can do that.

The next morning my troubles began.

Bad luck's a part of travelling. In maritime terms, ship happens, and there's not a lot you can do to change it now that human sacrifices are frowned upon. (They might not help much, but I can think of times when they would have relieved *my* feelings.) With that option closed, there are three ways you can look at luck. There's the rational: 'this is just a random concatenation of unfortunate events which I will survive'. Practically nobody thinks that way, especially using the word *concatenation*. There's the Viking: 'my luck's changed, I'll have to be tough'. Fine in most circumstances. And then, most traditional of all, the Homeric: 'oops, I just offended the Gods'.

I save *that* superstition until I really need it.

It started when I rang the Oslo engineers to get my motor fixed.

'*Hej. Förlåt, men snakker du engelsk?*'

'Yes. How can I help you?'

'I need help to change a starter motor.'

'No, you don't.'

'Yes I do.'

'You don't, it's easy. You've just got to change four bolts and two wires.'

Should I explain the location of the demon motor? I decided I couldn't be bothered. 'Just send someone.'

'Yes, sir,' he said in a voice which meant, It's your funeral.

Half an hour later the mechanic arrived, a short, swarthy man in overalls. He came aboard grinning, looking for the imbecile who couldn't change a starter motor. His English was as bad as my Norwegian, so I pointed him to the problem. He looked at the motor. He craned his neck to see the starter. He crawled in behind the engine, grappled with the air filter, scraped past the exhaust, bashed his head on Attila the Hull, and looked. A muttered word which sounded curiously like '*¡mierda!*' filtered up from the depths. When he reappeared, the grin was gone.

'Now I get it,' he said grimly, and rolled up his sleeves.

The first two hours passed with monosyllabic grunts and the clang of tools and curses. Then his mobile rang, and he answered '¿Sí?', followed by a long burst of fluid Hispanic. Subsequent conversation – in high-speed Spanish and accompanied by much arm-waving – established that he was a Cuban engineer who'd studied in Russia, fallen in love with a Norwegian and moved to Oslo to fix engines. After another hour, with the engine lying in oily pieces all over the deck, his boss rang to ask what the delay was. Listening in, I picked up the Norwegian for 'You're not going to believe this, *jefe*'; half an hour after *that* the boss turned up in person to see this starter motor from hell.

Five hours after rolling his sleeves up, Hermes tightened the last connection, climbed out of the engine pit, threw the key in the ignition – and nothing happened.

The starter motor had nothing wrong with it. It was the relay leading to it which was faulty. The fact that the motor started just as we hit it that first time in Stavanger was pure coincidence. That evening after work, Hermes dropped in on his way home with a replacement relay, fitted and tested it in thirty seconds flat, gave me a friendly grin and departed, leaving me one working motor better off and several hundred pounds' labour charges poorer.

Ship happens.

The next day I went shopping. My camera had broken a week before, so I needed a replacement. The salesman – yet another mad Norwegian, whose favourite hobby was driving a truck around Rwanda – found me a decent SLR for a reasonable price, and I cycled home content, right up until the moment I hit a stone, came off my bike, split my shin open to the bone and broke the new camera. It took two days and a fortnight's budget to get bike and camera repaired; the wound on my shin took weeks to heal.

I swore for a bit, then hobbled on. Things like that happen. It could have been worse.

The next day, after ten days in Oslo, I set off down the fjord, expecting the forecast light winds and sunshine, and ran into the worst storm I'd ever experienced.

It came out of nowhere, a black squall blowing up from the south, channelled by the narrowing walls and the rising seabed of the Oslofjord into a storm of hail and a barrage of two-metre waves. Within half an hour the weather had changed from summer to winter, and I was battling to make headway against it. I was heading for Sandefjord, the next inlet west of the Oslofjord, and to get there I had to leave the shelter of the fjord and head across a mile and a half of open sea. Even behind the sheltering rocks, the sea was bad. Outside, it was appalling. Great, foam-edged rollers were sweeping up from the south, their dark faces streaked with white, and when *Peregrino* lurched down into the troughs my eyes were level with the wind-lashed crests. I'd never seen waves bigger than the boat before, and for a second I was terrified. Then there was no more time to be scared: we were out in the open, and the wind was screaming, the spray rattling on the windows, and the roar of the engines rising and falling as we climbed up the face of the waves and surfed down their backs. Ahead and to the right the sea was a pale fury of breaking spray, great swathes of foam swirling and flooding across granite reefs. Even going head to wind, it took all my skill to hold the boat steady. Turning east across the wind, with those breakers heaving her bodily at the shore, would have been suicide. There was nothing for it. I waited for a gap between two breakers, spun the wheel, felt her turn, felt the next wave kick us further round, leant on the throttles and drove for the nearest safe haven.

The storm lasted a week, a miserable, rainy week in a grim

concrete harbour. At first I was resigned to waiting. Then I got annoyed. Patience is all very well as long as you don't have to be patient for too long. In my case, that's usually counted in hours. After a week the weather was still filthy, but it was nowhere near as foul as my temper, so, in the best traditions of the Viking berserker, I went out to meet my doom, steaming southeastwards across the fjord in the teeth of the gale. It wasn't pleasant by any stretch of the imagination, but it didn't look like it was going to sink me, and by that stage, that was all that counted. I spat into the wind (a stupid idea, it blew back in my face), raised two fingers to Fate, and lurched on across the waves.

That afternoon I came into sight of Väderöarna, the Weather Islands, a collection of granite skerries separated by narrow channels, the Swedish equivalent of Blindleia and just as beautiful. There's only one harbour there, accessible via a narrow granite-fanged fairway. The wind was blowing hard across the entry as I approached, so, acting sensibly for once in my life, I slowed right down to give myself a better look at the situation, then stopped to practise the necessary manoeuvres outside the harbour.

At this point my starboard gear-shift jammed.

You *can* steer a large boat into a narrow stone channel with only one engine working, but only if you don't mind swimming the last bit. Boulders break boats. That's all there is to it.

I sighed, turned away, made for a sheltered bay, and anchored for the night.

Next morning, after a wonderful night's sleep in which I only got up a dozen times to check that I hadn't drifted, my magnificent high-tech anchor winch seized up. A relay in the control-box had blown, and I didn't have a spare. What I did have was forty metres of anchor chain and a fifteen-kilo anchor to hoist up without mechanical assistance. The only way to get it in was to stand in the anchor locker and pull, with my legs braced against a steel girder which was welded in at exactly the right height to open the wound on my leg. It took a long, long time, and when I say it bloody hurt, I *mean* bloody. I was starting to feel that I had a Jonah on board. This was worrying seeing as I was alone.

Standing on one leg to relieve the pain, I steamed over to the legendary tourist port of Smögen, the Cowes of Sweden, and looked for a mechanic. None was forthcoming: the holiday season was over, and now everyone was busy repairing all the stuff they should have fixed during the summer. I spent two and a half hours in Scandinavia's boating capital, then lost my temper again. Four hours' drive away was the harbour of Henån, the only generator-repair centre in Sweden. *Sod it*, I thought. *I'll get there and get everything fixed.*

I reached Henån just after sunset, having steered in fetching curves all down the narrow fjord, and docked, one-engined, near a warehouse. Several answerphones later I discovered that the generator guys could send me a mechanic in the morning, but there were no gearbox experts in town. For that, I'd have to go to Gothenburg. At least it was in the right direction. I'd just have to manage with a dodgy engine. Steering in circles can get you anywhere, it just takes longer.

The mechanic played with my generator for all of ten minutes, shook his head and said, 'We'll have to send it back.'

'Send it back? It's only just been installed!'

'Sorry. There's nothing else we can do. I'll winch it out of the boat and send it to Germany. It'll only take a couple of weeks.'

'A couple of *weeks*?' It was late September. Between storms and starter motors, I was already a clear fortnight behind schedule. There was no way I was going to make it through the canals to Stockholm and back round the coast before the winter. So I hit the mechanic over the head with a spanner, tied him down on the quarterdeck, sacrificed him to Odin, poured his blood overboard to placate Aegir the sea-god, burned his liver as an offering to Thor, dedicated his heart to Thrym the ice giant, drank a libation to the whole Norse pantheon out of his skull, grilled the rest over a slow fire and ate him for dinner. Well, okay, I didn't, but it was very tempting.

Instead, I quickly changed my plans.

'If you take the generator out now, could you deliver it somewhere else?'

'Where?' he asked cautiously.

'Hönö.'

'No problem.'

'Right.' Two hours later the generator was on the jetty, and I was on the quarterdeck, heading out to sea. As night fell I wove my way between the treacherous rocks north of Marstrand and lined up on the first of the Gothenburg channel lights. Shortly after nine o'clock I curved my way under the Fotö–Hönö bridge, swung into the long, rocky harbour and tied up, once more, to the quay.

Jan and Anita were waiting for me with beaming smiles, a huge plate of fried herrings, and a tumbler of lemon vodka, Swedish to the end.

'How are you? And how's the boat?'

'I'm fine. As for the boat, right now I'd be better off with a kayak.'

So the next morning I caught the ferry into Gothenburg and hired one.

9

GÖTA ÄLV

'At the very end of summer, King Harald sailed south
to Kungälv. He gathered all the light ships he could
find and rowed up the river; he had them carried up
the falls and on into Vänern.'

Saga of Harald Hardrada

It wasn't madness.

Honest.

I'd decided that I wanted to see the Swedish waterways.
Peregrino's hard-worn hardware needed fixing, so the boat was
going to have to stay in harbour under the mechanics' tender
mercies. And given all the stress I'd had with said hardware,
going on in a vessel which had no moving parts whatsoever
seemed like a cunning plan. After all, I was going to be on
canals for most of the trip, so it wasn't as if I'd need big
engines, was it?

Sometimes I wonder how I've survived this long.

On 26 September 2000, I climbed into the touring kayak I'd
baptized *Peregrino II*, paddled out of Lilla Bommen harbour,
and headed up the Göta Älv. It's the most famous waterway in Scandinavia. Which *part* of Scandinavia it's the most
famous waterway of has always been an open question: for
a large part of the peninsula's history it formed the boundary

between Norway, Denmark and Sweden. Its reed-girt islands saw more parleys, battles and ambushes than anywhere else in Scandinavia. Every hero in the sagas ended up there at some point. As far as rowing upriver was concerned, I was in good company.

It's just as well, because I was in appalling weather. It was tipping it down when I left, sharp, straight, cold sheets of greyness sweeping across the scenery, but since the scenery in question was the industrial heart of Gothenburg, I wasn't missing much. From Lilla Bommen I paddled up under a huge steel flow-control system, past long lines of mouldering river-boats and heavy industrial barges, all welds and wiring, past factory wharves and green-streaked piling and looming steel pipes, and into a narrow river-valley fenced in behind wide bluffs. Rain-flattened swathes of rank grass spread out between cancerous industrial estates, and behind them the road and railway together roared into the heart of Sweden, a constant aural assault. I stopped a couple of times for a leak – well, see what a constant drip of rain-water and river-water along both wrists does for your bladder – grounding the kayak on narrow beaches of shattered bricks overgrown with slime. Each time, as I climbed back in, I nearly capsized. It was not, on the whole, an auspicious start. I only saw one sign of life all day: a decoy duck bobbing forlornly on the waters. I camped in the rain by the village of Kungälv, once the north's most fought-over border fortress, and dreamt of the olden days. At least my problems didn't involve homicidal relations and berserk marauders. Oláf Tryggvason was less lucky. In 998, his work in Norway barely begun, he sailed here to propose marriage to the widowed Swedish queen, Sigríd. One of his conditions was that she accept baptism. She refused, and in his anger he slapped her face. 'You might just die for that,' she told him. Within a year she'd married Oláf's great rival, Svein. Denmark and Sweden allied against Norway. Eighteen months later, Oláf was dead. Don't mess with Swedish girls.

Next morning brought me relief; it was a bit too late for Oláf. Before setting foot in my Ship of Folly I walked into the village up a steep, winding road, past snug wooden houses and well-tended gardens full of apple trees. It was good to move and stretch, good to smell the autumn air, good to see the sun slowly breaking out of the clouds. Quite suddenly a little well of *joie de vivre* bubbled up inside me. Whatever else might be bothering me, mechanical breakdowns and unreliable equipment couldn't be part of it. How – short of sinking – can a kayak break down? As the sun broke through the clouds, I felt thoroughly happy.

On the way back through the village I saw two old men working in their orchard. I stopped to say hello, and to beg for some water to refill my bottles.

'No problem,' said one, in calm, melodious Swedish which even I understood. As his companion took my bottles inside, he added, 'Do you want an apple?'

'With pleasure,' I said. He swung the gate open.

'Help yourself.' He pointed towards the windfalls scattered across the mossy grass. 'Take all you can carry, we've got far too many.' And, as I hesitated, 'And take the best ones. No, no, not that one, the best ones.'

Gothenburg was left far behind.

The river may not be prey to marauding longships any more, but don't let anyone kid you that it's safe. It's the main trade artery linking the lake of Vänern with the sea, and the four-thousand-ton freighters which make the trip don't stop for anyone: one grey giant swept past so close and so fast that the wash almost capsized me. (If anyone ever sees the freighter *Vänerland*, torpedo the swine.) Then, there's the current which is fed by the biggest lake in Scandinavia. It's terribly pretty to look at from the shore, rippling and rolling in strange, swirling feathers of oily movement. It even sounds cheerful, chuckling and bubbling and gurgling to itself; but not when you're waist-deep in a skinny eggshell of a kayak, trying to paddle against it. What you notice then is that it's *fast*. It doesn't want to go the way you're going, and when a billion tons of water decide to go in a certain direction, they don't hang about. I'd been relying on six hundred horsepower to get me around for the last four months. Doing it myself was a whole new experience.

Gradually my body woke up to the fact that I wasn't on *Peregrino* any more and adapted to the novel conditions of actual work. My arms found a rhythm of paddling, and my lungs eased out the wrinkles of four months' idleness. An hour before I camped that night, on a grassy bank between sweeping willows, I found myself singing Nina Simone songs to the paddle-stroke, and knew that I'd be okay. Things weren't perfect. My seat was wet, my backside itched, one heel was rubbed raw from sitting in the half-crunched kayaker's position for so long, and I was definitely starting to smell; but I'd got my good humour back. I'd stopped worrying about breakdowns and timetables and mechanics. It was worth a little discomfort for that.

I left my campsite just before eight o'clock on a gloriously sunny autumn morning. The trees lining the river were ablaze in their richest colours, from palest yellow to burning crimson, rising behind the stilt-like channel markers in pillars and plumes of fire. I paddled slowly upriver, keeping close to the bank, and in the clear water beneath me I saw the ghosts of rocks and treestumps floating past. Two swans went drifting by, arrogance personified, then took fright at something downriver and suddenly lumbered across the water and into the air. As they beat by above me, I heard the wind crooning in their feathers. Clusters of ducks and geese were scattered broadside over the water: as I came closer the ducks shot straight into the air like Harrier jump-jets, the geese paddled calmly away. Overhead a buzzard mewed. Beside the river, broad green fields led down to willow-screened banks, and the cows stopped grazing to watch me paddle by. Once a lone jogger waved to me from the footpath.

'Where are you going?' he shouted.

'Stockholm!' I replied.

'Good luck!' he called, and pounded on downstream.

Then the Lilla Edet lock loomed ahead, a solid wall of steel and concrete across the river. There was no way I was going into that dark basin, built to hold the giant cargo ships: I turned towards the bank, aimed my bow between two rocks, felt a sudden bang jar the kayak, and as I looked round saw the feather-like rudder hanging useless from the stern-post.

A kayak has *almost* no moving parts to break . . .

I hauled my kit out of the boat, hoisted the kayak itself onto the bank, and carried the lot around the lock and deposited it back in the water on the far side. By the time it was done I was sweating like a reindeer in a sauna (a very Swedish concept), so I walked up to the lock to sit in the sun and steam. It wasn't a scenic, grass-and-honeysuckle lock like Heybridge. This was a commercial lock beside a giant, scum-bedecked weir, and in days gone by some mad industrialist had built a colossal red-brick factory right across the lot. As an aesthetic phenomenon it left a lot to be desired, so I turned my back on it and peered down into the deep, slimy basin. A floating platform was anchored in a corner, and two workmen were busy doing something noisy to the walls.

Workmen = tools = welding = repairs: the equation popped

up in my brain with a ker-*ching*. Before I quite knew what was happening I was rifling through my Swedish dictionary, and a minute later I called down to them, 'Sorry, gentlemen, but is there somewhere round here I can get my stern-post welded?' Try finding *that* in a phrase book.

They looked up, waved, then both scrambled up one of the lock's ladders. I'd be happy to stop for a chat too if I had to spend all day counting bricks.

'What kind of welding?' asked the younger, a lean, smiling man with a coppery tan. 'Stainless, iron, or aluminium?'

I showed him the offending rudder. He prodded it thoughtfully. His partner slapped his hand away, grabbed it and held it up to the light. A rapid altercation ensued while I watched, entranced. It ended with the elder – a stocky man with a huge white beard and numerous smile-wrinkles – holding the rudder above his head out of Junior's reach, turning to me and saying, 'Come to the factory.'

We crossed the lock by the 'Strictly no entry' bridge, clattered down a stairway labelled 'Authorized Personnel Only', rapped on a door marked 'Protective clothing to be worn at all times', and were granted admittance by a lad in jeans and T-shirt. He took some convincing – possibly he hadn't expected to see a kayaker in Gore-Tex top, spray-skirt, swimming-trunks and bare feet at that time of morning – but he led us into a high brick-vaulted room marked 'Danger: work in progress' where six overalled workmen were busily playing cards. My guide explained the situation, the foreman took the rudder, examined it briefly and shouted 'Tommy!' (I should have guessed), and one of his henchmen took it, held it up to the light, said 'One point six mil, thirty-three point three' or something like that, and vanished into a back room. Two minutes later he was back, the repaired rudder gleaming like new in his hands.

'No cost,' said the foreman. 'Have a good journey.'

A chorus of good wishes followed me back to the lock. I gave the thumbs-up to the lock-menders, already back down in their dungeon, strolled across the grass, and re-fitted the rudder. It never troubled me again.

From there it was a four-hour paddle to Trollhättan, through the most beautiful bit of river I've ever seen. The forests seemed aflame. The current was thick with fallen leaves, golden reefs drifting down to the sea. Gradually the banks drew in, until I was paddling between jagged-edged cliffs topped with pines. Once a heron took off from the water's edge and flew past me, upstream. Twice flights of swans soughed through the air above. A cormorant swam by, dived and came up with a wriggling flatfish. I cut across the winding river from side to side, seeking out the backwaters and eddies, flying upstream with them, then biting my way across the weight of the current to find the next. The air was cool and brilliant. A faint mist rose from the water. Just after five o'clock, an hour before sunset, I rounded the last corner and came out into a great dark glass-smooth pool between rearing cliffs, a bowl full of drifting wisps of mist like a vision of King Arthur. To one side the current poured past a long, high wooden jetty. To the other, the deep basin swept around towards the vertiginous cleft of the Trollhättan river. In between, a sheer cliff loomed over the water, pine-crested, ragged-faced. Beside it, a steel door heralded the first of the fabulous Trollhättan locks.

Once, on a long-ago raid into Swedish territory, Harald Hardrada had carried his boats up that cliff, but he'd had an army to help him, and they were all mad Vikings anyway. I was alone and arguably sane; at least, nobody had told me I wasn't recently – one of the advantages of solitude. I couldn't carry the kayak around that lot. I pulled in behind the jetty, tied up to a convenient tree and scrambled out into the brambles. There was no path, but a seven-foot paddle makes a great machete. I bashed my way through to the foot of the lock, and there I found a narrow metal walkway leading upwards. Up I climbed, past one basin after the other, and at the third I saw the lights of the control tower gleaming above me. A swinging gate with 'Authorized personnel only' blocked my way, but I was growing used to local customs. I shoved it aside, went up to the door, and rang the bell.

A young man opened the door. His reaction might have been copied from the Lilla Edet factory: stare, pause, think, grin.

'Excuse me,' I said. 'I'm trying to get my kayak from Gothenburg to Vänern. Can I come through the locks?'

He hesitated, then ushered me up the stairs into the glass-walled control tower. Radar and TV screens stared down on two great grey desks studded with flashing lights. A VHF radio hissed static in a corner, an FM one played quiet music. I repeated my request to his superior, another bearded veteran, and was relieved to see him react as if it were the most normal thing in the world.

'There's a freighter coming through in an hour,' he said. 'You can come in after him.'

'What, you mean at the same time?' Twenty-kilo kayak meets four-thousand-ton freighter, it was an entertaining prospect.

'No. We'll lock him through, then you can go.'

Slowly it dawned on me that they were going to open the four locks and shift a hundred and ten thousand tons of water just for me and my kayak. I tell you, public service really *means* something in Sweden.

I stayed up there for an hour, enjoying the warmth and chatting about their job. It was a good position to have, they told me; at least everyone else there looked up to them. At this time of year they were passing a dozen freighters a day, wood going downstream from the great sawmills of Värmland, containers going up to the towns of Vänern. In summer, pleasure boats were their main customers, a dozen at a time, though *pleasure* was the wrong word to describe it: few of the skippers had any experience of locks, and you can't sail up a learning curve. They sat me down in a comfy chair and regaled me with coffee and stories while the sunset turned the sky crimson behind them.

'Okay,' one said at last. 'Get ready. As soon as he comes out, you can go into the bottom lock. We'll take you straight through.'

'Thanks,' I said, and went back into the cold.

The jetty behind which I'd left *Peregrino II* was built of giant wooden beams, the cross-pieces starting a metre above the water, with long braces running off into the woods behind. I slipped backwards from my mooring and pulled myself along a strut, sitting with my bow pointing at the lock gates and the water lapping gently all around me. I felt like an outlaw in the gathering dusk, hidden and watching, a silent raider on the quiet waters. My heart was pounding. My only experience of canals had been with *Peregrino I* in Belgium, and I knew from that how strong the currents in a lock could be. What it would be like in a kayak, I shuddered to think. My heart gave a lurch as the freighter's bows appeared above the lock gates. Metal boomed and water roared, and great, circular ripples washed outwards against the jetty. Slowly the towering barge sank out of sight. Then, with a still greater boom, the gates shivered and opened, and the huge rumbling brightly-lit mass inched forwards out of the lock and into the fairway. It passed me with a grumble of engines and a stink of diesel. Slap-slap-

SLAP ran the wake along the pillars towards me, lifted gently under my hull and passed. I shoved off and paddled for the lock.

Cool air. Darkness. The smell of weed and the music of dripping water. Then I was gliding to a halt beside a ladder, my bow scraped the concrete, I grabbed a dripping rung, and behind me the lock gates groaned and began to shut. The keepers were wasting no time. With a clang the doors closed, and at once a sound rose and swelled, a deep grumble like the flushing of the world's largest toilet. The water in front of the gates blossomed white in an eruption of bubbles. The kayak bumped backwards. I tightened my grip on the ladder, swung the bow back in to the wall, felt my arm drop as the water rose, snatched for a new grip higher up. A second rose of bubbles blossomed behind the first, then a third, wild water growing nearer and nearer. Behind me the water heaved upwards and creamed, and the kayak tugged forwards again. Gently, gently I rose. Drips and burps, hisses and gurgles surrounded me as cracks in the stonework filled. The acoustic was astonishing. I couldn't help it, I *had* to try it out. I was halfway through 'Old Man River' when my head rose over the coaming and I came eyeball to eyeball with a staring tourist.

'*Hej*,' I said weakly.

He backed away.

'Nice day . . .'

He left hurriedly.

'Philistine,' I muttered, and shoved off from the wall.

Luck was with me. It was dark by the time I passed the fourth lock, but there at the very exit a side-channel led into a tiny guest harbour with water-level pontoons and an open shower-block. A friendly passerby pointed me to a stretch of grass by the old lock gates where I could pitch my tent. Warm and clean at last, with my washed gear draped across the shower-block radiators, I sat in my tent and cooked by candle-light, then lay back in my sleeping-bag to write my diary. Not quite a thousand years before, Harald Hardrada had camped here on his way to yet another bloody battle. I bet I was having more fun than he did.

Next morning I awoke to glorious sunshine. Hurrying onwards in weather like that would have been a crime, so I ate and packed at a leisurely pace, then left my kit in the kayak and went to explore. Three different waterways lead down through the Trollhättan rock: 1800, 1844, 1916, each set of locks longer and broader than the last. They were, without exception, obsolete before they were finished, which shows how much traffic planners have learned in the last century or so. The antique locks are no longer used, their gates leaning open, their scarred rock sides hung with moss and fern. Above them pine trees cling to the top of the cliff, and a viewing-point thickly carpeted with fallen needles looks down over the lower basin. As I awoke, a giant freighter was pulling into the upper lock, its bridge looming over the surrounding houses, its engines shaking the air. As I reached the look-out point, it was just leaving the basin with its funnel gleaming in the daylight and its decks shrouded in shadow, and the sight of that monstrous ship caught between wooded cliffs under the sunlit sky is one of the enduring memories of my voyage.

As I slid into the kayak with barely a wobble and wriggled into position, a woman out for her morning stroll stopped by the jetty and looked down at me, smiling.

'Where did you come from?'

'Gothenburg.'

'Where are you going?'

'Stockholm, I hope.'

'What a wonderful day for it. Enjoy it!'

So I did.

The canal took me into a narrow, sheer-sided gut blasted out of the rock, along which I paddled at top speed: meeting a freighter at the halfway point would not have been entertaining. It was a Saturday morning, so the water was littered with floating beer bottles. I started collecting them – I hate litter – and by the time I reached Trollhättan town they were piled so high on my spray-deck that I could barely paddle. I tied up by a convenient flight of steps at the old town quay, dumped them onto the stones, pulled myself out, and went looking for a bin and a food shop.

The first shop I came to had 'corner store' written all over it. In Arabic. Egyptian pop music drifted out through the open door, packets of henna depicting buxom red-haired seductresses were stacked on the shelves, and beside them were jumbled sacks of rice, two-minute noodles, tins whose labels were all in Arabic, hard flaps of bread, packets of strange powders. The air was full of the dry, dark-red smell of mingled spices. Behind the counter, a plump, gentle-eyed man smiled at me. He was wearing an England football shirt. When he turned round later I saw that it was David Beckham's. Any British ambassadors who think they're the public face of the UK overseas, guess again.

'*Ya saba'h in noor*,' I said cheerfully. I'd picked up a little Arabic in Egypt, and it's amazing what I'll do to get a discount. His face lit up.

'*Ya saba'h il yasmin! Izzayak?*' he answered. I'd just wished him a morning of light; he'd replied with a morning of jasmine, and asked how I was. The conversation continued in that vein for some time. Arabic's a glorious language for poetic extravagance, and we made the most of it. Mind you, when I got round to doing the shopping, it was in Swedish; my Arabic is strictly for showing off. By that time my new friend had offered me a cup of mint tea, told me his life story, and shown me a picture of his son, a twelve-year-old waif in what looked like an Arsenal soccer strip.

It was an Arsenal soccer strip. He was currently vice-captain of the county under-fifteen side, had been dreaming of playing for Arsenal ever since he kicked a ball, had recently been over to London for trials, and was hoping to start playing for their youth team the following season.

'Not Manchester United?' I asked, indicating the shirt.

'No,' he said firmly. 'I don't approve of Ferguson's style.'

There followed a long discourse, in Arabic-accented Swedish, on the rights and wrongs of the English Premier League. It was great. All I'd wanted was a tin of tuna.

I left just before noon. Soon the canal widened into a broad lagoon, scattered with polished islands and patches of reeds, through which the marked channel wove a devious course. I took the straight route between two islands and past an immense flotilla of geese, skimming over rocks so shallow that my paddles grazed them, then turned a corner and saw the great bridge of Vänersborg, with the town and the lake beyond. A stiff breeze was blowing straight at me, shivering the reed-beds and kicking up little waves, and it was an effort to make headway against it, even hunched forward in the cockpit to minimize air resistance. Slowly, slowly the bridge crawled by overhead, and I turned towards Vänersborg, took a short-cut under a railway bridge so low I had to genuflect, drifted out into the harbour, and saw the waves breaking against the harbour wall, brilliant in the sunshine.

Vänern is Sweden's biggest lake. It's *huge*, an irregularly shaped inland sea left over from the retreat of the glaciers and fed by just about every river in the country. Its long axis runs from northeast to southwest and stretches almost a hundred miles; if all Yorkshire were covered by water it would be that big. Like every other body of water in Sweden, it boasts an archipelago, low, rounded islands half-covered in reeds and trees, and its sandy fringe studded with tourist villages and clusters of summer homes. Standing on the beach at Vänersborg and looking out, it might as well *be* the sea. To the left the beach runs round to a low cliff, sweeping back to the right and vanishing into blue haze. To the right a wide bay swings round to a sheer distant headland as stubborn as a whale's brow. Looking northeast, across the bright blue water and the white-capped waves, the horizon comes down to meet the lake. It might go on for ever.

The problem, of course, is that when a force-five wind blows down across a hundred miles of open water, the waves tend to get rather big. Not, perhaps, in comparison with the four-teen-metre monsters available in a hurricane, but quite big enough to make any kayaker with his head less than a metre above the water wish that he wasn't there.

I paddled out of Vänersborg's little harbour.

I turned round and scurried back.

I sat in the lee of the breakwater getting my breath back. The spirit was willing, but the flesh was frankly terrified.

I tried again. The first wave slapped my bow sideways, dumping me into its trough. The second one broke over the side, dumping a demijohn or so of water into my lap and setting me rocking wildly. By the time the third rose, I was scuttling panic-stricken into the shelter of another breakwater with all the grace and style of a water-beetle.

There, to the music of the crashing waves, fear held a stern debate with determination.

Fear won hands down. There's a time and a place for brav-ery. It's anywhere you're not going to have to swim home from if things go wrong.

I surfed the breakers back to the beach and reconsidered.

I was still deliberating when yet another smiling matron passed by on the path.

'Where are you going in that?' she asked me with some amusement.

'Well, I wanted to get to the Göta Canal . . .'

She stared at me, caught between sympathy and laughter.

'But it's closed!'

'You what?'

'It closed on the first of October! I thought everyone knew that.'

'Ah.'

'Safe journey!'

'Thanks,' I said weakly. This was going to take some thought.

I presented myself at the information office. They confirmed it. The Gota Canal was, indeed, closed.

'But you can still kayak it,' added the assistant brightly. 'You just have to carry your kayak round the locks.'

'How many locks are there?'

'Fifty-eight.'

I went back to my kayak and stood looking out at the bright white waves on the bright blue water. Hamlet might have recognized my dilemma: to sea, or not to sea? Give up and paddle back to Gothenburg, and wait for the mechanics to finish their hacksaw job? Or brave the waves and battle onwards to my fate? A very wet fate, probably . . .

Go on?

Go back?

Go on?

Go back?

I set my jaw and came to my decision. It would take a brave man to carry on across the lake in those conditions, knowing full well that a gruelling fifty-eight-lock ordeal lay ahead; but I'd learned a thing or two on my travels.

Like when not to be brave.

So I went into town to hire a bicycle and carry on on that.

10

SWEDEN

'He moored in Stock Sound; he pitched his tents in
meadows to the south of it.'

Ynglinga Saga

It wasn't that easy, of course. How could it be? There were
five bike shops within striking distance of Vänersborg. Three
were shut for the winter. One was open, but only between
four and seven p.m., at which point it turned out to have
nothing for anyone over the age of twelve. The last shop I
tried not only had one bike available for hire, but it was built
for adults. Unfortunately it was built from cast-iron drain-
pipes. It had gears (three, broken) and brakes (one, operated
by back-pedalling). The ideal vehicle for a five-hundred-mile
ride, it wasn't.

That afternoon I caught the train and ferry back to Hönö,
collected my bike from the boat, and took the bus back to
Vänersborg. It took the best part of the following morning to
pack my panniers and arrange to leave the odd, minor item
of equipment in storage; the kayak, for example. Just before
noon, with the sky a bewildered mass of flying clouds and
the ground fading in and out of shadow, I heaved my bike
(*Peregrino III*) upright, clambered aboard, and wobbled off
eastwards.

It was the first time in my life I'd attempted cycle touring. Under normal circumstances I would never have considered setting off on a five-hundred-mile ride without the least practice, but then, under normal circumstances I wouldn't have ended up dressed in swimming-trunks and Gore-Tex on the beach of a Swedish lake wondering why small waves were so scary. Besides, I'd been alone on the road in Sweden for four whole days, or at least on the river, so I was starting to feel at home.

I hadn't learnt much Swedish while I was with the Freds, nor in the time I'd spent with Jan: their English was so good that there was no point even trying to communicate any other way. Nor had my time in Gothenburg improved things much, since the only friends I'd made had been Tommy and his drunken crew, and Mia, the red-headed shopkeeper, all of whom preferred practising their English. But as soon as I left Gothenburg behind the whole cultural climate changed. Gone was the big city, the port, cosmopolitan, self-assured and oblivious to newcomers. I was out in a land of villages and small towns, strung out across a great waste of forest: not blind to the outside world, nor hostile (far from it!), but with no experience of meeting foreigners face to face. In every village I found somebody, somewhere, who spoke broken English and was proud of it; but for my everyday communication I had to rely on remembered phrases and a quick-draw dictionary. There's no better teaching method. No language exam ever set would have passed me, since not many language systems put much emphasis on asking strangers about rune-stones, front-fork suspension and spot welding, but I was proud of my progress.

I fell in love with the language. Swedish belongs to the Scandinavian branch of the Germanic language family, great-nephew of old Icelandic, and cousin to both modern German and that half-Romance bastard, British English. It's retained some grammatical features alien to either of its cousins, and a system of pronunciation entirely its own, where the letters *skj, sj, ski, ki, kj, kö* and *tj* all signify the sound 'sh' or 'hw', but apart from that – well, it's family. Take the verb *att köpa*, to buy. Its written form looks like, and is related to, the modern German *kaufen*, to buy. Its pronunciation, 'shöpa', gives the modern English 'shop' and 'cheap', and the element *-köping* ('market') in placenames is a direct equivalent of the English Chipping, as in Sodbury. Many words are close to identical with both cousins – *skip* for ship or skiff (German *Schiff*), *båt*, pronounced 'boat', German *Boot, kyrka* for church, *Kirche, kung* for king, German *König, styrbord* for starboard or *Steuerbord*. (The term comes from the days before rudders, when ships were steered with a giant oar attached to the right-hand side of the hull. This was the steering side – the literal translation of *styrbord* – and since the steersman faced the oar, his back was to the other side of the boat; hence Swedish and German *backbord*. When coming into port, it was advisable not to crush the steering-oar against the jetty, so vessels always moored with their left-hand side to the quay, and thus invariably loaded and unloaded over that side: the Middle English *lade-bord* or larboard. When, in 1844, the Royal Navy realized that 'starboard' and 'larboard' confused their merry matelots, they adopted the traditional variant, 'port side'. So now you know.)

Svein's Nordic forebears settled most of northern England, and our placenames show it. *Grimsby* (Grim's farm), *Tranmere* (the sandbank of the cranes), *Snaefell* on Man (snow mountain), *Scarborough* (the hill with the gap), *Harrogate* (cairn street), *Lockerbie* (Locard's dwelling), *Mull* (the snout) are all of impeccable Scandinavian origin. The three Ridings of Yorkshire are a Scandinavian creation, from *thrithiungr*, a third. Dingwall, in Scotland, the parliament plain, has exactly the same meaning and origin as the Icelandic parliament-place of Thingvellir. Even British northern dialects are half-Norse. Look at the Scots words *bairn*, 'child', *skerry*, 'rock in the sea' and *kirk*, 'church'. In Swedish they're *barn*, *skär* and *kyrk*.

I pedalled across Sweden in a state of linguistic delight. Every day I listened to the news on my pocket radio, straining to make out the headlines. Every evening I lay in my tent by candlelight and read through my secret weapon, *Härsskarringen*, *The Lord of the Rings* in Swedish, a book which I've read so often in English that I didn't have to look up the vocabulary – a great advantage. My dreams were a jumbled mass of half-remembered conversations and random words afloat on a storm-tossed sea of grammar. Every morning I awoke wondering, 'What the hell does *sommarstuga* mean, anyway?' (Summer house, actually.) Some people say that dreaming in a language shows that you've mastered it. My dreams just proved that my memory didn't function when I was asleep either.

Maybe language skill made a difference; something certainly did. I'd found the Swedes of Gothenburg pretty unapproachable. Meeting strangers there, at least sober ones, had proven close to impossible. Beyond the city, the situation changed. Perhaps small-town dwellers are simply friendlier than their big-city counterparts. Perhaps it was that I was living out of a tent, rather than an apparently luxurious motor-yacht, and therefore less formidable. Whatever the reason, something worked.

On the first afternoon I stopped in a little village on a hill-top south of Vänern to ask for directions. I'd been following a long-range cycle path, and had temporarily lost the waymark. On one side of the road was a tiny village playground, a sand-pit with two swings and a merry-go-round beside a phone-box with broken windows. Behind it was the village church, a gleaming white wooden building with a high, conical spire, the churchyard (*kyrkogård*) surrounded by beech trees, the pathways deep in leaves. On the other was a large house attached to an unfenced orchard, where a man was standing in the lifting-bucket of a small JCB, calmly picking pears.

'Excuse me,' I called. He glanced down and smiled. 'Which way to Katrineborg?'

He thought for a second, then pointed straight ahead. I waved my thanks and was about to head onwards when he shouted, 'Want a pear?'

'Love one!' I replied after an instant's hesitation.

'Helmet!' One after the other he lobbed four freshly picked pears into it. 'Safe journey!' I ate them at my next stop. They were delicious.

That evening I was looking for a campsite. The sun was close to the horizon and my legs close to exhaustion, but there was nowhere to stop. Sweden is famed for the *allemänsrätt*, the law permitting travellers to walk and camp anywhere in the country unless the landowner specifically forbids it, but I was passing through a patchwork of dense woods and ploughed fields, neither of which looked particularly inviting places to sleep. At last I stopped at a roadside house, leant the bike against a fence and rang the doorbell.

'Excuse me,' I said to the master of the house, who was looking at me with some suspicion. 'Is there somewhere near here where I can camp?'

His face cleared. 'Certainly. If you go on for half a mile, then turn left and follow the trail, it'll bring you to the lake. There's a good campsite there.'

'Did you say half a mile?'

'Yes, five kilometres.' Being sensible, Swedes use traditional measures, like the mile; being fundamentally odd, they use it to mean ten kilometres. I didn't really fancy pedalling another five kilometres, but there didn't seem much choice. I plugged on past field and wood, turned down the side road between the trees, came to a fork in the road, sat, and dithered. He hadn't mentioned any fork ... I was still trying to make up my mind when car headlamps shone behind me and I pulled off the road. The car stopped beside me and my guide poked his head out.

'I thought I'd come and check to make sure you'd found it. You want to take the left-hand fork. Go ahead, I'll follow you.'

Five minutes later, lit from behind by my guide's headlights, I pulled off the road onto a grassy lawn beside the reeds of Vänern. The sun was setting in crimson splendour to my left, pillars and battlements of rose-gold cloud shone in the water, and on my right a long series of little boats rode serenely by a jetty. The lawn was smooth, deep and sheltered from the wind by a screen of young birches.

'You'll like it here,' he told me. 'If you're lucky you might see an elk. Sleep well.' And he reversed back the way we'd come.

I didn't see any elk, but five minutes later a trio of deer trotted out of the woods behind me and went down to the water to drink. They stayed there for almost a minute, drinking, looking up, drinking again, ripples spreading out in dark circles across the glowing water. Then an engine growled in the distance and they rocketed away.

Lights jolted along the road and a battered 4×4 came out of the woods towards me, half-blinding me. It stopped a courteous distance away, the lamps winked off, and two people got out: an elderly man and a woman my age, both wearing boots and dungarees.

'*Hej*,' said the father. 'I own the farm along the road there.' I'd passed it on the way. 'Henryk told me you were here. I just came to see if there was anything you needed.'

Cool! I'd been half-expecting a 'Get off my land'.

We stood and chatted for a few minutes, discussing the weather (a good autumn after an awful summer), his business (mainly pigs – I could smell them from there), the number of summer houses in the area (hundreds), and the effect of tourists (litter). His daughter stood looking around. She was a short girl, stocky and dark-haired, with a long, intelligent face. After a short silence she spoke.

'How long have you been travelling?'

'Over three months.'

'Don't you get lonely?'

'Sometimes. But the people are friendly here.'

'What about your job?'

'This is my job.'

For a while they digested that. Then the father said, 'Can you give my daughter a job, then? There's not much money in farming.'

I tried to explain that, as a fledgling travel-writer, I wasn't exactly a major player in the international employment market, but my Swedish failed me.

'Oh well,' said the father. 'Sleep well.'

And they left me to my cooking.

The two days which followed were harder. I'd run through the first burst of energy which always accompanies the beginning of a voyage. Moving hurt, and pedalling hurt, and my legs had decided they weren't playing any more. At the same time, the weather changed, from the glowing autumn which looks back to summer, to the grey, cold emptiness heralding coming winter. It rained nonstop for two days, by the end of which I was thoroughly wet and miserable, half-wishing that I'd never left the boat which, for all its sins, was drier and more comfortable than my weather-weary tent. Just. Nevertheless, the human warmth continued unabated. I stopped at one house to ask for water and spent half an hour chatting with the owner, a retired telephone engineer who was servicing his hunting rifle when I arrived, preparing for the beginning of the elk season. When I rang the doorbell he opened the door with weapon in hand, which rather took me aback, but he turned out to be the soul of courtesy, filling my bottles from his spring (he was too far from any town to receive piped water), telling me about the joys of elk-hunting, and asking me as a favour to climb his apple tree and help myself to the crop, since he was too stiff to climb himself.

The following day, in the worst downpour so far, I stopped in a village whose streets were an inch under water and made for the shelter of a combined news-stand and hamburger stall, the community's only retailer. The lady in charge took one look and ordered me to take a seat while she brought out a gallon of scalding camomile tea, on the house, then repositioned her electric heaters so that I received the maximum benefit, all the while discoursing volubly on that day's gossip. Village life? No, it was the day Milosevic's government fell, and she was speculating as to how the ethnic power balance in the Balkans would change. Two days after that, in a one-street village almost swallowed by fallen leaves, I chatted with a delivery trucker outside the local general store. He was a keen cycle tourist, and regaled me with tales of the round-Vänern tour, an annual event in which a hundred lycra-clad maniacs race around the lake's three-hundred-mile perimeter for no other reason, as far as I could tell, than sheer masochism. He, too, was a hunter, and his main lament was that he'd come to it too late in life. Behind him, stapled to the village notice-board, was a government notice advising those aged less than twenty-five to register for the professional hunter's exam at the state's expense. He'd started hunting at twenty-six. Fate can be cruel sometimes.

Though the people and language no longer struck me as strangers, I found it hard to get used to the countryside. No amount of looking at maps could have prepared me for the sheer size and wildness of Sweden. I was currently trying to cross the country on its shortest axis, taking a somewhat winding line between Gothenburg and Stockholm. The distance I was planning to cover was close on the distance from London to Edinburgh. If I'd tried it the other way, from Finnmark in the north to the southern tip of Skåne, it would have been the distance from Copenhagen to Palermo. Sweden, put bluntly, is *huge*, and most of it is covered in trees. When I was a boy I'd read Laura Ingalls Wilder's *Little House in the Big Woods* and *The Last of the Mohicans* by James Fenimore Cooper and they'd left me with an abiding impression of vast oceans of trees interspersed with isolated settlements. Sweden was just like that. Cycling across it, it felt like I was crossing the sea again, lost and alone in a spreading expanse of vegetation. Beside every road were thickets and ranks of birch, their leaves lying in wet golden drifts between the skeletons of rosebay willowherb. Behind them reared dark ranks of pine trees, thick and black and silently menacing. Everywhere I looked, the trees were there, circling round farms and settlements, hemming in the fields. Never in my life have I had such a feeling of wilderness as when I came out of the woods into a heavily farmed area, rich, fertile fields turning from gold to black under the ploughs, and looked down across the bowl of the valley and up the far side, to see the forest starting again. It might have been American frontier country. It didn't fit into any of my preconceptions of Europe.

Not that the countryside itself was predictable. The first two days, south of Vänern, were delightful for cycling, long, flat roads running from farm to forest and back. From there the route began to climb in long, strenuous zigzags, up onto the heights between Vänern and Vättern, a gorgeous country of dry-stone walls and winding lanes, fallen leaves and quiet villages, each with its own wooden church. Somewhere amidst those heights I crossed the Göta Canal at sunset, camping on its banks and watching the colours blaze and fade in the water, and the next morning I free-wheeled five kilometres downhill with a grin of reckless delight. That led me into the *trolliga skog*, the haunted woods of central Sweden, a broken country of granite mounds, twisted trees and mist-wreathed lakes, generally dimpled with rain, and thence to the relatively flat land of the east coast, where for the first time I saw brick houses again. For Sweden is covered in trees, and its geology is predominantly granite beneath thin drifts of topsoil: wherever you go in the woods, rock reefs jut through the earth like old bones. This has had a strong influence on local building practices: why break your back quarrying when you can fell a couple of trees and get all the timber you need? Swedes like wooden houses. They're sensible people.

The country feels ancient. Partly it's caused by those low, rounded, glacier-ground rocks. The stone here isn't jagged, vigorous, all saw-toothed edges and gouged-out valleys like the Alps or the Pyrenees. This is stone which has spent a million years being ground under ice. It's *weary*. And for all the country's frontier wildness, the human elements are similarly ancient. On the coast north of Henån is the Bronze Age settlement of Tanum, where, centuries before the Romans reached Britain, coastal settlers ground their totem images into the smooth rock-faces: ships, sledges, warriors, lovers, a six-foot-tall god wielding a massive spear, a figure in a chariot pulled by goat-like creatures who, according to some, is the first known representation of the thunder-god Thor. Scattered around the country under trees and by roadsides, great flat standing stones carved with pre-Christian runes serve as memorials to the dead of the Viking past: 'Armod raised this stone in memory of his brother Thormod, who died in the west,' reads one inscription, a reminder that not all Svein's followers made it home. Behind it a low, rocky mound is said to be the eighth-century burial-place of a local chieftain, no doubt hallowed in folklore as the home of some troll or undead wanderer. (Grave-mounds always are.) There was nothing like the overwhelming presence of the past that can be found in Spain or Italy, a bombardment of Roman and Romanesque memorials. This was more subtle, a feeling of age emanating from the ground itself. Sweden, the land seemed to whisper, is very big, and its history has been going on for a very long time.

So's this chapter. I'll get on with the story.

Five days before I was due to return and face the mechanic, I climbed a steep hill and looked down for the first time on the Baltic. The rain had blown away the clouds, and sea and sky were a brilliant blue, flecked with white waves and whiter clouds. Below me was a stately home overlooking the rocky bay, with a handful of boats beside a wooden jetty; miniature wooden Viking boats, unless my eyes deceived me. Curious . . . Behind lay an eyesore of a building, a concrete oblong mercifully half-hidden by trees. According to my guidebook, this was Stensund youth hostel. I cycled down to have a look.

The reception area was closed, but the main door, swathed in ivy, looked open, and I was about to go and investigate when two middle-aged men came out, arguing in voluble Swedish. They stopped dead at the sight of me, as well they might.

'Can I help you?' asked the elder after a second, in excellent English: a tall, stooped man with a hooked nose and thinning blond hair.

'I was looking for the youth hostel,' I said, bewildered as

much by the language change as their sudden appearance.

'Ah.' He gave me a measuring look. 'Well, I'm afraid the youth hostel only operates during the summer. This is a school.' And, before my face fell too far, 'Why not come in and have a coffee?'

They led me into the elegant grand hall, all wooden panels and carpeted floors, the view stretching over a formal garden to the sea. From there we went down a narrow passageway into a stainless-steel industrial kitchen, where my interlocutor, Tommy (seriously!), opened a thermos of coffee and poured out three generous mugs. I gave him a coffee-potted history of my voyage, and he nodded and grunted affirmation. Then, pondering, he slurped his brew, and when he came up for air he said, 'Well, officially the youth hostel's closed, but . . . You said you've got a tent?'

I nodded. My legs were aching.

'Well, if you pitch your tent down in the valley, nobody will mind. In return, how do you fancy giving an English lesson tomorrow? Everyone would appreciate it, and the boat-builders might take you out sailing.'

Boat-builders?

I'd stumbled, by sheer luck, on one of the finest schools it's ever been my privilege to encounter.

Stensund school is, broadly speaking, a further-education college for mature students who want help to change their careers. It acts as a boarding school, that concrete horror behind the main house being accommodation, teaching block, gym and social centre, while the administrators hog the good rooms in the stately home. Pupils board during the week; most go home for the weekend. The difference between Stensund and every other school I've ever visited is the range of subjects taught. Drug therapy (most of the students are reformed addicts, dealers or both, so the entire campus is a strictly no-drugs, no-alcohol area). Public health (a distinctly Swedish idea, it trains its students to act as health-and-happiness advisers to large organizations. The course includes sport coaching, nutrition and psychology). Professional-level sports coaching. And boat-building. In the valley below the school, just behind the soccer-pitches, three long, low sheds house the tools, frames, easels and wood-stores of a fully-functioning boatyard.

That evening, my tent set up, I went for a walk, and felt my original plan of proceeding on to Stockholm the following afternoon vanishing. The reception hall of the main building had been converted into a common-room, complete with log fire, and there the students had gathered to chat, eat bananas and drink coffee. (The Swedes claim to eat more bananas and drink more coffee than any other nation on earth.) They were a very cosmopolitan crowd. One of the sports coaches was a Ghanaian former international soccer player, a drug psychologist was a Paris-born Algerian, a Chinese lad was studying English and computing, an American my age with a beard my father's age was building a boat. Then there were the Swedes: a carpenter, a pre-school teacher, a nurse, a former drug debt-collector, a reformed addict who talked a lot about it but wouldn't meet my eyes, two Swedish-American alumni who'd come back to visit, and the entire public-health faculty: twelve girls brimming over with health, enthusiasm and good looks and two muscular lads who couldn't believe their luck.

Everyone knew about the stranger who was camping in the woods behind the school – the Irishman cycling round the world, according to the normal Chinese whispers – and everyone was keen to meet me. Before I knew it I was planted in a deep armchair holding a stumbling conversation. Where had I come from? What was I doing? The public-health group pricked up their ears when I mentioned cycling and kayaking;

the boat-builders at the mention of *Peregrino*. When I told them that I'd be giving an English lesson in the morning, they were thrilled. How about talking to the public-health group about my journey? suggested one girl with pigtails and melting eyes. Twist my arm . . . Would I like to come and see their boats? added a builder with blond hair, bulging forearms and the brightest blue eyes I've ever seen. I was still agreeing enthusiastically when the American announced that he and his friends were going sailing the following afternoon and there was room for another in the boat. Then, the one-time hardman of the Stockholm underground told me that the community would be taking a sauna the following day and invited me to join them. Pretty girls, wooden boats and a sauna at the end of the day. Hopefully, Heaven will be like this.

The English lesson was not a great success. Tommy had asked me to get the students talking. This meant, in practice, that I spent lots of time listening to embarrassed silences. I did, however, manage to winch out of them the views that they had of Britain: beer; the buildings of Oxford; fish and chips; red buses; red phone-boxes; black taxis; and the fact that the English, 'like the French and Germans', want to be kings of Europe. They themselves felt Scandinavian, not European: Sweden's history has always been seen in relation to its immediate neighbours, so they looked on continental Europe with a 'them–us' suspicion. It made me feel quite at home. After that it was uncomfortable silence again until I started telling travellers' tales. At that point, to my gratification, they woke up. We passed a happy twenty minutes until the bell released them. Who knows? Perhaps they even learnt something.

The bell led to *fika*, the thrice-daily coffee-break which is a pillar of Swedish society. I ate with the boat-builders and when the bell went again they showed me into the workshop. It was, in its way, beautiful: a long, low-ceilinged wooden hall lined with work-benches, sunlight streaming in through the wide windows. Dust danced in shimmering spirals, slanting pillars of gold, and the warm tints of wood and varnish glowed in the autumn light. Walls and benches were cluttered with glinting tools, but the floor was bare save for four long, low cradles. On each one, tensely braced, was the keel of a new-laid boat, a long straight central section clamped and glued to the curving stem and stern. Above them a cat's-cradle of glittering wire supported plumb-lines and measuring-lines, needle-tipped pendulum weights that swayed gently as we walked past. In one corner a long box emitted puffs of steam: as I watched an alarm-clock rang, and a single student raced over, opened it, pulled out a plank, ran over to the fourth boat, laid the plank on the half-built stern, slid three screw-clamps into position and wound them up with ferocious haste, bending the steam-softened wood into shape, glaring along the line of the stern all the while. Within two minutes of the alarm sounding the job was done and he stood back, mopping his brow.

'Do you have to do it that fast?' I asked curiously.

'I don't know,' he replied, 'but I never felt like experimenting.'

I watched them work, taking pleasure in the patterns of light and colour, the perfume of wood and tar. Teams of three were working on three of the boats; the fourth, whose stern I'd watched being bent into place, was the responsibility of a single student, a graduate. Around the floor lay portfolios of blueprints, some machine-drawn, some handmade: the school's philosophy was that each boat be made according to a traditional design, and one of the students' greatest pleasures was trawling for rare plans in libraries and archives around the world. Most came from registered boatyards, but Patrick the graduate had created his blueprint by measuring the remains of a wrecked nineteenth-century Norwegian dinghy. Each trio was bent over its skeletal ship, measuring, calculating, sometimes stopping to point and argue. They were a fine bunch of dreamers. One wanted to build his own yacht, sail it around the world until he found someone to buy it, use the money to build another, and so ad infinitum. Another had already bought a wooden boat of his own. He was planning to restore it using the skills he'd learnt here, and sail away. 'But wooden boats take a lot of work, it must be easier with steel,' he said, and wondered why I laughed. Another did it simply because it was fun.

'Do you want to work with boats later?' I asked.

She shrugged. 'That's next year's problem.'

That afternoon, as promised, they took me sailing. In fact I took them sailing, since we had two boats to play with and only one experienced sailor, Gerald the American. 'You're a seaman,' they told me eagerly, 'you can handle a dinghy,' which is like assuming that all pilots are good parachutists. Their enthusiasm waned somewhat when I clambered aboard our Viking skiff and began my normal pre-cruise checks.

'Oil.'

'Nope.'

'Water.'

'Nope.'

'Power.'

'Nope.'

'Ignition.'

'Ben, this is a *sailing* boat.'

I hadn't sailed a dinghy since I was fifteen, and this square-sailed pocket longship was nothing like the fibreglass bath-tubs I'd messed around in before. It turned out to be just as well, as someone who actually knew what they were doing would have had more to unlearn. Henryk of the brilliant eyes and bulging forearms rowed us out into the bay while I hoisted the sail by the simple process of plonking the mast into its socket and shoving the boom upwards and sideways into the top corner of the sail. At once the wind filled it with a clap, the boat rocked violently, we blundered into one another and fell over. The boat turned head to wind and sat there with the sail flapping like a distressed tent, I grabbed for the tiller and main-sheet, Henryk pushed the boom out with his foot, the sail snapped open again, and we were off, slapping across the wavelets while Gerald's crew watched open-mouthed. I hoped that they were admiring our style.

The old skills came back quickly. Keep the breeze on your cheek, keep a little pressure on the tiller to stop her coming head to wind, miss the rocks ... The wind was blowing straight down the bay, so we had to tack against it to reach the open sea, and after two fumbling attempts we got the hang of it and started enjoying ourselves. After so long on the water surrounded by gleaming steel and the rumble of engines, it was a tactile delight to be aboard a handmade boat, rough and fragrant and somehow part of the elements. After half an hour my conscience twinged and I asked Henryk if he wanted to steer, but he was happy in the bow, humming to himself and staring out to sea. We lapsed back into companionable silence. Only when the sun dipped to the horizon did we turn and run before the wind back into harbour. We'd missed the sauna, but who cared? I'd always hoped to sail on the Baltic. Doing it this way, I didn't miss my boat at all.

I left Stensund the following morning, sun- and wind-burned. The fresh breeze had developed overnight into a full gale, so it was just as well I'd abandoned the kayak when I had. Pedalling against it was hard, but paddling would have been a nightmare. It took five sweaty hours to reach Stockholm, and when I got there my plan was simple: get to the station and get the first train back to Gothenburg. The mechanic was due to finish in three days' time, and I still had to collect my kayak and paddle back down the Göta Älv. So, having defied adversity in a manner worthy of an Anglo-Saxon hero to get to Stockholm, I had to defy it again to get home. It made sense at the time.

The station ticket office was hideously crowded. I took my place in the queue, leaning against my laden velocipede, and watched the world hurry by. After a while I picked up the distinctive nasal tones of an Australian accent, and looked round to see an attractive young woman buying a ticket. It was a month since I'd spoken English with a native, and by the look of the queue it wasn't going to be my turn for half an hour, so when she walked past me I stopped her and said, 'Sorry, I couldn't help hearing you speaking English.' As a chat-up line this is never going to reach the top ten, but it did the trick: she stopped, looked me over, decided that I wasn't a threat and became sociable. She'd only been in Stockholm for a month, so perhaps she, too, felt the need for company. When my turn finally came she accompanied me to the ticket office.

'*Hej*, can I get the train to Gothenburg with my bike?'

'No.'

Frosty silence.

'Erm . . . There's no way at all?'

'No.'

'Not even if I . . .'

'No.'

'How about . . .'

'No.'

'Thank you.'

I turned to my new friend. 'This could take a while.'

She smiled. 'I've got a bit of time.'

She accompanied me to the bus terminal. It took some finding: Stockholm Central is more complex than Heathrow Airport and the signposts are not outstanding. At last we tracked it down.

'*Hej*. Can I get the bus to Gothenburg with my bike?'

'No.'

Cold silence.

'Er . . . can I send it freight?'

He looked annoyed. 'Go and ask at the freight office.'

I waited. Nothing more seemed forthcoming.

'And the freight office is . . . ?'

'Down the hall, second on the left,' he said shortly, and turned his back.

We trundled on to the freight office.

'*Hej*. Can I send my bike to Gothenburg by freight?'

'Yes.'

'I *can*?'

'If you put it in a cardboard box.'

I stared at him, then started to rummage through my pockets. No, there didn't seem to be a mountain-bike-sized cardboard box there.

'Can I buy a box here?'

'No.'

'Do you know where I can buy one?'

'No.' He looked at the clock on the wall. 'And we're closing now. You'll have to leave.'

We walked out. Small gouts of steam were popping from my ears and my eyes were glowing red. I was about to do something regrettable when my fair companion smiled and, metaphorically, took off her hat to reveal a halo.

'Look, I've got to go and meet a friend now, but I'll be home at eight. You go and try the railways again, and if it doesn't work, get the underground out to this tube station. I live five minutes' walk from there, straight down the road. Number 113, you can't miss it. We'll find you a place to stay and sort it out in the morning. Here's my phone number. Maybe see you later. 'Bye!'

'Can I get my bike on the tube?' I called after her.

'Sure, everyone does!' floated back down her slipstream, and she was gone.

The railway staff hadn't grown miraculously human in the last half-hour, so I thumped and banged my bike down into the underground and went in search of a ticket office. When I located it, I received the first friendly smile I'd seen on a uniformed Swede. The lady was about to sell me a ticket when she noticed the bike.

'Were you wanting to take that on the underground?' she asked. No sentence starting 'Were you wanting' ever bodes well.

'Well, I was . . .'

'I'm sorry.' She sounded genuinely sympathetic. 'It's not allowed.'

'Ah.' I grabbed my patience with both hands before it could get away and throttle someone. 'Is there anywhere I can leave it?'

'You could ask at the information desk. It's just round the corner.'

I hauled self and bike back against the rush-hour commuter tide. The young man behind the information counter was industriously picking his nails. I cleared my throat.

'Yes?' He didn't look up.

'Is there anywhere I can leave my bike here?' I asked.

'I don't know.'

I waited, but that seemed to be it.

'Would you mind asking?' I said sweetly. He looked up,

astonished that someone actually wanted him to do something. Something in my eyes must have registered. He hauled himself out of his chair and went to find his supervisor. Five minutes later he was back.

'There's nowhere you can leave it, and you're not allowed to have your bike here, so you'll have to go away now,' he said.

I stared at him, Hannibal Lecter style, until he began to stammer apologies, then very carefully turned my back on him and walked away. It was that or feed him to the pigeons, and you don't get many pigeons underground. I padlocked the bike to the railings outside the station, heaved my panniers onto my shoulder and caught the tube out to Shanel's place.

Which was locked, with no signs of life.

It started to rain.

I sat in the vestigial shelter of the garage wall and said rude words.

Just as I was building up to a sulphurous crescendo, an engine roared and a car swung into the drive, and Shanel staggered out, laden with shopping-bags, followed by a lanky young man. Her face lit up when she saw me.

'Hi, you made it! Sorry we're late, we had to go shopping, this is Jad, come on in, have a seat, how did you get on?, have a cup of tea . . .'

The hospitable bustle swept me into the house. Soon I was showered and shaved, sitting down to a hot meal with two Australians, a German and a Frenchman, all graduate students, while my washing gurgled in the machine and the rain hammered on the window. The house, the décor, the random distribution of souvenirs of all nations, the piles of dirty dishes, the scattered books and papers, the empty bottles and beercans, it might have been a student house anywhere in the world. Stockholm and the Station from Hell seemed a million miles away. I told them the story of my happy day. By the end, even I was laughing.

'What you need to do,' Jad the Lebanese Australian told me solemnly, 'is go to the station tomorrow and say "I want to send my bike to Gothenburg via SJ Express". I know it works, I found out the hard way last year.'

I repeated the words like a mantra. 'I want to send my bike via SJ Express . . . I'll try it.'

At crack of dawn the next day I was in the ticket office again, pronouncing my mantra to a draconian female. Her brow furrowed. Was that a glint of chagrin in her eyes?

'Take it down to the SJ Express office, one floor down, outside, second right,' she said rapidly in a last-ditch effort to throw me off the scent. I walked out loftily, went down one level, outside, took the second right into a crowded and smelly back-alley, and saw a gleaming sign ahead, 'SJ Express.'

An hour later my bike and I drew out of Stockholm Central Station with a sigh of relief. As we left, a text message appeared on my mobile from the Angel Shanel: 'Hope U made it!'

I replied, 'Victory!'

Three days later, bang on schedule, I paddled back into Lilla Bommen, left *Peregrino II* with the owner, collected *Peregrino III* from the station, and pedalled back to the Hönö ferry. *Peregrino I* was waiting in harbour, gleaming and serene. I let myself aboard, dropped my panniers on a bench, turned, looked down into the engine compartment, and saw the echoing gap where the generator had been. And still wasn't. I may have been bang on schedule. My mechanic wasn't.

'Well, I'm back,' I sighed, Sam Gamgee style, and walked up the hill to Jan's place.

11

DENMARK

> 'While Oláf lay with his ship off Bornholm he experienced a sharp gale and great seas and could not hold his ground there, so he sailed south to Wendland, where he found a good harbour.'
>
> *Saga of Oláf Tryggvason*

Summer was well and truly over. Ever since I'd left in my kayak, storms had been battering the coast of Hönö. The day I returned the sky cleared and the sun came out, and Jan and his family took me into the woods to share the traditional Swedish autumn sport of mushroom-hunting, the vegetarian-ecological-anti-bloodsports equivalent of elk-shooting. Though, presumably, without the macho image. Next morning the clouds returned, and through a driving wind I headed up to Lilla Bommen for the last time. On the way back downriver, a small white gull came whizzing over my head and dived for the wave-tops. Behind it, wings flashing, was a great, dark-arred falcon. I throttled back and stood enthralled, watching the chase swoop and flicker over the water. Just on the edge of sight the black dot and the white merged, and then the black dot lifted and clawed heavily away against the clouds. Grey sea and grey sky were heaving and flying, and between them the falcon laboured landwards. And I didn't care any more that I was heading for Denmark six weeks later than planned.

I'd learnt a lot about Denmark on my travels. Scandinavians treat one another much the same as Brits do: when they're abroad they huddle together, and when they're at home they laugh at one another. Where the English have Irish jokes, the Norwegians have Finnish jokes, the Finns have Swedish jokes and the Swedes have Danish jokes, so my cruise had been a reintroduction to the art of international slander. The Freds had told me that all Danish cheese smells and all Danes live on *pølse* sausages – not a fabulously useful insight into a nation's culture, but it was a start. One of the friends I'd made in Stavanger claimed that, while Norwegians eat to live, Danes live to eat; the calumny was reinforced in Stensund, where I was told that the Danes never became a Great Power after Svein's day because they were too busy eating. I'd also been warned that Danes have a real problem welcoming strangers; this, coming from a Norwegian, was a fine case of the pot calling the Ketill black. Finally, I'd been told time and again that 'Denmark's more European than the rest of Scandinavia'. It made sense until I thought about it. More European? So Copenhagen is more like, say, Nice? Barcelona? Bratislava, Munich, Split? Europe's a big place. Which bit did they have in mind?

However, first of all, Denmark reminded me of Wales. This may be pulling another slander out of the valise, but I spent my first eighteen summers in Gwynedd, and I *know* how much it can rain there. Not the hammering, stair-rod rain of the tropics, just grey, drifting veils trailing across the landscape. I love it, actually; but the voyage from Gothenburg down the Øresund to Copenhagen was a celebration of Welsh-style rain. I barely caught a glimpse of the Swedish coast to port, and when I finally entered the jaws of the Sound all I could see of it was my radar picture. A twelfth-century book of Viking sailing directions advises the young navigator to stay off the seas between October and April. I was beginning to understand why.

Prejudices are a peculiar thing. I'd expected the Swedes to be Volvonic and unwelcoming, and received my first invitation within four hours of landing. Having been warned that the Danes were a hostile lot, I went one better, and walked into an invitation before I'd actually reached the country.

I'd stopped for the night in a little harbour on the Swedish side of the Sound; running down one of the world's busier shipping lanes at night in foul weather didn't really appeal. Just above the harbour a blunt promontory stretched out across the mouth of the Sound. The rain stopped just before sunset, so I decided to walk up to the lighthouse on the headland and watch the sun go down. It was cold up there, so I didn't linger. Halfway down the hill I found two women standing looking southwards. They stood aside to let me go past, and as I went on I heard one say to the other in English, 'And *that's* the lights of Denmark.'

With my normal subtlety I turned, walked back up to them and said, 'Excuse me, I couldn't help hearing you speaking English.'

They turned and smiled at me, a middle-aged woman with greying hair and a kind face, and a young, black-haired, black-eyed woman who radiated energy even when she was standing still. 'Yes, we were,' said the elder, with what looked like pleased surprise. 'Why, are you English?' It works every time.

'British,' I said. 'I'm sorry to interrupt, it's just nice to hear my own language.'

She laughed. 'I can imagine.' And, looking at her companion, who was still smiling at me, 'We were just going up, would you like to join us?'

I hesitated. 'Well, I was heading back to my boat . . . I'm moored in the harbour here. Would you like to come for a cup of tea, if you've got time?'

The grins flashed out again like a happy lighthouse. 'We'd love to,' said the younger woman in a strong Spanish accent. 'Wheech boat ees eet?'

I gave them directions and swung on down the hill, hoping that I'd got some biscuits left, and that they wouldn't change their minds. It takes a special person to accept an invitation from a complete stranger.

I had.

They didn't.

They were.

After an hour and a half of tea and gossip, I'd learned that the elder, Hanne, was Danish, worked for the Danish environmental agency, lived north of Copenhagen and had a part-time job as a tourist guide, and that the younger, Martha, was a PhD biochemist from Madrid who'd come over for a year on an exchange programme to see what Danish fungi were like. She was renting a room in Hanne's house; Hanne had recently separated from her husband and was having problems making ends meet. Hanne was quiet, calm, friendly and understated. Martha was Spanish. Their reactions to the boat showed their personalities perfectly. Hanne looked around the cabin, ran a finger absent-mindedly along a shelf, smiled at me and said, 'Nice boat.' Martha erupted in squeaks of delight and ran around like a child at Christmas.

When they left to catch the last ferry back to Denmark, Hanne said, 'Why don't you come round for supper one day this week?'

'Oh, *sí!*' Martha added, bobbing up and down.

I accepted with pleasure, making the mental note that Danish xenophobia wasn't all that legend portrayed.

Within forty-eight hours I was forced to reassess: Danish xenophobia doesn't *exist*.*

It started when I moored up in Copenhagen marina. To be honest, my arrival was something of a disappointment. I'd been looking forward to a romantic city worthy of Hans Christian Andersen. What I got, of course, was a working port: cranes, chimneys, flame-stacks and refinery towers, with, cowering beneath them, a tiny glint of gold which might have been a cathedral dome. Ships criss-crossed the water: tankers, freighters, a Russian tramp steamer streaked black and red with rust, white-hulled ferries plying the waters to Sweden, where the cranes and refineries of Malmö seemed almost within spitting distance. The legendary Øresund Bridge, crown jewel of Danish architecture and the latest in a long line of Famous Danish Bridges, resembled nothing more than two shocked millipedes standing face to face. No offence to Danny Kaye, but it wasn't much to sing about.

Just north of the city centre, the legendary statue of the Little Mermaid leans on her rock, looking sadly out to sea. Just behind her is a tiny guest harbour, where, under a sunset of stormy gold, I tied up in an empty berth and stood on deck to stretch. I was still there when the harbourmaster walked along the jetty.

'Hi, welcome to Copenhagen,' he said cheerfully. 'Rough day, isn't it?'

'Lumpy,' I agreed. 'But not too bad.'

'Are you staying long?'

'A couple of days.'

'Do you need electricity?'

'No thanks, I've got a generator,' I said proudly.

---

* Not as long as you're white, self-supporting and not planning to immigrate anyway.

'Do you like fish?'

'Sorry?' That wasn't a normal harbour question.

'Do you like fish?'

'Well, yes . . .'

'Good, I went out fishing this afternoon, I'll bring you a couple of mackerel. Enjoy your stay!'

He smiled and left me. As I gazed after him, an elderly woman out for an evening stroll slowed down, looked up at me, smiled, and walked on. It was possibly the first time since leaving the UK that a stranger had smiled at me without my smiling first. *I'm going to like it here*, I decided with a sudden rush of warmth.

I retreated to the quarterdeck, humming and thinking positive thoughts. At that moment, my mobile rang.

'*Hey, hier ist Helena*,' came the familiar voice. I hadn't seen her since setting sail. It felt like a long time.

'Hey, I was just thinking of you,' I said happily.

'I can't talk for long. Where are you?'

'Copenhagen.'

'Cool! When are you coming to Germany?'

'Two weeks. Are we going to meet up?'

'Would I have asked otherwise?'

I laughed. 'I'll call when I'm there.'

''Til then!'

''Til then!'

I put the phone down, smiling, swung down into the cabin, and started wondering what to cook with the promised fish.

The third thing I noticed about Copenhagen was its size. It's huge, a magnificent city of stately boulevards, far too big for the country it represents. But when it was built Denmark ruled western Sweden, the whole of Norway, Iceland and Greenland, so that's hardly surprising. The second thing I noticed was the number of British tourists: they were everywhere, filling the cafés along the old canals, swarming in churches and galleries. But the *first* thing I noticed, uniquely in any capital city I've ever visited, was the locals.

They were friendly. They were smiling. They seemed happy to see me, happy to make eye contact, happy when, dazed, I smiled back at them. Perhaps my sensibilities were sharpened by staying so long in the north, but I felt I'd never been in such a friendly place. It started right outside the harbour, as I stood gazing down at the Little Mermaid. Behind me a pair of American tourists stopped to take the obligatory photo, then remarked in dissatisfaction, 'Gee, I didn't think she'd be so small.' A passing businessman carrying a lap-top overheard the comment and noticed my amusement. He winked at me and walked on. It continued on my walk along the stately waterfront – beautiful town-houses, churches and palaces on the right, wind generators and oil refineries on the left – where joggers and dog-walkers seemed to be making a special effort to brighten my morning. It even lasted in the city centre itself, where a wizened old lady bumped into me, turned round and, rather than withering me with the invective you'd get in London, apologized, asked if she'd hurt me and went on to say that it was nice weather for the time of year, wasn't it?

In many ways, Copenhagen reminded me of London. If you ignore the word 'European', which is meaningless anyway, it really is like London or Amsterdam: the same ponderously magnificent architecture, the same stone statements of power and wealth, the same impression that this city grew rich on overseas trade. Which, of course, it did. But wherever I went there were smiles. I saw them in the pavement cafés, where locals and foreigners had sat down for a pint of beer (at ten in the morning!); in the pedestrian zones, where lean, hunted-looking men ran pea-and-shell gambling games while their friends in the crowd kept watch; in the one-time hippy commune of Christiania, now a sad monument to vanished ideals, where every former squat boasts a satellite dish and the few fading posters proclaiming liberty and revolution are obscured under a thick layer of adverts for mainstream pop CDs; in the Church of Our Saviour with its famous twisted spire. Looking down from the spire over the fume-wreathed city, the sound that pierced the roar of traffic was the shouting and laughter of children, playing in a school below. It seemed appropriate.

Even the choir of evangelists I saw in a quiet pedestrian street fitted the friendly atmosphere. They stood singing hymns, then circulated among the listeners, offering cakes and coffee with rum. It was a very cold day. I chatted with one for a while, until she gave up on me as a heathen. Before we parted she asked if she could bless me, warned me that she spoke 'in tongues, the language of Heaven' and, brilliant blue eyes staring into mine, she put one hand on my head and repeated, 'Amana-amana zhovin mana zharata ma ana-ana-zharata-zhovin . . .', and with variations on this unfamiliar theme, continued for quite some time. This too is not something which happens every day.

It was a far cry from the Viking tradition of conversion. Oláf Tryggvason, enthusiastic Christian that he was, patented the peculiar Norse technique for evangelization which continued for most of the next two hundred years: 'The King went north and bade all men accept Christianity; and those who spoke against it he punished severely, killed some, had some maimed and drove others into exile.' His five-year rule of Norway was a succession of massacres, murders and grisly torture scenes. In similar circumstances his successor Saint Oláf was murdered by his own people. The same might have happened to Tryggvason, but his other enemies were already waiting for an opportunity. By the time his policy of forced conversion was properly launched he'd managed to anger Svein Forkbeard, Eirík Hákonarson, and Sigríd of Sweden, all of whom were far more politically astute than he. His fiery temperament proved his death warrant. In all, I was glad my Copenhagen lady hadn't adopted his techniques.

I walked back to the boat, pondering the change in Scandinavian evangelism. As I passed the Little Mermaid I heard a dissatisfied German photographer remark to his wife, 'It's a bit small, isn't it?' Mermaid. Little. Little Mermaid. How difficult can it be?

I'd arranged to go and see Hanne and Martha two days later, and there was a gale blowing up the Sound, so cruising seemed best avoided. Instead, I hoisted my bike off the quarterdeck, caught the train to a rural station, and went exploring.

Historically, linguistically and culturally, Denmark is a part of Scandinavia, but its architecture and landforms are British. All the houses I saw were brick, with red roof-tiles and privet hedges, as solidly British as could be imagined, a far cry from the wooden towns of Norway and Sweden. The countryside, a pleasant mixture of field and woodland, gently undulating and scattered with small villages, looked like the best bits of Shropshire. Unsurprisingly, given that they're on the same latitude and share almost identical climates, the vegetation mirrored that of the Scottish Midlands, with its hedges of thorn and blackberry, oak and beech trees hung with rooks' nests, lush tufted grass in the fields, willows beside lake and pond. The postboxes were a friendly red, not the yellow of everywhere else in Europe. It was so like home that I had to force myself to look for differences: streetlamps and pylons the wrong shape, traffic on the wrong side of the road, shop signs and street signs in Danish. Even the tabloids advertised in newsagents' windows were full of illicit pictures of the royal family, although it was the princess of Sweden they were following. On the evidence of that day's ride, if ever a country was closely related to the UK, it's Denmark.

Two evenings later I went to dine. Having already confirmed that Norwegians and Swedes are still closely related to the British, I was eager to see if their southern, more 'European' neighbours would live up to my hopes. If anything, they exceeded them. Norwegians live in a land made almost exclusively of mountains. Swedes have a country so big it looks like the American West in the days of the first European settlers. Both lie so far to the north that winter lasts half the year. Inevitably, their environment influences them; you don't see many happy faces in Gothenburg in January. (Or any other time of year.) Denmark, on the other hand, might as well *be* Britain. It's on the same latitude. It's surrounded by sea. It's similarly rolling (the highest point in the country is a towering 400 metres above sea level). It lies to the east of a large body of water with prevailing winds coming from the west. It even has a language which isn't pronounced anything like the way it's written. How much more similar can you get?

Denmark's main problem is being famous for not being famous. (Name five famous Danes, anyone?) As in so many other countries, this is because it's only actually known for its chief export – bacon. Whether this is worse than Sweden's stolid cars is open to debate, it depends if you prefer breakfasts to fast brakes, but neither really qualifies their country for international glamour. It's a shame. Any country which prides itself on high-quality food has the right attitude as far as I'm concerned. The Danes know that they're never going to rule the world again. They've had their empires, once in the days of Svein, once in the days of 'the Valdemars' (Kings Valdemar the Great and Valdemar the Victorious, who conquered large territories in Germany and Estonia in the late twelfth and early thirteenth centuries), and again during the period of the fifteenth-century Kalmar Scandinavian Union. Imperially speaking, things have been going downhill ever since. The Swedes broke away from the Union in 1523. In 1659 they annexed the Danish provinces of Halland and Skåne and the island of Gotland. In 1801 the Danes allied themselves with anti-British Russia to protect their overseas trade, and were promptly bombarded by Nelson. Six years later the British decided that the Danish fleet was too great a threat to national security, sailed back to Copenhagen and demanded its immediate surrender. The Danes refused, so the British spent three days fire-bombing Copenhagen, then took the fleet anyway. Not entirely surprisingly, the Danes allied themselves with Napoleon, so at the end of those wars they found themselves on the losing side *again*. That misjudgement cost them Norway, which had been a Danish province since the 1540s. Fifty years later the newly appointed Prussian Chancellor Bismarck annexed the southern provinces of Schleswig and Holstein. Finally, in the closing days of the Second World War, Iceland decided that it no longer wished to be united with Denmark, and declared its independence. All that remains of the glory days is the county of Greenland. Denmark's still big, but it's no longer a major international player.

It makes me wonder if Britain will be like Denmark in a couple of hundred years' time. We're still trying to kid ourselves that we're a great world power, much to the annoyance of China, Russia, and the USA. The Danes have got over their post-imperial complex, and have sensibly re-adjusted their view of their history to point out what a nice little country they have. Not for them the gorier excesses of a glorious past. They concentrate on the establishment of an absolutist monarchy in the seventeenth century: as the rest of Europe wallowed in blood and fire the Danish king, Frederick III, decided that his nobles were so incompetent that it would be better for him to rule alone. The national response ran along the lines of, 'Oh, all right then.' In 1848, as every throne in Europe was rocked by popular uprisings, a group of Copenhagen notables went to Frederick VII and asked for a constitution, please. His response – quoted to me by various Danish friends – was 'All right, my children, if that's what you want.' They concentrate on the fact that Denmark was the first country in the world to abolish slavery, on its long history of consultative government, on its immensely durable royal family (the present queen is a direct descendant of Gorm the Old, Harald Bluetooth's father), on its high standard of living and its cosmopolitan atmosphere. They're proud of being a leading exporter of dairy products. Absurd or admirable: the choice is yours.

Dinner at Hanne's was a lesson in hospitality and history. From the moment I stepped through the door of her snug brick bungalow to my staggering out to retrieve my bike, she pressed food and drink on me. (The dry-cleaning bill was awful.) Preprandial snacks led to two whole roast chickens, stuffed with garlic and garnished with potatoes, which led to salad, which led to ice cream, which led to coffee, which led to the biggest bowl of fruit I've ever seen: at least one Swedish prejudice seemed justified. Danes might not live to eat, but if I'd had any more I might have died of eating. Both Martha and I were intrigued by the Danish view of history, so the questions kept flowing, and Hanne, flattered to be asked, responded with an affectionate overview of her country's background.

It wasn't until we came to her own lifetime that the affection waned. She was born in 1938, and her first memory is of a German armoured car squeaking past her house, rattling the cups on the hooks. The Danish take on their history might be light-hearted and tolerant, but this stops abruptly in 1940. On 9 April Hitler's armies invaded Denmark on the way to Norway. The Danes took one look at the battle-hardened veterans of the Polish *Blitzkrieg*, and surrendered. April 9 remains a day of national mourning. The memory of the surrender is a painful one. No matter how sensible a move it was, Hanne and her generation seem embarrassed by the fact that they didn't fight. It was a relief when Danish Resistance groups began to operate in September 1943.

For the Danes, Sweden was the Haven over the Water during the war years, where they could send their refugees, their Jews, their dissidents. Whilst Norway has never forgotten that the 'neutral' Swedes allowed the Wehrmacht to use their railway system in the invasion of Norway, the Danes remember that by the time the war ended there were so many Danes in southern Sweden that they'd formed their own Freedom Army, equipped with Swedish arms. It was the country where the lights still burned, even when Denmark was under a blackout. Those lights had an immense impact on Hanne's generation. When the Armistice was declared, she ran into the kitchen to light candles and stick them in the window, to show that the blackout was over. Most of her neighbours did the same. Fifty years later, she was one of thousands of candle-carrying Danes who formed a human chain from Helsingør to Copenhagen to celebrate the anniversary of the peace. Sweden, for the Danes, meant hope.

The ones they really don't like are the Germans. Once, in a Danish harbour, I was talking with a forty-year-old mechanic about Copenhagen. I said the name with a flat 'a', 'Copenhaagen', as I always have. He bridled and gave me a ferocious stare.

'If you call it that,' he said coldly, 'everyone here will think you're a German and they'll hate you. Call it Copenhaygen. We don't like Germans here.'

When I told Hanne that, she said it was rubbish.

'So what do you think of Europe?' I asked. It was like throwing a cigarette-butt into a petrol tanker. Two weeks before my arrival, the Danes had voted 'No' in a referendum on joining the single currency. The memory was still vivid.

'I think it's a disgrace! The government tell us that if we don't join the euro the economy will fail, the world will come to an end, but they haven't given us a single good reason why we *should* join! What they mean is that their careers will come to an end. Why should we worry about that? We're a small country! If we join the euro we'll be flattened by the French and the Germans! We'll end up paying extra taxes to send money to Spain and Turkey!'

She shouldn't have said Spain. Not when she was sitting next to Martha.

'You think Spain has it easy?' Martha turned on her landlady, her black eyes spitting fire. 'We've had problems with Europe too! Did you realize that olive oil has doubled in price since we joined the euro?' I'd never thought of using olive oil as a standard of international financial comparison, but then, I'm not from the Mediterranean. 'But we're trying to make the world better!'

Hanne's face grew red. I sat back, hardly daring to breathe. This was better than Wimbledon.

'So you think we should pay even more taxes, just so we can give free hand-outs to countries like Greece and Turkey?' With admirable tactical awareness, she left Spain out of it this time. It didn't help. 'This isn't a charity!'

'Well, it should be!' Martha flared. 'If everyone in power thought like you do we'd never stop fighting wars!'

They stopped, glaring at one another. I decided to intervene before blood was shed.

'So you don't like the idea of a single currency wherever you go?' I asked Hanne.

'Why should I? I don't travel that often, and I certainly don't want a foreigner's face on my money.'

Martha opened her mouth. I had to move fast.

'What about Leonardo da Vinci?'

'Or Cervantes?' Martha chimed in.

'Or Beethoven?'

'Or Voltaire?'

'Or Shakespeare?'

Our hostess was definitely feeling got at. 'That's the problem with the younger generation,' she muttered. 'You've been brainwashed by the politicians. You don't even know how to question them any more.' And, quickly, before we could protest, she added, 'Now, who wants some cognac?'

Peace was restored with true Danish flair. By the end of the evening we were happily giggling away together, all hostilities forgotten. Perhaps the EU should bear that in mind the next time they plan a summit.

Next day I headed south. The gale was still blowing, bringing waves up all the way from Latvia, but I was starting to fret. Time was ticking away, and I wanted to get down to Germany and see Helena. From Copenhagen to the southern tip of Denmark should be an easy run in the shelter of the country's hundreds of islands, but from there I'd have to cross the exposed neck of the Baltic down to Rostock. It was going to be a challenge. First thing that morning I walked over to the

Little Mermaid and, copying her pose almost exactly, looked out to sea. We would have made a fine pair if only I'd been born with a tail. The wind had turned easterly, blowing straight off the Swedish coast. That meant that the waves should be diminishing, and it's waves which kill ships, not wind. I decided to risk it. Half an hour later I was heading out into the Sound.

I'd been optimistic. The conditions were hideous, a jumble of grey, cross, bursting waves, the 'crab sea' of the Baltic. Soon my glasses were dotted with spray and I was forced to reduce speed, climbing and falling and rolling across the bay. South of Copenhagen the coast bends in to the west, juts out into a long, low headland, and then sweeps in again to a second bay, opening at its southwestern corner into the shallow lagoon between the great islands of Sjaelland, Lolland and Falster. I had been hoping to make that lagoon in a day; soon, as the waves and the wind increased, I abandoned the idea and concentrated on rounding the headland. Just on the far side was a fishing harbour: if I could get that far I should be able to dash across the second bay the following day. *If* I could get there ... Every few minutes the sea blackened and broke as the waves ran together, and I'd throttle back and turn to meet the chaos, feeling the daylight draining away. All the while the wind was rising, up towards a gale, jabbing the waves in short punches against the hull. As the headland came up on my radar, the sky was already dark. I double-checked my charts and GPS, switched power to the searchlight, re-checked my position and hoped like hell that the harbour lights were working. Approaching an unknown port single-handed in the dark is the most dangerous act of pilotage you can attempt. All day I'd been racing the sunset. As the last light burned the clouds blood-red, I knew I'd lost.

Night fell as I lurched towards the headland. Everything

was black, black cliffs, black water, black sky, and my heart beat like a trip-hammer. Where was I? Where was I going? What was that shape ahead? I jumped at shadows and the heave of waves, half-expecting to see the surf breaking under me, the rocks dead ahead. I throttled right back, hearing the spray rattling on my jacket and the wind snapping my flag, feeling my way through the darkness. Suddenly the GPS beeped, warning me that I'd reached my turning-point. At once I swung the wheel over, away from the wind, feeling the waves lift and roll her. I braced my feet. A cupboard burst open below. Now I was running due west along the land. Slowly an inlet opened beside me, and at the bottom I saw the winking lights of harbour and town. I was past the worst. Safety was in sight. I nudged the throttles forward and stared towards shore, straining my eyes for the pilot lights.

God knows what reflex saved me. Something made me look down, and in the same instant I shouted and jerked back on the throttles and slammed into reverse as a line of buoys appeared out of nowhere and slid under my bow. I threshed backwards, sweating and panicked, praying that they hadn't caught in my propellers, unable to believe that someone had set nets right across the harbour channel. Two seconds slower in my reactions and I would have run right over them, my props tangled in half a mile of cable, engines stalled, transmission wrecked, a lump of useless metal heaving up and down in a gale. My heart pounded at the mere thought. I flicked on the searchlight, and through the driving spray I saw the line, tossing on the waves, right across my path, sliding back out of view. Shaking, I turned seawards, crawled south to head round the obstruction and try again. My legs were quivering. How close had that been? I went a full mile out to sea, turned west, and inched forwards with searchlight blazing. Just when I thought I was clear, the buoys appeared again. I swung south again, eyes and lights glued on the deadly line, intent on swinging around the danger and heading back into shore.

CRASH! and before my brain had registered the impact, my hands had snapped the gears back and swung the searchlight forwards. There above my bows loomed a dozen posts joined with a maze of sagging nets, smoking in the bursting storm. I'd run right into them, and my bows were caught fast.

I can't even say that I thought about what to do. I was running on fear and gut instinct, caught fast on the open water with a gale blowing up from the worst possible direction, and running through my veins was the knowledge that things could turn out very badly indeed. It probably wouldn't have been fatal: even if the ship had been overwhelmed in the storm I had my life-raft ready, my diving gear and breathing equipment, and a sloping shore a mile and a half away, downwind. But in the blackness of the night, with the solid spray flying through the beam of the searchlight, the sea wild and the wind howling, I wasn't thinking about that. I wanted out.

I ran to the quarterdeck and jammed the props into reverse. The boat shuddered and groaned, but nothing moved. I applied more power. Could I pull out of the trap? The engines roared and foam spat from under the stern, and then with a jolt and a clang *Peregrino* shot backwards. For half a second I thought I'd done it. Then I heard the death-rattle of anchor chain spewing out of the locker, and hope died. *Peregrino* jerked to a halt on the waves, nodding like a dog on a rope, held in the trap by my anchor and forty metres of chain.

I flicked power through to the anchor winch (mended on Hönö), pressed the switch to reel it in, nudged the boat forwards, waited for the winch to work – and nothing happened.

I swore, stumbled forwards along the deck, yanked the anchor locker open, and was met with the stink of smoke and burnt plastic. Automatically I hit the manual override and tried the winch again. Nothing. This wasn't a faulty component, this was meltdown. A wave crashed over me, drowning the locker and foaming out through the scuppers, but I hardly noticed. I grabbed the kicking anchor chain, braced my legs against the iron bar, and pulled. The chain jumped in my hands, ripping the skin off my palms and twanging back into the locker, bar-taut. That wasn't an option. Measured thought vanished. I had only one idea: dump the lot. I forced myself down into the locker, gasping as another wave cascaded over my back, switched my torch on and jammed it into my mouth, stretched down to the shackle holding the chain to the hull, wrenched desperately and failed to open it. Suddenly the words of a maritime uncle came back to me, 'Always attach your anchor chain to the boat with a rope so you can cut it,' and if I hadn't been in such an awkward position I would have kicked myself. I fumbled a shackle-key over the shackle and wrenched again, and the thing slipped, sliced another gash in my palm and clattered down into the bilges, out of reach.

There was no time for dismay. Yet another wave broke over the bow, and I fought my way back out of the locker and hobbled into the cabin. I wrenched the tool locker open, leaving blood on the mahogany, and scrabbled through masses of metal to find my hacksaw. My torch blinked and started to fade as I ran forwards, clutching the saw in one hand and the guard-rail with the other, the kick of the sea almost knocking me off my feet. Then I was back down in the anchor locker, hewing away at the chain. As the saw-blade slipped and slid, my heart sank: surely the chain wasn't hardened steel? Then it bit. I heaved and hacked like a madman. Panic is a great motivator. Almost before I knew it, the chain had parted. The boat jumped and, with a last vicious rattle, the whole lot spat out of the locker and dropped into the waves.

I flung the saw into the locker and stumbled back along

deck, slamming the boat into gear and swinging the bow wide of the obstruction. The posts rocked by overside, besieged by the reeling sea, and I swung round past them and set my head for the harbour. I was shaking and sick. All I wanted to do was collapse, and still I had to steer, navigate, watch out for yet more nets, locate the harbour lights and handle the boat through a wicked following sea. It seemed endless. By the time I swept in by the Rødvig harbour wall my legs had given out and I was holding myself up by the wheel. The harbour was tiny, half-abandoned, an unlit mess of mooring-posts and trailing ropes: too complicated for me. I swung in alongside a moored fishing boat, dropped a rope over his forward bollard, hurried astern to make all fast, dropped down onto a deck-box, and stared out to sea, shivering.

The gale blew all the next day, driving bursting spray high over the harbour wall. I slept like the dead that night, and spent the day staring out over the grey wilderness of the waves, towards the long lines of nets jutting out into the bay. With day-light and hindsight it was easy to see my mistake: I'd allowed the swell to push me closer and closer to shore, out of the normal fairway and into the fishermen's zone. *That's the last time I try a night approach*, I thought. The mistake had cost me an anchor and a chain. I was lucky it hadn't been worse.

That night the wind lessened to a mere force six and, as dawn turned the sky grey, I set out into it, steering so wide of the nets I was practically driving along the beach, aiming for the safety of the lagoon. The first hour was a nightmare, a wild rough-and-tumble ride slewing across the waves, but then I came into the lee of the islands, and almost miraculously the waters calmed. As the sun came up red I started threading my way between the buoys of the shallow channel, eyes flicking from compass to chart to buoys to depth-gauge, barely two metres of water under me, and low green islands all around.

The scenery was fabulous. Here and there the sea's grey mirror-like surface was powdered black and white with an amazing number of birds, swans, geese, ducks and gulls, and to the side of the channel the black flags of lobster-pots nodded in the wind. Little motorboats spread long, blade-straight ripples across the water, and out of the haze loomed enormous bridges, the life-lines of Danish transport and a monument to the creativity of their architects. I would have loved to explore in *Lilla Blån*, the Stensund sailing boat, shallow-keeled and slow, but here and now my thoughts were fixed on survival. This beautiful lagoon hides a thousand shallows and sandy reefs. I forced myself to go slowly, measuring, checking and double-checking. I'd had enough excitement for a while.

I steered past the pastures of Falster and turned south across a wide, shallow bay. Ahead of me opened an inlet between green banks, a high bridge spanning it: the four-metre channel between the islands which leads to Gedser, Denmark's southernmost headland, the jumping-off point for Germany. Four metres is not a lot of water, and the chart warned that it could be a metre shallower in southerly winds, but that still left me a lot of clearance. I throttled back and started to follow the buoys, eyes on the depth-gauge. Three metres under the keel, no problem. Two, still no problem. My eyes flickered to the chart. I should cross a depth contour in the next two minutes, and then the bottom would level out. There it went, one and a half metres ... one and a half ... one ... one ... nought point seven ... I throttled back, my throat suddenly dry. That was two metres shallower than the charted depth, surely the wind couldn't have had such an effect? Nought point six ... I looked around. The channel I was in was barely ten metres wide, a narrow double line of buoys across a featureless grey expanse. There wasn't even room to turn around. If it got too shallow here I was going to have to reverse out of the trap. *Keep going*, I told myself grimly, and went on, eyes on depth-gauge and hand on gear-lever.

Nought point five . . . point five . . . point five . . . suddenly it jumped to nought point two and an alarm started beeping in the cabin. I wrenched the engines out of gear, let her drift forwards, sweating. At least it was a sandy bottom here, covered in weeds: if I touched gently I wouldn't stick . . . Point two, point one, and then suddenly point five again. I waited for a minute, pushed back into gear, nosed forwards. Point five, point six, point five, point one, out of gear, drift, sweat, wait for the end, point five once more, point four, point four, heart pounding, the buoys drifting past, point two, out of gear, point one, point one, wait for the crunch, point nought, what's happening?, point nought and still drifting forwards, no sign of collision, point nought, and suddenly the depth jumped to one point two and I was drifting forwards, shaking, but triumphant, heading southwards.

I pulled into Gedser harbour just before five, killed the engines and looked over the side. There was no damage there, no sign of trailing weeds, and though my engine-cooling water filters were thick with green scum there was no sign of trouble or overheating. I'd been driving for ten hours without a break. When I came back on deck and tipped a bucket of slime overboard, the sun was going down in ruby splendour.

I looked out across the Baltic. Surely, surely those waves weren't as heavy as I'd expected? I looked up, checking the breeze. Surely it had turned, blowing up from the south? I stood still, calculating. Southerly. A wind off Germany. The closer to land I came the smaller the waves would become. Even if it was rough here, it wouldn't get worse. If I set off now I could be there in four hours. For a second the fear of the night engulfed me. Could I do that again? But my nearest landfall was Rostock, the biggest port in eastern Germany. No fisherman would set nets across the main ferry route . . . Then the thought came in, *If you get there tonight you can be in Berlin in the morning.* Berlin meant Helena. I gave one last, long look at sky and water. *It'll be rough, but I can do it.*

I swung back into the cabin to switch on my instruments.

It was a magical night. As I drove out of the harbour and into the pitching swells the last crimson rim of the sun ducked under the horizon. The sky was clear, a piercing blue on my left hand arcing through turquoise to tangerine on the right, and here and there the first stars pricked through the emptiness. Swiftly night fell, cold and clear, and behind me I saw Polaris grow to a brilliant spark, its light splintering along my wake. Ahead the channel beacons danced and winked, and the ships around me moved in endless chains of lights. Gradually, as I'd hoped, the waves diminished, the wild swings of the compass decreased, and I settled to my course between the blackness of the water and the burning brilliance of the stars. After an hour and a half a faint white light began glowing on the horizon dead ahead, and as I wondered if it could be the loom of the lights of Rostock so soon the half-moon rose out of the waves and turned my track to a swaying mesh of black and silver.

Four hours after leaving Denmark I slipped along the slick dark waters of the Warnow river among the myriad lights of Rostock and tied up at the town quay. As I shut the engines down, the sound of sirens came to my ears, the unmistakable music that pervades all German ports. An hour after that I was in the station, finding out train times to Berlin. At dawn the next day I was on the train, and just before noon I stepped out into Berlin station and walked out into the busy streets. I'd been trying to call Helena all morning, but the phone was permanently engaged. Feeling slightly light-headed I walked into the courtyard of her block of flats, pulled out my phone and dialled her number. For a wonder, I got through.

'Hallo?'

'Hey, it's Ben.'

'Hey! How are you?'

'Fine. Are you busy right now?'

'No.'

'Will you do me a favour?'

'Maybe . . .' She sounded suspicious.

I grinned down the phone.

'Go down the stairs and open the door.'

'Are you crazy?'

'Go down and open the door.'

She put the phone down. I walked up to the door. A window opened above me. Helena looked out. Her face lit up. Fifteen seconds later footsteps thundered down the stairs, and the door burst open.

12

SLAVIA

'Slavia is a very large province of Germany ... It is said to be ten times bigger than our Saxony, especially if you count as part of Slavia Bohemia and the expanses across the Oder, the Poles, because they differ neither in appearance nor in language.'

Adam of Bremen, *History of the Archbishops of Hamburg-Bremen*

So I reached Germany. Or, as it used to be called, East Germany. Or Prussia. Or Slavia. Or Heathen Wendland. Home of the Germans, or East Germans, or Prussians, or Wends, or – as modern German slang has it – fish-heads. As you may have guessed, it's an area with a lot of history.

It's mainly a history of racism. In the wild and marshy land between the Elbe and the Oder, the Slav and the German met. They remain enemies throughout time; anyone who thinks that that's historical rhetoric might wish to consider 1 September 1939. Throughout the Viking era the German emperors fought to establish their power on the Elbe's right bank, and the Slavs fought back. In 983, as the civil war between Svein and his father was brewing, the Slavs rebelled against their oppressors, swept across the Elbe and sacked Hamburg. In 1002, as Ethelred ordered the massacre of Danes in England, the German Emperor declared war on the Christian Duke of Poland, the greatest power in Slavia. The struggle went on for a generation. All the while Danish and Swedish raiders and traders were sweeping down on the coast to burn or barter, carving out independent territories of which Jómsborg was only the most renowned. The borderlands where German and Slav met were not a good place to be.

And it was here that Oláf Tryggvason's saga came to an end. Contemporary history says little about his fall; the chroniclers can't decide on when and where he died, but where history fails, legend takes up the story.

It happened in September 1000, a millennium and a month before I reached the Slavic shore; and it happened because Oláf, impulsive to the last, couldn't resist interfering. The problem started in Poland. As part of the long-ago settlement with the Jómsvikings, Bolesław of Poland had arranged to marry Svein's sister Thyri. She objected on the not unreasonable grounds that he was not only a heathen, but old. Svein, acutely aware that he needed Bolesław's support to keep his Baltic borders quiet, ordered her to shut up and marry the man. She fled to Norway and asked for Oláf's protection. As the saga relates, 'He asked if she would marry him. She said it was too great a matter for her and asked him to decide for her.' (With a flutter of eyelashes and a giggle, one suspects.) 'And the way they worked it out was that King Oláf took Thyri as his queen.' Astonishing.

But Thyri pined for the royal lands she might have held in Poland. Oláf, anxious to cheer her up, offered her a stalk of celery instead. (It's true! The saga says so.) Unsatisfied with this – how unreasonable women are – she accused him of being scared of Svein, and therefore afraid of sailing to Poland to claim her territories there. Oláf promptly summoned a small fleet and sailed southwards towards the lands of *all* his mortal enemies. As I may have mentioned, cold-blooded calculation was not his strong point.

His enemies heard that he was coming, let him pass, and set an ambush for his return.

It was the greatest battle of the age. Not until the autumn of 1066 would the fate of so many kingdoms be decided in a single fight. Svein and his allies – the Swedes under Queen Sigríd's son Oláf, the Norwegians under Eirík Hákonarson – stood massed on the shore of an island which historians have yet to identify, watching Tryggvason's fleet approach. As the first ship went by, grander and more stately than any known in Denmark, Svein called for his arms. Eirík restrained him. Ten ships followed, each more imposing than the last, and each time the kings clamoured for action. Then Oláf himself came into view on his ship *The Long Serpent*, the greatest longship ever built in the North. There could be no mistaking it. One after another, the kings went to their ships and rowed out to meet him.

Oláf saw them coming. Outnumbered five to one, the heroic tradition of resistance against impossible odds and famous last stands had sunk right into his bones. When his men begged him to sail away – the attacking kings having lowered their masts as a preparation for action – he replied in true Viking style, 'I never yet fled in battle, and I never will!' And he commanded his men to lower the sail, lash their ships together with *The Long Serpent* foremost, and attack.

The men in the bows of *The Long Serpent*, less whole-heartedly empty-headedly heroic than their king, were dismayed. Perhaps Oláf's nerves were as strained as theirs: he accused them of cowardice. It was too much. Ulf the Red, his leading forecastleman, fired back a retaliatory insult. Oláf set an arrow to his bow and aimed it at Ulf.

'Shoot the other way,' Ulf told him, 'that's where it'll be

needed!' And then, beating Bryan Adams by a thousand years, 'Whatever I do, I do for you.'

Vikings always die in style.

Oláf went through a characteristic mood swing. He sprang onto the steersman's platform and eyed his opponents.

'Who's that?' he shouted, pointing at the leading ship.

'Svein Forkbeard!'

'We're not scared of those cowards, they're Danes!' and laughter went up. This was a king that men would die for. 'Who's that lot?'

'Oláf and his Swedes!'

'They'd better go home while they can! Whose are those large ships?'

'That's Eirík and his Norwegians, Sire!'

'We might have to have a proper fight, then! They're Norwegians like us!' His men cheered. The king stood high and exposed in the stern, visible to all, shining in his armour. This was Oláf at his glorious best. Whatever his faults, his courage and charisma were unforgettable.

But the battle was Svein's. He was a man who never wasted an effort, never risked a loss, never forgot his long-term goals of survival and power. He sent the Swedes and Norwegians against Oláf's linked fleet, keeping his own men in reserve, bombarding the defenders with arrows and javelins. Cunning played little part in Norse battles; generations of poets have grown up on tales of Svein's cowardice. But his strategy worked. Under cover of his bombardment, Eirík and his Norwegians boarded Oláf's flanks. Hand to hand on the defenders' decks they fought, swept them clear, used the bloodied hulls as bridges to swarm in on the little fleet. Behind them stormed the Danes and the Swedes. Surrounded and outnumbered, as they had surrounded and outnumbered the Blackwater Saxons a decade before, Oláf's men hurled defiance, and built their shield-wall, and went down fighting. An iron pincer closed on *The Long Serpent*.

One man might have saved the day. In the stern of *The Long Serpent* stood Einarr Thambarskelfir, youngest of Oláf's men and the finest bowman ever to live in the Northlands. He shot at Eirík as he came rampaging across the decks, and the arrow passed through the Jarl's hair and embedded itself in the ship's timbers. Again Einarr shot, and the arrow flew between Eirík's arm and his ribs.

'Shoot that archer!' called Eirík; and a man called Finn, a bowman and warlock (as all Finns were), loosed just as Einarr was drawing again. Finn's arrow struck Einarr's bow an inch above the hand-grip, and the bow burst in two.

'What cracked so loudly?' called Oláf over the battle.

'Norway out of your hands!' answered Einarr.

'Nothing so serious,' laughed the king, looking out over the wreckage of his fleet, and tossed Einarr his own bow; but even in his youth Einarr was too strong. At the first attempt he drew the bow so far back that its timbers warped; and so he drew his sword instead and fought hand to hand as Eirík's men swept in.

Ship by ship the enemy advanced. Crew by crew they cut down Oláf's men or hurled them into the sea. The defenders' swords were notched, their edges blunted. Oláf threw open his own treasure chest and hurled new swords to all who could still use them; but as he did so they saw blood gushing out of his sleeve. Nobody knew where he was wounded. Twice Eirík stormed the bulwarks of *The Long Serpent* and charged in among the defenders. Twice he was repulsed with heavy losses. The ships behind were littered with his Norwegian followers; but always more reinforcements came, Danes and Swedes, as Svein coolly sent fresh squadrons into the battle. The most daring Viking in the history of Norway was battling the most cunning general in the North. There could only be one outcome.

No saga records Oláf Tryggvason's death. At the third charge Eirík broke the defenders' shield-wall, and his men came pouring onto *The Long Serpent*'s deck. Hemmed in to stem and stern the last of Oláf's men stood and fought and died as the men of Maldon died; and seeing that the fight was lost, Oláf dived overboard, plunging into the sea in full armour. At once a shout went up from the attackers. All eyes were turned to the blood-stained waters, littered with splinters and fallen arrows; but no bright head broke the surface. Then all those of Oláf's men who still could leapt overboard after their master, swimming for safety. Few broke through the encircling Danes. As Eirík's Norwegians rested on their blood-ied swords, Svein rowed over to *The Long Serpent*. Standing amidst the carnage, he and Eirík struck hands. The Norwegian had the glory, but the victory was Svein's. His last great rival was defeated. Rumours of his survival would continue to cir-culate for years; but Oláf never returned to the North. In his place, Svein would set up Eirík as his regent in Norway. It had taken him fifteen years; but the Jómsvikings were broken, Oláf was gone, and Norway was his to take. Even the Swedes were his allies. At last his position was secure.

Two years later Ethelred ordered the massacre of the Danes in England, and the Scandinavian juggernaut turned west. This time, Danegeld would not be enough.

In time, the Baltic power balance shifted. After Cnut's death, Danish power waned, whittled away in Scandinavian feuds. Headed by the Crusading Order of Teutonic Knights, the Ger-mans expanded eastwards along the Baltic coast, conquering and converting the Slavs. The Hanseatic League became the area's Great Power, challenging Denmark for control of the Øresund, then declined as Europe's trading interests moved from the Baltic and the Mediterranean to the East and West Indies. Sweden enjoyed a brief century of glory, altering the course of the Thirty Years' War and threatening to conquer Russia, before collapsing. Caught between the hostile powers of Prussia, Russia and Austria, Poland was stripped of its budding empire, robbed of its richest provinces and then, in 1795, divided and destroyed. It only regained independence in 1917, to lose it once more in September 1939. Hitler saw his war as a crusade against Bolshevism and the Slavs. The Russian response was to annihilate him. The post-war division of Germany was the Slavs' last attempt to break the old enemy's power.

I'd never been to East Germany. I'd been to East Berlin to visit Helena, but that's got nothing to do with the rest of the old DDR: the few parts of the city which haven't been yuppified beyond recognition are now hippy communes with all the vitality Christiania lacks. When I was growing up in the seventies and eighties all East Germans were steroid-swigging athletes who cheated at the Olympics (they must have cheated, they beat us), androgynous cyborgs with moustaches and no sense of humour. Their country was a wasteland of concrete and industrial slag, their roads potholed and chaotic and their cars, the legendary Trabants, powered by lawnmower engines. All scrupulously rational stuff drawn from the observations of those noted anthropologists, Le Carré, Ian Fleming and Biggles.

Then the wall came down. I remember sitting at home on New Year's Eve 1989, watching the choirs and orchestras of East and West Berlin combining to perform Beethoven's Ninth Symphony, the Ode to Joy. Even then I noticed that they'd changed the words. The invocation to 'Freude', Joy, was changed to 'Freiheit', Freedom.

So I was looking forward to Rostock. I wanted to see how the city looked after forty-five years of communist rule and a decade of capitalism. Seen from the water, it was hardly prepossessing. Rostock lies on the river Warnow (a Slavonic name, incidentally), a few miles from the coast. As is so often the case in Baltic rivers, the estuary is almost blocked by a long sandbank with a marshy lagoon behind it: great for shipyards, great for tourism, less good for building anything you want to remain standing. In communist times, the Rostock shipyards were the biggest facility on the Baltic coast, and the fishing village of Warnemünde with its long sandy beaches was the country's premier resort. As with the rest of the East German economic miracle – arguably even greater than the Western one, given the lack of US support and the hindrances of communism – business boomed. All along the river, from the towering sea wall to the *Speicher* warehouses in the old town, the banks were built up into concrete wharves. Cranes stand black against the grey winter sky, gas towers and fuel containers squat, warehouses and hangars and railway-tracks gleam brown-black in the drizzle. Once it must have been an imposing sight. Now most of the wharves are closed. The hangars stand empty and rusting, weeds crowding up to their walls and broken windows. Not far from the estuary a huge new crane marks a wharf revived with EU assistance. Apart from that, rust lies everywhere.

Then you reach the old town, and you might be on any waterfront in the western world. Nothing will ever make an old port a joy to behold: ports mean transport, and transport means roads and railways, and whatever narrow-gauge fanatics may say, neither create much of an ambience. The Rostock waterfront, a beautiful new yachting facility with security gates and hot showers, suffers rather from a large, hideous wine bar on the waterfront. (It also suffered, while I was there, from not having a winter harbourmaster: I spent a week climbing over security fences to get from boat to shore and back.) But behind the waterfront water-hole and the inevitable road, the town has been restored in a way which architects everywhere should be obliged to study; restored, be it noted, by the communists. I spent a happy afternoon chatting with a motherly lady in the town information centre, who, true to her task, informed me that Rostock's main street and harbour area had received prizes for the high standards of their restoration. Not only had the surviving *Speicher* – typical North German warehouses, red-brick, tall and narrow, with stepped gables and wooden cranes projecting from the gable-ends – been rebuilt using original materials and techniques, but some of the post-war era's more lamentable concrete errors of taste had been removed to create *Speicher* that hadn't been there in the first place. Later, walking through the town, I had to agree with her enthusiasm. The shops on the main parade were all major West German chains (Peek & Cloppenburg was a particular favourite of mine, simply for the name, though it was no match for Prang's Driving School, which I discovered later in Kappeln), and their ground floors were a mess of plate glass and platitudes, but the upper storeys were pure nineteenth-century decoration, coloured tiles, carved gables, and all. Once, just after 'the Change', a western architect had come to town with the intention of suggesting 'improvements' to the restorations. He hadn't been able to think of a single one.

One block away from the centre, though, the standards dipped sharply. From what I'd heard from (West) German friends on my travels I'd been half-expecting desolation, dirt and neo-Nazi graffiti. Desolation there was aplenty – splendid town-houses and even a brewery which in the West would long since have been converted into a theme pub, slumped behind rank nettles, their windows broken and ground floors filled with rubbish – and the streets were no cleaner than in any other city, but what surprised me was the graffiti. It was everywhere, and it was all anti-Nazi. In a quick half-hour swoop through the city I saw 'Nazis go home' (tricky, in Germany), 'Fuck the Nazis' (in English – the international language of obscenity), 'Nazis are killers' and, simply, 'Nazis out'. I didn't see one pro-Nazi item. That, in a town which has lost a fifth of its population in the last ten years to unemployment and urban drift, was impressive.

I liked Rostock. The people were friendly, even by Danish standards. Admittedly it helped that I speak the language, which hadn't been a major feature of my voyage so far, but I grew used to drifting through streets and into shops and striking up conversations with strangers. A little old woman pruning geraniums in her window-box one cold morning called out that I must be a gardener because I was wearing gardening gloves, and would I give her a hand?

'What, with my high-fashion, high-performance yachting gauntlets?'

'What?'

I gave her a hand.

One afternoon I climbed over the fence to get into town and discovered the centre full of policemen. It's a small centre, with the main square at one end and the University square at the other, green and pleasant and backed by a delightful corner of medieval wall which must be glorious in summer, and there was a policeman every two metres.

'What's going on?' I asked a leather-jacketed, flat-capped giant who was resting one hand negligently on his gun-butt. The uniform wasn't unusual. Every man in Rostock over the age of seventeen wears a leather jacket and flat cap.

'Some foreign president's coming.' He glanced at his watch. 'He'll be here in five minutes, then we'll be gone.'

'Who is it?' I asked curiously. Astonishingly, he bit his lip.

'Erm . . . I'm not allowed to say. In fact I shouldn't have told you that much.' He looked at me in consternation, and I realized he couldn't be more than twenty. Then he grinned. 'Don't tell anyone, or I'll have to shoot you.'

I grinned back. 'I take bribes.'

He laughed, and we stood in comfortable silence until the cavalcade went by. It was the Icelandic president, by a bizarre quirk of fate. I should have asked him if he'd heard any good sagas recently.

'That was boring, wasn't it?' said the giant.

'What were you expecting?'

His officer called him away before he could answer. He gave me a grin and trotted off to the police-wagon. I saw him in town quite often after that. Every time we saw each other we'd smile. If you ever go to Rostock, *don't tell him about this book*. He might shoot me.

After a week there I took the train down to Berlin to see Helena again. Why waste the opportunity? Besides, I love German trains. The second-class carriages are still divided into little five-seat compartments, three passengers ('Fahrgäste' is the German word, 'travelling guests', which gives you some idea of the service) facing two, with glass luggage racks above their heads, backed with mirrors, just in case your rucksack wants to admire its reflection. Now you might suppose that five Germans in a second-class compartment would travel in icy silence. I did. When we rolled out of Rostock – slightly late – I was alone with a little old bespectacled lady in her seventies surrounded by shopping baskets. She was reading, of all things, *Harry Potter and the Prisoner of Azkaban*, which had just come out in German. I sat admiring the cover art, which had carefully made Harry look German – spiky hair, narrow cheekbones, pointed chin, wire-rimmed octagonal specs – then settled back to enjoy the winter scenery of green pastures, low hedges and leafless trees. After a while my companion put down the book and looked at me cautiously.

'Does this train go to . . . ?' I've forgotten which station she asked.

'I'll check.' I picked up the 'today's journey' leaflet from the neighbouring seat; another German masterstroke, it tells you the train's name, why it's called that, where it's stopping, when it's due to get there and what connections you can make when you're there. They don't always live up to it – German trains do get delayed, on one occasion because I was kissing Helena goodbye and the guard decided to give us a couple of extra minutes – but it's a nice thought.

'Yes,' I said, and was just wondering how best to break the ice her question had cracked when she asked, 'Where are you going?'

'Berlin.'

'Ah, Berlin!' She smiled. 'I haven't been there for years. Everyone tells me it's changed so much, it must be wonderful to see now. Do you know it well?'

'Well, no, but I've been there a few times . . .'

And she started asking me about her capital city. I replied as well as I could – yes, there were lots of building works, yes, the Potsdammer Platz looked wonderful, yes, the East Berlin TV tower was still the finest landmark for miles – and in return, began to ask her about herself.

She'd always lived near Rostock. She grew up there during the war years, and remembered standing outside watching the flashes on the horizon as the RAF came calling. (Heinkel's main aircraft factory was outside Rostock.) She remembered when the border between East and West was established: there had been a country lane leading to the West which she'd always loved to cycle along, and suddenly, one day, it was barricaded. She kept on going there, but the road surface grew worse and worse and in the end she had to stop. 'What's the use of a road leading nowhere?' she asked me. 'I'd love to cycle out there now, they tell me it's been opened again after the Change' – they call it 'die Wende', the Turning Point – 'but I'm too old.' In that one sentence I felt all the sadness of the generations that had grown up behind walls.

'Do you think the Change was a good thing?' I'd always wanted to ask someone.

She beamed. 'Oh, yes! It's the best thing that ever happened.' She saw my surprise. 'Of course, we've been lucky, my husband and I. He retired just before the Change, and his pension is secure. It's been terrible in Rostock. Our eldest son left to go to Frankfurt, and our second is in Lübeck, doing something with computers. It's been awful for the young. No jobs, no prospects, no money . . . There are quarters of Rostock which are empty, the young go looking for jobs and the *really* old people go West to the retirement homes. It's better for the old, over there. I hope I never get like that,' said my septuagenarian. 'My sons look after me.'

'But it's a good thing?'

'Oh, yes! We're free now. You can't imagine what it was like, not being able to cycle down the lane I knew as a girl, not being able to go where we wanted. And then there was the atmosphere, you know? The State encouraged people to inform on each other. If a farmer kept a pig for himself and didn't declare it his neighbours could denounce him and get a reward, and he'd go to jail. For a pig! It was awful. You never knew who was working for the Stasi, the security police. Oh no. It's much better now.'

'But haven't there been lots of problems with neo-Nazis?'

'Not in Rostock,' she said firmly. 'We don't have anything like that here. People work. The EU has paid to rebuild the shipyards by the Warnow, and jobs are coming back. Billions, they've spent on it. But it's funny. It's such a success that the EU says it's going to fine the business because they made too many ships this year. They've got a quota, they're not allowed to go over it. The EU gives us money, then tries to ruin us. Does that make sense to you?'

She pierced me with a bespectacled glare, and I had to admit that it didn't.

We were talking travel when we pulled into the next station, and three more passengers climbed in. One was a woman of my age, in jeans and a heavy sweater; the others were a retired couple, the very image of rich refinement. They exuded the sort of affluent arrogance that kills conversation at fifty paces. My companion gave them a tolerant smile and carried on asking me about Provence.

Appearances can be deceptive. After three sentences I noticed that the plutocrats beside me were listening with close attention, exchanging smiles that spoke of old, shared memories. When I paused, the lady – their spokesperson, a woman whose husband was called 'Don't we, dear?' – leaned across and said, 'Excuse me, we couldn't help overhearing. Was that France you were describing?'

I toyed with the idea of saying that no, it was Provence, New Jersey, but decided against it.

'Ah, France!' Evidently it was the day for saying 'Ah, Placename!' 'You know, we always wanted to go there, but somehow, ever since the Change, we haven't managed it. Too busy ... What's it like there?'

Where do you start?

'Hot,' I said, looking out at the winter landscape, where patches of old, grainy snow lay in the cuttings. 'Hot and blue, with a brilliant sharp-edged light ... and full of tourists.'

They laughed, and their air of being armoured in inch-thick wads of D-Marks abruptly vanished. Within five minutes we were laughing and chatting as if we were family. Within twenty the Young Woman with Jumper had graduated from watching warily to listening eagerly to joining in tentatively to story-telling happily. When my pensioner got out we all kissed her goodbye and waved from the window. Passersby in the corridor looked on in shock; surely that's not German ... When we finally pulled into Berlin Spandau, the first of the Berlin stations, Jumper Woman stood up, collected her bag, looked down at us, said, 'This is too much fun! I'll get out at Ostbahnhof instead,' sat back down, and continued the conversation. We were all disappointed when we reached the end of the line.

The Rich Retirees had told me one anecdote I'll never forget. They'd taken their first holiday In the West soon after the Change. (It says something that they'd been able to afford it so quickly. I don't know what Don't-We-Dear's line of business was, but he must have been good at it. And no, it wasn't hers. She wasn't that kind of wife.) They'd flown to the Canaries; I forget which island. 'It was wonderful! So warm, so clean and so blue. We'd never had a holiday like that before, had we, dear? There was only one problem.'

'Really? What was that?'

'The German tourists. Do you know, they even collected stones off the beach to mark out their territory so nobody else would go there. Isn't that awful?'

After Rostock, I had to go to Lübeck. The two cities have had an almost identical history as leaders of the Hanseatic League, and an almost identical position at the head of a river some miles from the sea. The only difference between them is that Rostock lay to the east of the Iron Curtain. A visit to both cities now gives a chance to compare the effects of forty years of free-market capitalism with those of forty years of communist dictatorship. It's hard to tell who wins.

Lübeck lies on an island in the Trave river, its red-brick medieval heart connected to the outside world by a series of bridges. 'Medieval' is a loose term here. Between the ravages of RAF bombers and post-war architecture, Lübeck's heart is decidedly non-historic. Narrow streets of traditional *Speicher* break out in a sudden rash of squat concrete bunkers, like matter and anti-matter and just as bad for the watching eye. The medieval market square, a symphony of red- and black-glazed bricks around the Marienkirche, leads down to a series of plate-glass-and-pillars shopping arcades almost entirely indistinguishable from any others in the western world. At the river's mouth, the beach resort of Travemünde curves along the sandy bay, the exact equivalent of Rostock's Warnemünde. Neither has been spared the indignities of modern development, but where Warnemünde's pride and joy is a domed two-storey concrete café-cum-dancehall, which at least looks strikingly original and has the inspired name 'Die Teekanne', the teapot, Travemünde's landmark is a colossal tower-block. It's visible for miles, which is very nice for benighted mariners, but in terms of aesthetic appeal it lacks practically everything.

On the other hand, it's open. The Warnemünde Dome has been closed for the last two years because nobody can afford to maintain it. In this case, the East has the style, but the West has the money. Rostock's city centre has been beautifully restored, but in the rest of the town smartness and dereliction stand side by side. There simply isn't the money to restore everything. Lübeck has rich districts and poor districts, but there's never the impression that the money isn't there. It just doesn't get distributed very evenly. Which is what capitalism is all about.

I felt at home in Lübeck: bored. It's a western city like any other. There was nothing exciting about walking down the street picking out signs that things were different here, so I concentrated on monument-hopping. It was a wet, blustery winter's day, a fine day for being indoors. Fortunately, Lübeck has a wealth of medieval churches to visit, and they *have* been restored. They needed it. Lübeck was the first German city to feel the weight of Churchill's displeasure after Hitler unleashed his Blitzkrieg on Coventry: the RAF bombed the medieval centre to pieces. The most impressive war memorial stands under the belltower of the Marienkirche. It's the remains of the church's bells. On the night of the bombing, incendiaries smashed the nave, and the billowing heat from the flames set the bells ringing of their own accord. Then, inevitably, the supports gave way. Tons of metal crashed down onto the brick floor. When the rubble was shifted, workmen found their warped remains, bent and ripped like half-melted Easter eggs, and left them in place as a memorial. The bricks underneath them are shattered, pulverized. It takes no effort at all to imagine the impact that did it. Most war memorials remind you of what happened. This one shows you. It's hard to forget.

Lübeck is full of strange memorials. The one which affected me the most lies in a side chapel in the Jakobikirche, the church of the mariners' association. Just in front of the chapel is a model of a four-masted square-rigged grain ship, the *Pamir*, very like the *Viking* in Gothenburg. The real *Pamir* lies at the bottom of the Atlantic. Commissioned in 1911, she served as

211

a grain freighter on the Cape Horn run, then as a sail-training vessel. In September 1957, three days out of Buenos Aires on the way back to Hamburg, the ship ran into a hurricane. Nobody knows what happened. Of a crew of eighty – boys and young men from all over North Germany – seven survived, in a single lifeboat. All they knew was that, at the height of the storm, their ship began keeling over, gently at first, then ever more violently. Slowly the deck shifted from horizontal, to tilted, to crazed, to vertical. Fourteen-metre waves came smashing in on the deck, driven by a hundred-mile-an-hour wind. The ship went down in seconds.

One other lifeboat was picked up days later by a search vessel. Its side had been stove in, its rescue equipment ripped away, but, waterlogged and empty, it remained afloat. And *that* is the memorial in the Lübeck chapel. It lies tilted to one side, surrounded by tributes and wreaths for the crew who never came home, a fifteen-foot rowing boat with two-inch-thick sides. It's almost hidden, a little to one side of the main altar up a few brick steps, and it seems somehow lonely and uncared-for. The model gets more attention. But looking at it, and touching the splintered timbers which had felt the full shattering weight of a South Atlantic hurricane, was perhaps the most moving moment of the entire voyage. I'd had my own brush with ship-wreck. I'd got away with it. These German boys, ten years younger than I was, studying for a career in the merchant marine, had seen the sky blacken, seen the smoking footprint of the wind race towards them, felt the swells rise to immensity and thunder by in the insanity of a full hurricane, known that heart-stopping moment as their ship began to roll, tasted the worst fear in the world, and never come home to tell of it . . .

If you ever go to Lübeck, light a candle for them.

I'd left *Peregrino* in Travemünde. The harbour there runs along both sides of the river. Beyond it the water flares out into an immense lagoon studded with banks and reeds and a million water-fowl, and at that time of the year mine was the only boat in sight. Everybody else in the Baltic had been sensible. The wind was howling up from the southeast, a booming wall of air from the icy heart of the continent, and the pleasure-boaters had long since hung up their oilskins for the year. I found a prime berth just opposite the town's colossal multi-storey retirement home – which turned out to be scandalously noisy at nights, though whether the thudding music was the result of disco fever or deafness I'm not sure – and spent a couple of days looking at charts and planning my next move. Winter was upon me, and I wanted to stay in sheltered waters as far as I could.

I was flipping through my address-book in an idle moment when an entry caught my eye: a scrawl of faded ink on a rain-stained page, 'Flemming (Clervaux) – Flensburg, Germany'. I'd barely thought of him for a year and a half, but as I read those words my memory went back to a spring day at the beginning of my walk, and a monastery garden in Luxembourg where I'd met a Danish teacher and jazz fan and exchanged addresses. Flensburg? That wasn't far . . . I pulled out my Western Baltic chart. From Lübeck the coast runs due north to the island of Fehmarn, bends sharply west to the right-angle of Kiel, Germany's great naval base, and thence runs north again, forming the base of the Jutland peninsula. Three long fjords pierce the peninsula. The northernmost is the Flensburg Fjord, and forty miles in along the winding waterway is the town of Flensburg itself. Perfect! I thought. I even had Flemming's number. I phoned him at once, and as soon as he answered I could see him perfectly in my mind's eye, a middle-aged man with dark hair and an absurdly youthful face, chewing on a pipe.

'Do you need somewhere to sleep?' was his only question.

'I've got the boat,' I replied.

'See you soon!'

I hopped onto the jetty to go food-shopping. I'd grown addicted to German bread, moist, dark, flavoursome loaves made of a thousand different grains, the best in the world. As I hurried along the green-tinged planks, scaring the gulls and slipping on the carpet of guano (nobody bothered cleaning the jetty in winter), I tripped over an unexpected mooring line.

'Watch it!' shouted the Ancient Mariner angrily as his rowing boat rocked. He was well past retirement age, but still fit, a tall, powerful man in a leather jacket and Russian fur hat. A fishing-rod lay in the filthy bilge behind him.

'Sorry!' I called, and he grinned.

'Not a problem. You could make up for it by giving me a hand.'

I obliged, helping him lift his gear onto the jetty. He wouldn't let me give *him* a hand up. Age hath its pride ...

'Thanks,' he said. 'Is that your boat? She's nice.'

'She is,' I agreed. 'Cold, though.'

'I wouldn't live on board at this time of year. Fishing's bad enough.'

'Catch anything?'

'A few, but that's not the point. It's nice to get out for a bit. I live in there,' nodding at the retirement home behind me, 'but I need to get out somewhere. You can't imagine it, all these fat Westerners in their best clothes arguing about what's on TV ...'

I looked again. Leather jacket, Russian cap ... 'You'd be from the DDR, then?'

'Well done. Retired now, but I come from Rostock originally. I used to take people out for fishing trips in the summer. It was a good job.'

'Hard work?'

'Hard enough, but it got me out on the water. I liked that. I loved being out there at dawn, watching the sun come out of the waves, watching the lights fade, the waves change colour . . . I still do it sometimes. Don't go to sea, it's too dangerous with all these sport boats, and there's no fish left, but the lagoon behind us is wonderful in the mornings. Sometimes you get a mist over the water, and then the sun comes up and turns it to gold, and you see the shapes of other boats like black shadows, and everything's silent. Not even any sirens,' he added drily as a police car tore by on the far side of the river. 'Then the birds wake up and start flying, it looks like whole patches of the water take off all at once, and they fill the sky above you . . .' His eyes were far away. 'Yes, it's better than my last job.'

'What was that?' I asked.

He looked around carefully.

'Chief of Police in Rostock. I gave it up in the end. I couldn't stand all the informing. Don't tell anyone, will you?'

'Don't worry, I won't.' (I'll give you a hint: I did meet him, but not in Travemünde.)

He reached down into a bucket. 'Here. Have a fish. And remember, East Germans can be nice too.'

'I know that already.'

He smiled. 'Good. Have the fish anyway, they'll go mad if I take it inside. And safe journey.'

He shook my hand and strolled home.

13

SCHLESWIG

> 'As the German Emperor was leaving Denmark, Harald Bluetooth met him at Schleswig and gave battle. The Saxons gained the victory . . . Not long after, Harald himself was baptized together with his wife, Gunnhild, and his little son, whom our King raised up from the sacred font and named Svein Otto.'
>
> Adam of Bremen, *History of the Archbishops of Hamburg-Bremen*, record for AD 974

Three days later I reached Flensburg.

It had been a tough voyage. The southeasterlies which had been messing things up for the last month were still blowing strong, bringing great, grey, rolling seas up from Kaliningrad: it was a time of ice and battering waves. The clocks had changed to winter-time while I was in Denmark, and the cold and the dark and the solitude of the abandoned yachting harbours were depressing. The seas were almost empty. I saw two fishing boats just north of Lübeck and a navy frigate east of Kiel. That was all.

My first sight of Flensburg didn't help much. The firth itself is beautiful, a winding inlet sheltered by rolling green hills, but the approach to the city runs past a series of wharves and grain elevators with all the charm of a cigarette-butt. *Don't think I'll stay here long*, I thought with sovereign inaccuracy, staring across the water at a long row of plain-faced houses. Flensburg was the economic powerhouse of the region in the nineteenth century, flamboyant apex of a trading triangle which ran from the Baltic to the Slave Coast and thence to the sugar plantations of the Caribbean, but its prosperity died with the collapse of the slave trade, and since then its spirit seemed to have deserted it. It wasn't even that the waterfront was spectacularly dilapidated: it was simply boring, a mish-mash of old half-timbered *Speicher* and new brick structures with a main road running across one side and the railway line crossing the other. Of all the cities I'd seen on my travels, this was the least appealing. The only unusual feature was that the small, grimy harbour was full of yachts. I was the first time since leaving Oslo that I'd seen pleasure boats in bulk. When I asked why, I was told that the stream which decamped into the head of the fjord came straight from the nearby paper factory, creating a warm current which kept the harbour free of ice. *How delightful*, I thought, and wondered how long I'd bother staying.

My first encounter made things even worse. On the far side of the harbour was a long line of wooden sailing ships. On one of them, a man was swinging about the mast, doing some-thing with a coil of rope. It looked fun. I decided to go and watch. As I passed one of the narrow alleyways leading up from the quay, a large black dog emerged from the shadows, drooling in a friendly manner. I crouched down and started scratching his ears. Just beside me a ground-floor window opened and a young woman looked out.

'He often comes here,' she said cheerfully, smiling at me. 'I've no idea where he's from, but he's friendly.'

So was she, and I was delighted. My first local contact, and I'd only just arrived! It made up for everything. We chatted

217

for a couple of minutes about inconsequentials – the dog, which was making determined efforts to lick my glasses off, the weather, my journey – and I was just wondering if I should suggest adjourning somewhere for a drink when she smiled and added, 'Do you want to come in?'

Brilliant, I thought happily, *a cup of tea*, and was about to accept when she added, 'It costs a hundred Marks.'

My eyes, which had been preoccupied with the dog, began to register other significant details, like the red lamp over the window, the ultraviolet stripper-light below, the sheen of her Day-Glo underwear, and the tiny room behind her almost filled with a double bed. And nothing else.

'Oh,' I said.

She gave me a cool look. 'Now you get it, right?'

'Have a nice day,' I said weakly, and retreated to look at boats. How was I to know that I'd been hounded into the most notorious red-light street north of Hamburg?

Things picked up on the docks (much better than someone picking me up there). As I was admiring the wooden sailing-barge *The Two Sisters*, the skipper looked down from the mast-head and called a cheerful 'Moing moing!', which is how good Flensburgers say hello.

'Moing!' I replied, getting into the spirit of the thing. 'Nice boat!'

'Thanks! Want to come aboard?'

He slid down the mast, and soon we were sitting in his cabin, sipping tea with rum and swapping yarns. (Flensburg is famous for its rum as well as its Leasehold Ladies. It's very popular among seamen. I can't think why.) A cast-iron stove roared merrily, the kettle bubbled, and he sat back in his rocking chair, puffing on a carved pipe. He must have been in his late forties, and looked like every Viking should, with a thick blond beard and twinkling blue eyes hidden in a network of smile-wrinkles. The cabin smelt of wood and tar, varnish and pipe-smoke; pictures in brass frames screwed to the golden wooden walls showed photos and paintings and diagrams of ships. He'd built the boat himself ten years before from the blueprints of a 1794 vintage sailing freighter, retiring from a full-time career as a street musician. Now he divided his time between boat, music and his wife and teenage daughters: most of his income went on mobile phone bills. And strangely enough, with so little in common, we got on like a house on fire: I was delighted when he invited me to drop in later that week. As I staggered back along the jetty, I decided I was going to like Flensburg.

It was a short walk from the harbour to Duborg, the Danish school where Flemming taught English. Everything in Flensburg is a short walk from the harbour: the town follows the hillsides on either side of the fjord, so it's steep, narrow and long. To get to Duborg from the quay you walk up the red-light street – where the houses have carved gables and decorated upper storeys, though remarkably few of the visitors look at them – turn right along the main street, and then drag yourself up a flight of about a million stairs to the school's red-brick turret. The view back over the town and along the fjord is beautiful in summer, or so they tell me. I wouldn't know. It was chucking it down by the time I got there, and I could hardly see out of my specs.

I was nervous when I entered the school. I wasn't sure if Flemming had told anyone else I was coming, and I hate walking in on groups of complete strangers. Naturally, it was break time, so the corridors were full of curious teenagers, all staring at me. A helpful janitor directed me to the staffroom. As I dithered outside the door, a short, bright-eyed lady came up to me.

'Are you Flemming's friend?' I sagged in relief.

'Yes.'

'Wonderful! He said he'd be a little bit late, there's something he needs to finish off. I'm teaching an English class next lesson, would you like to help me?'

I'd barely agreed when a tall, lean, amused-looking teacher limped over. 'Are you doing anything in lesson seven?' he asked.

'I'm sure I could be.'

By the time Flemming arrived five minutes later, I was booked for the rest of the day.

Flensburg is Germany's northernmost city. It wasn't always that way. Until the middle of the nineteenth century it was one of Denmark's southernmost cities. Then it was German. Then Danish. Then German again. Now it's German, but with a strong Danish flavour. Like the local bacon. And just as nice.

It started, like so much else, with Harald Bluetooth. During his father's reign, the southern Danish border was a hazy concept. The towns and villages of North and South Schleswig – roughly the area from Esbjerg to Kiel – were fiercely independent, loyal only to their local magnates. Chief among the towns was Hedeby, at the head of the Schlei fjord south of Flensburg, the richest trading settlement in the Baltic: ships coming from the east would unload their wares there and send them on overland rather than risking the passage round Jutland. South of Schleswig lay the county of Holstein, nominally a part of the German empire. West of Hedeby, the *Dannevirke*, a defensive dyke, marked the notional end of Danish territory, but throughout the area the Danish and German populations mingled. So Harald decided to conquer Schleswig.

The German Emperor, Otto II, was not amused. (It's a German imperial thing.) He attacked Schleswig in 974, but failed to gain a decisive victory against the coalition of Harald Bluetooth, Mieszko of Poland (Bolesław's predecessor), and Jarl Hákon of Norway. So to pacify the Emperor, Harald accepted Christianity and began converting his people. Schleswig remained Danish, Holstein remained German, and the population kept on mixing.

The problems really started in the early twelfth century, in the reign of Svein's great-grandson Niels. To strengthen his grasp on the southern border, Niels made his nephew Duke of Schleswig. The Duke promptly declared his independence, invaded Holstein, and was ultimately confirmed Count of Holstein by the German Emperor. His son Valdemar the Great kept both titles and fought his way to the throne of Denmark, and for the next eight hundred years Schleswig and Holstein formed a semi-independent annex to the Danish kingdom. (Holstein remained officially German, but with the King of Denmark as its Count.) In 1460 the Danish king tried to strengthen his claim by declaring that Holstein and Schleswig should be for ever united, 'up ewig ungedeelt'. This worked for almost four hundred years. The king failed to foresee Bismarck, but you can hardly blame him. Nobody in the whole of Europe could have foreseen Bismarck.

Then came the Napoleonic wars. Denmark was on the losing side, and bankrupt. At the same time, Germany, on the winning side, flourished, and began to call for national unification. Holstein – still technically a part of Germany – decided that it wanted to play too. And, since Schleswig and Holstein were permanently united, the Holsteiners decided to take Schleswig with them. In 1848 a rebellion started in Holstein and spread right across South Schleswig, which by then had a German majority. Denmark declared war on the rebels. The Danes won, but German popular opinion ran high. And in 1863 Prussia and Austria invaded Schleswig and conquered the lot. North Schleswig, never hugely pro-German, now became vigorously anti. After the First World War the League of Nations put the whole question of nationality to the vote. North Schleswig opted to return to Denmark. South Schleswig remained German.

Happy so far?

Hitler, of course, Messerschmitted everything up. His occupation of North Schleswig caused all the civil strife you might expect. At the war's end, Germany's ruin made the people of South Schleswig think hard about their allegiance to the Fatherland. Up went the cry, 'We want to be Danes again!' To which Denmark replied, 'Well you can't.' The Danish and German governments signed a treaty fixing the border along the 1920 lines, and in order to avoid future civil war, they agreed a far-reaching package of minority protection measures. Danish schools were established in Germany, German schools in Denmark. Both speech communities were guaranteed full legal, political and cultural freedom. Of course, by then the populations had been mingling for so long that there was no way of telling who was 'really' German and who was Danish, so the only way of finding out who was on which side was to ask people, 'Which side do you *feel* you're on?' Which meant that geographical or linguistic considerations had nothing to do with it. You're from Bavaria and you feel Danish? Right you are. Welcome in.

Ethnic affiliation in South Schleswig is a question of pragmatism. Just after the war, the province was crammed with German refugees. It caused severe shortages, so the Danes north of the border started sending food packages to the

Danish community in the south. Guess what? The number of officially registered Danes trebled practically overnight. (They're still referred to as *Speckdänen*, 'bacon Danes'.) Nowadays Duborg is generally reckoned to be one of the better schools in the province, and parents who want their children to receive both a superior education and an in-depth knowledge of another language and culture seldom hesitate to declare their Danish affiliations. Chatting with an official in the Danish Bureau in Flensburg, I learnt that fewer than ten per cent of the 'Danes' in Flensburg actually speak Danish at home. At Duborg itself, the language they use in the classrooms and staffroom is Danish, but the kids speak German in the corridors. The official – who, with true Danish hospitality, offered me coffee, biscuits and a cigar, told me to drop in whenever I felt like it, and was wounded that I waited three days before doing so – admitted that, by any measure of language or parentage, the Danish minority is extinct. Ethnicity in Schleswig isn't a matter of birth, it's a club.

One minor side-effect of all this cultural mingling is that Flensburg is the friendliest city in Germany. Germans aren't exactly unwelcoming anyway, but Flensburg has raised hospitality to an art form. It must be the Danish influence. Flensburg is as friendly as Copenhagen, *but in a language I understand*.

It started with Üze, the smiling Viking from the harbour. He spends a lot of time on his boat – a wife and two teenage daughters can have this effect on a man – and I got used to seeing him clambering around the rigging, fixing ropes and incomprehensible wooden things, pipe clamped firmly between his teeth. Whenever he saw me he'd invite me on board for *Tee mit Rhum*. I must have spent hours in that golden cabin watching the patterns of water reflected across the ceiling through the stern windows and swapping stories of street music. After a few days he invited me up to his house. There he introduced me to his wife and daughters, and the daughters introduced me to a couple of their school friends, who promptly took me under their collective wing and decided that I needed showing a good time. Being teenagers, that involved talking about going out to get hideously drunk, deciding that we couldn't really be bothered, and sitting around in somebody's bedroom with the lights off and the lava-lamps glowing, listening to weird music, drinking peculiar mixtures that no sane adult would ever contemplate, and talking about life, love, travel and parents. It was like being a teenager again. I loved it.

Üze, meanwhile, introduced me to his favourite bar, Columbus. It lies just behind the harbour, a wood-panelled, half-timbered barn of a hostelry, all German beers and Spanish olives. The manager, Albert, was a raving eccentric in an open-necked shirt and silk cravat, whose hairstyle was never the same two days running. He was a people-watcher and an armchair philosopher, so we got on fine. He'd attracted a whole network of like-minded individuals who propped up the bar and over the next few days I met practically all of them.

It started on my first evening there. Üze had gone home, and I was sitting with Albert discussing – if I remember correctly – the art of customer relations as applied to petrol-pump attendance. Abruptly he stood up and waved to a jovial middle-aged man whose balding dome gleamed with sweat, and a soulful-looking woman in a black great coat. Introductions were swiftly made and beers ordered, and then the conversation turned weird.

The man, Rüdi, started it. 'Ah, you're English! God shave the Queen,' he exclaimed. 'She needs it. We hate her here, I'm a Nazi myself.'

I looked at the glass in my hand. Had I really heard that?

'Shush, Rüdi,' Maren reproved him. Then she turned to me, and I saw that she was holding a pen and a post-it note. 'He's only joking. What did you say your name was?'

'Er . . . Ben . . .'

She looked at me with long-suffering patience. 'And the surname?'

'Nimmo . . .'

'Spell it.'

Rüdi sat back, watching with a smile, as I wrote my name down. As soon as I'd done it she wrote a single-digit number under each letter, added the digits, wrote the totals under the original numbers, added the totals, wrote the new results underneath them, and carried on until she had a little pyramid of numbers under my name.

She gave me a piercing glance. 'I knew it! You're a seven!'

'I am?'

'That means you're adventurous.'

'It does?'

'Of course! And . . . let's see . . .'

'Hang on,' I said, getting my wits back with an effort. 'Do you have to use my real name or the name I use?'

She gave me a withering look. 'Your real name, of course! This is a precise science! Shut up, Rüdi.'

'Ah.' So I told her my full name. Another pyramid of numbers formed.

'Aha! You're a three! That means you're kind to people.'

'Well . . .' Modesty forbade.

'And you're going to be famous. But . . .' Her face fell, and then she looked up and stared straight into my eyes. 'I want you to be very careful from the ages of thirty-five to fifty-six. There'll be a lot of danger in your life,' she said insistently. Her eyes were hypnotic. I swear my mouth went dry. 'Promise me you'll be careful.'

225

She looked down before I could. 'But you'll have someone looking after you after that. All the time. Someone who cares about you. You'll meet her when you're . . . fifty-six. Look out for her.'

Rüdi burst out laughing. Maren kicked him. Albert poured beer on the troubled waters. We moved swiftly onwards to a less fraught subject, and peace descended.

Temporarily.

Somehow we ended up talking about the British national psyche. Rüdi, who was far more perceptive than his good-humour-beer-and-sausages demeanour indicated, asked why it was that Britain has such a massive inferiority complex.

I thought hard. 'Perhaps because the only things we've won in the last fifty years have been the Falklands War and the 1966 World Cup.'

And my genial friend froze, turned scarlet, leaned across the table, and levelled a furious finger at me, grinding out, 'That ****ing ball never ****ing crossed the ****ing line, all right?'

Ladies and gentlemen, it *still* hurts.

I spent a lot of evenings in Columbus. It was warm and friendly, the staff soon got to know me, and anything was better than sitting on *Peregrino*. No matter how good the heating, a steel-and-glass boat is never going to be luxurious in sub-zero temperatures. One by one I met most of Albert's crew: Fiede, a small, dapper journalist who interviewed me for the local paper; Rasta-Arne, who was restoring the sailing freighter in the berth next to Üze's; Matthias, a management consultant from Hamburg who managed to find an excuse to come and drink in Flensburg at least twice a week; Lothar, a friend of his who specialized in turbo-charging second-hand cars. We'd sit in the candle-lit darkness sharing wine and olives, looking out over the cold harbour and putting the world to rights.

In the daytime, I went back to school.

I hadn't seen much of Flemming. Just after I arrived he fell ill, although I don't think there was a connection: he left me in the capable hands of the rest of the staffroom. They decided that a native English speaker with a story to tell was a godsend, and turned over their classes to me. One, who shall remain nameless, even left the class to me entirely 'so they wouldn't feel intimidated about talking English' and bunked off for a coffee. Evidently Danish casualness was well-established there. I wondered what the parents who'd sent their little darlings to the school for its educational superiority would think.

The didactic aim was to get the kids talking English. It wasn't easy. Being a teenager is all about being terrified of embarrassing yourself in front of your peers, and to start with the only way of getting a word out of them was torture. We finally hit on an arrangement whereby I'd ask them a question, and then they'd ask me one, which at least got them talking.

'So,' I began, 'are you Danish or German?'

There was an awkward pause; then someone muttered, 'I'm from South Schleswig.'

'Explain,' I said, which was rank cheating, but I was intrigued. The class ignited.

'The Danes up there all think we've got funny accents! They don't think we're proper Danes at all.'

'And the people down south think we're odd for going to school in Danish.'

'Nobody else knows what it's like!'

'This is the only place we feel at home.'

'And what about our question?' asked a bright-eyed girl pointedly. The class laughed and the ice was broken.

'Go ahead.'

'How old are you?' she asked.

'Twenty-eight,' and there was a ripple of surprise.

'Cool!' she exclaimed. I was flattered. I hadn't realized it was cool to be twenty-eight. It was only months later, on another visit to Flensburg, that I learned that the teacher had introduced me with, 'This is Ben, he looks fifty, try and find out how old he is.' I'll get him for it one day.

'What's your favourite sport?' asked a bulky lad in the back row.

'Rugby.'

'That's the one with horses, isn't it?' asked the bright-eyed girl.

Before I could reply, her neighbour snorted, 'Rubbish! That's cricket!'

Who says culture's globalized?

In time, we got on well. About a quarter of the Sixth Form pupils came from 'Danish' families in the Schleswig hinterland, too far to commute daily: during the week they boarded in a breeze-block bunker at the top of the hill. After a few days they decided that I was a human being rather than a teacher, and invited me to visit. There they whiled away the winter evenings playing pool, sending each other text messages and smoking far too much. I upheld the pride of Britain by being soundly thrashed at pool. Being nice kids they gave me the chance to redeem myself by showing how good I was at the games on my mobile phone. It might even have worked if I hadn't answered, 'Have I got games on it, then?' As they looked at me pityingly I could see the word 'Dinosaur' forming in their eyes. Twenty-eight will never seem cool again.

At the end of my first week in Flensburg the weather turned really foul, with long trails of sleet lashing down from a black sky; the final proof that I'd missed any chance of getting home before the winter. It was just the excuse I needed to hang around the town. I'd belatedly discovered the joys of Flensburg's urban architecture, and pottering around an endless succession of covered passageways warmed by efficient German gas heaters seemed just the way to pass a few happy days. Üze's daughters decided that I was the ideal companion for town, being old enough to be trusted by their parents without being parental enough to stop them eating pancakes. They led me through an endless succession of fashion boutiques, CD stores and computer-game arcades, chattering inanely all the while. Evelyne, my bright-eyed interrogatrice, decided that I needed a social life, since I was so pitiably far from home, and organized trips to the cinema to see *Gladiator* (much more grimly realistic in German), to the skating rink, and to the pedestrian street where the Christmas market was in full swing, a mile of mulled wine and pancake stalls. If anyone from Flensburg reading this saw a loud group of teenagers and a regressed Brit oscillating along the street arm in arm doing the Monkees' walk – sorry.

During school hours, I explored the town alone. Flensburg might not look like much from the harbour, but once you're in the *Speicher* district it's a treasure trove of hidden courtyards, narrow alleys, covered boutiques and unexpected short-cuts. I spent one morning poking around a record shop specializing exclusively in pre-1980s LPs, another admiring the displays in a decorative glazier's studio – he might not have been a genius, but he certainly had an infinite capacity for making panes. There were second-hand bookshops and alternative clothing stores, waffle shops and sports boutiques, a mobile phone store with queues a mile long and one harried assistant (it's universal), tattoo studios, ethnic craft stalls, everything's-a-Mark shops, and restaurants, restaurants, restaurants, all hung with evergreen branches and vines of Christmas lights. The whole town smelt faintly but agreeably of mulled wine. The only disappointment was the pancake stalls. I went to every one in town, but could I find a pancake with lemon and sugar? They offered cinnamon, chocolate, jam, liqueur, even Nutella and After Eight pancakes, but sugar and lemon were not to be found. In the end I bought a lemon in a supermarket and did my own. The stall-holder looked at me as if I were mad. I'll be going back there next winter to see if it's caught on.

One day Evelyne came down to visit me. I'd told all my friends that they were welcome to drop in, never expecting that any of the teenagers would actually take me up on the offer. I was therefore delighted but shocked when she scrambled aboard one day with boyfriend in tow and found me eating peanuts in the cabin with my feet propped on the steering wheel, listening to music. It was rather embarrassing, there were holes in my socks. However, despite my sartorial shortcomings, she got into the habit of strolling down after school to make sure that I wasn't getting bored, and I got into the habit of making sure that the kettle was on when she got there. Normally we'd have a cup of tea and then go on into town to meet the rest of the mob, but on one occasion she lingered. There was something on her mind.

'Er . . . can I invite my parents here this weekend?' she asked suddenly. 'They really like boats, and I think you'd like them.'

'Sure,' I replied. 'Will they want to go for a cruise?'

'Oh, can we?'

'It'll do the boat good. Keep the engines warm.'

She pulled out her mobile phone, and the date was made.

Sunday dawned bright and cold. Her parents and sister came up laden with presents for the lonely foreigner: lots of chocolate, a huge tub of meatballs, and even a blue plastic rose. I'd been shopping to provide a proper lunch, so the table was piled high, and by the time we trundled out of the harbour

our stomachs were exceedingly full. Of course, as soon as we were well into the fjord, the weather turned cold and miserable, sleet-squalls following one another down the water. We didn't stay out for long. Soon we were back in harbour tucking into more meatballs. They were delicious.

'I'm glad you like them,' said Evelyne's mother, watching me tuck into my third plateful. 'I made them myself.'

I made enthusiastic noises and waved my fork up and down to indicate an even greater degree of approval.

'It's good meat, too,' added her father. 'A friend of ours runs the farm. It's not far from here.' And then, just as I swallowed, 'I hope he survives. They found mad cow disease at his slaughterhouse the other day.'

After two weeks in Flensburg, the weather changed. The southeasterly gales died away and were replaced by a windless, glittering calm. It was my hint to leave. More than once in the preceding fortnight I'd wondered about staying there for the winter. Flensburg felt so much like home . . . Only the suspicion that I'd never leave at all if I didn't leave now stopped me. I spent a day saying goodbye to my friends, and then, before dawn, set off northwards down the fjord.

It took me ten hours to get to England. I know, I didn't believe it either, but what is England? The Union Jack. The English language. Fish and chips. Cheery back-chat and beery faces. I found it all in Kiel.

What Hedeby was to the medieval Baltic, Kiel is to the modern sea: the crossroads of the sea lanes. Until the mid-nineteenth century it was literally a backwater, endowed with a splendid natural harbour so far from the main trade routes that few ships bothered to stop there. Then Bismarck backed a plan to dig a canal right through the base of Jutland to the river Elbe, and Kiel's fortune was made. In calm weather half the shipping in the Baltic heads for the Holtenau locks and the straight run through to the North Sea; in foul weather practically all of it. Not far from the locks lies one of the German navy's largest bases, and all along the Kiel fjord are warehouses, hangars, wharves and drydocks. Taking a small, slow yacht into the Kiel harbour area is like trying to cross the M6 on a pogo-stick. 'Heavy traffic' takes on a whole new meaning when the smallest vessels are five thousand tonners. Still, there's still courtesy at sea. As I was pulling into the main shipping lane a German frigate went roaring past me, ensign flying. Remembering a half-obsolete piece of naval etiquette, I lowered my flag in greeting. Twenty seconds later a sailor sprinted out of the bridge, scrambled up a ladder and flung himself at the flagstaff. Ten seconds after that the immense black, red and gold banner of Germany dipped in answer.

And then there's the yacht harbour: the Royal British Yacht Club, Kiel, inside a huge concrete basin just seawards of the locks. At the end of the basin a tall clubhouse flies the Union Jack, and a treble pontoon in front of it looks out over countless moorings. It must be madness in summer. When I got there at the end of December, it was almost empty. Two powerboats and a small racing dinghy sat looking lonely. I wish I knew how the British got their club there, having spent the whole war bombing the place. I asked, but the personnel told me they'd have to shoot me if they told me.

This is because it's an army base. I worked that out as soon as I walked into the harbourmaster's office and saw a small, wiry, short-haired man in an army sweater chatting with two well-groomed young ladies in regulation blue. A Royal Yachting Association calendar hung on one wall, and below it stood the first proper kettle I'd seen in months. And Tetley tea-bags. Only those who've lived overseas can appreciate the magic of those four syllables. *Tetley tea-bags!* Music to my ears.

'*Kann ich Ihnen helfen?*' asked the officer in remarkably German German. Justifiably. It can't be often that visitors walk into army offices and stand staring at the tea urn.

'Well, that's my boat over there . . .' I pointed out of the window. He looked across and thawed instantly.

'Aha, you're the chap! What are you doing here at this time of year?'

'Trying to get home.'

'Cup of tea?' The warcry of the British abroad.

'Love one.' The countersign.

'Milk and sugar?' One secretary was already on the case.

'Black, no sugar, thanks. I'm a poor mariner.'

I followed him into his office.

'So what have you been up to?' he asked, and I told him. He nodded abruptly from time to time and fired knowledgeable questions, but I had the definite feeling that his time was limited and I was in the way. I found out, for my part, that this was a British Army adventure training facility, that they'd been clearing away for the winter, and that there was a skeleton staff still on site. Then he dismissed me, courteously, but firmly.

So I went to chat to Linda the secretary instead.

Then with an engineer, two communications specialists, and finally a 'general technician' who ran everything from the air-compressors through to the skipper's cafetière. I asked if there were any way I could get my diving tanks filled; he grinned and said, 'Well, not officially, so leave it on deck and I'll sort it out.' It was the kind of morning that would increase anyone's patriotism.

That afternoon I biked along the back lanes to the Holtenau locks and went to chat with the lock-keepers. Compared with

Kiel, the Trollhättan locks are a drainage ditch. The Kiel Canal is built to take all but the biggest North Sea tankers, and it sees the passage of hundreds of vessels a day. There are three pairs of locks there: two narrow basins for sport boats, four vast excavations for the real men's ships. You probably couldn't get an aircraft carrier through there, but my kayak would have looked like a peanut in a squash court.

The lock-keepers, on the other hand, would fit in at Trollhättan easily. When I climbed the control-tower stairs I wasn't quite sure what to expect: after all, this was the living manifestation of German bureaucracy, that terrifying squareheaded beast. When I knocked, someone answered with a cheerful 'Moing!', and when I explained that I was a powerboat owner come to ask about their locking procedure, they were incredibly friendly. The only hard part was interrupting the flow of 'stupid skipper' anecdotes for long enough to get the information I actually wanted: radio frequency, light signals and lock etiquette. When, the following day, I glided into the lock and tied up to a slippery pontoon, both men rapped on the control-tower windows and waved down at me eagerly. Edging forwards into the canal not long afterwards, my radio crackled.

'*Peregrino*, this is Holtenau. Safe journey and come back soon.'

So I promptly went and almost sank myself.

14

SAXON SHORES

'He remembered his home though he could not drive
his curving prow on the sea (the stormy ocean surged,
battled the wind; winter fettered the waves in icy
chains) ... as men still do, endlessly awaiting their
chance, the bright clear weather.'

Beowulf, lines 1129–36

'And in the days of Martianus and Valentinus, Vortigern invited the English hither ... Those men came
from three German tribes: the Old Saxons, the Angles,
and the Jutes. From the Jutes came the people of Kent
and the Isle of Wight ... From the Old Saxons came
the East Saxons, the South Saxons and the West Saxons.
From Angeln came the East Angles, the Middle Angles,
the Mercians and all the Northumbrians. Their leaders
were two brothers, Hengest and Horsa ...'

Anglo-Saxon Chronicle, AD 449

I always used to wonder what it would be like to see a *real*
hurricane at sea. I've now decided that, really, I'd rather not.

After a slow and boring passage through the Kiel Canal,
which does rather lack the rugged glamour of, say, the Norwegian fjords, I reached the locks at Brunsbüttel, passed

through onto the broad and shining waters of the Elbe, and ran down to the port of Cuxhaven at the river's mouth.

Cuxhaven is the closest thing you'll find to a motorway service station on the water. The Elbe is one of Europe's great waterways, but just outside its estuary lie the nastiest sandbanks in the whole North Sea. Half the rivers of North Germany dump their silt into the Elbe, and the Elbe dumps the lot off Cuxhaven. West of the Elbe, the rest of the continent's waterways do the same: the Jade, the Weser, the Ems, the Ijssel, the Rhine. The European coast from the root of Jutland to the Hook of Holland is a mariner's nightmare, where sandbanks and mudflats drift and shift with every storm, and tide and wind and shallows create an ever-changing seascape that not even locals can navigate with confidence. Cruising there is a challenging business – you can't go out if the tide's too low, you can't go if the wind is strong onshore, you really, *really* can't go if tide and wind are cutting across one another. Cuxhaven is one of a select band of ports whose main function is to give yachtsmen somewhere to sit and be bored while they wait for the weather to get it right.

I got to Cuxhaven.

The weather was awful, a southwesterly gale laden with sleet. The rising tide was undercutting the waves and creating bursting havoc in the estuary.

The specialized yacht harbour with its guaranteed tideproof floating pontoons was closed for the winter, so I tied up to the quay in the non-specialized, non-tideproof fishing harbour, hurrying out on deck every hour to shorten my mooring ropes as the three-metre tide lifted me up the slick and slimy wall. The Baltic doesn't have tides, so it was a novelty. Then the novelty wore off.

There are two ways of surviving as a winter mariner. Either you develop a boredom threshold higher than your own mast-head, or you get extremely good at calculating risks. Sailors lacking both qualities tend not to survive very long. The ones who can't stand the boredom give up and take up something less weather-dependent. The ones who can't judge risks sink.

After twenty-four hours in Cuxhaven, my patience was exhausted. There may be a more grimly depressing place to sit out a winter storm, but I never want to see it. I checked the weather forecast three times that day, and each time it got worse. A whole series of hurricane-strength depressions was tracking eastwards across the Atlantic, and the wind for the next three days was expected to oscillate between force eight (gale) and force ten (storm). In those conditions, not even the big freighters would risk the Elbe estuary and its ship-eating sandbanks. Wherever else I might be heading, it wasn't going to be seawards. Just after dawn I scrambled ashore and went to stand on the sea wall, looking out across the water. The sky was the greyish black of filed iron, a flying tapestry of gun-metal clouds, and beneath it the river was flood brown, mud brown, and pitted with purple troughs. The gale came shouting up from the southwest, behind me; a handful of gulls were beating into it, veering and dipping as they fought to hold their station. Southeast along the river, the waves were stitched with crazy ripples where the wind rushed off the fields. It thrummed in struts and cables, slapped a flag-halyard against its mast. I could feel it yanking at my hat, buffeting my shoulders – I leant back into it, trying to imagine what it would be like on the water. *Wind alone doesn't kill powerboats*, I reminded myself, *it's only waves which do that*. I looked down at the waves. They didn't look impossible.

I went back to *Peregrino*, checked my charts. Upriver from Cuxhaven the wide channel leads southeastwards to the elbow of the Elbe, then turns northeast for the twelve-mile run to Brunsbüttel. There it curves slowly to the right, eastwards and then southeast, growing narrower all the time, and so weaves its way up the fifty-six-mile passage to Hamburg between banks no more than half a mile apart. With a southwesterly wind, that meant that only the stretch of river from the Elbow to Brunsbüttel would be vulnerable to the build-up of wind-driven waves. For the rest, the wind would be blowing straight off the banks, loud but impotent. *So what if it's a gale?* I thought. *It can't sink me.*

Things started well. I left the harbour with the wind behind me and turned right into the shipping lane. With Cuxhaven as a bail-out port in case of trouble and a second option upriver at Brunsbüttel, I was feeling confident. Outside the harbour wall the water was almost flat, darkened and frowning under the weight of the hurrying air. As I came out of the shelter of the towering docks the wind snapped and boomed in my quarterdeck canopy, heeling the boat over, but it was nothing that I hadn't seen before. *Is this all?* I thought. *It's not so bad.*

Then I reached the Elbow.

The change was terrifying. Nothing could have prepared me for it. The wave-crests were flying northeast, high and steep and violent, and their purple-shadowed troughs were so sheer they might have been cut by machines. The channel marker buoys were lying over almost horizontally, yanking at their cables as if desperate to escape. The second I nosed into that tumultuous water I knew I was in trouble. *Peregrino* leapt like a stung horse. Instantly I knew that I should have run for Cuxhaven, but it was already too late. Turning round in that barrage of waves would have been suicide. Nor was Brunsbüt-tel an option. If I made for safety there I'd have to wait on the river for the lock gates to open, sitting exposed at the wrong end of a twelve-mile wind tunnel in the full lunacy of the gale-force breakers. There was no choice. I'd have to ride the storm and the raging waves, trust to my reflexes and my boat's stability, hope that I could make it round the Brunsbüttel corner and on to Hamburg . . . I was alone on the water in the middle of a strengthening gale, and there was no safe port to run to. The crew of the *Pamir* must have known that feeling.

I drove. *Peregrino* surfed. I wrestled with the kicking steering-wheel as the waves rushed up under my stern and heaved me back and forth, slipping and sliding from crest to trough. Racing drivers on Grand Prix circuits struggle like that: hands and eyes fighting for control while their body jolts around the cockpit. All it would take was one wave to slew me round, and the next would roll me over and bury my engine-room vents in the water, and when your engine compartment floods you don't roll back up again . . . It took an hour to claw my way up to Brunsbüttel, and my only memories are of the ache in my wrists from clutching the wheel, the tension in my legs as I swayed from side to side, the frantic tattoo of metal on metal when the cockpit canopy ripped along the line of its eyelets and beat its end to pieces on the superstructure, and the drum-tight thrumming of the wind.

Then came the turn, a wide arc of water with the white horses sweeping across it in gleaming squadrons. On the far bank, half a mile away, the face of the Brunsbüttel locks was a grey cliff curtained in a bursting barrage of foam. Nobody would be coming in or out today. I headed towards it for a moment, steeling myself, then snatched one hand from the wheel, shoved the throttles forwards, grabbed the wheel again and swung it to starboard as the engines bellowed. Spray from my own wake rattled on my back then, as *Peregrino* heaved around, the wind scoured along my cheek, ripping my hood off. It boomed and tugged wildly, flailing at my left ear, but there was no time to deal with it. The boat heeled over and as the deck slipped under me I thought that I'd lost control; then it catapulted back the other way, and then, at last, ahead of me I saw smoother water. One more wave hurtled by, its crest lost in whipping spray, and I was past the worst. Ahead, great freighters sat snugly at anchor, wavelets breaking against their bows. To either side the low grey banks stretched away into haze, unbroken by hedge or tree, as if shaved bare by the gale. The breakers fanned out, shrinking, fleeing. Suddenly there was time to pull my hood up, tie down the thrumming canopy, and fasten a fender that had broken loose and gone careering round the deck.

Done it, I thought in relief; and then, with a touch of pride, *I judged that right after all*.

And then the wind got worse.

For half an hour it stayed at the pitch it had been; half an hour as I pushed upriver, and the banks grew higher and nearer, and the first trees appeared. The waves were no more than a nuisance, lifting me sideways as I steered, breaking against the hull and sending up a driven mist that clouded my glasses and chilled my reddened hands. Once a deep-laden freighter grumbled past me, ploughing its way through the swell, and the gunshot impact as it crossed the waves sent up clouds of spray that spread and drifted downwind from its bows as if in slow motion. The sky had lightened to burnished pewter, the dull water began to gleam, and the growing light brought out unexpected swathes of colour on the leaden banks. I was looking to windward, when suddenly the horizon vanished.

The clouds were black and trailed a grey mist of rain and sleet that swallowed up the landscape. One moment I was admiring a skeletal wood of winter trees, the next it was blotted out. The squall moved with appalling speed. I could see it racing down the sloping banks towards me. A hundred metres ahead of it the water darkened in racing semicircular ripples – the footprint of the wind. They fled across the water towards me. I braced myself. They were still fifty metres away when the gust hit.

Peregrino slewed sideways. The cockpit awning bulged inwards as if punched by a giant fist, shook, ripped clear from its remaining eyelets and went billowing across the waves, rolling and tumbling, then crumpled like a shot bird. The boat simply lay over, water creaming along the side. I'd barely begun to turn upwind when the sleet came. The Elbe disappeared. Chunks of ice like bullets stung my cheek, broke in a midge-cloud over the deck, whipped up the river in flying clouds, a thick haze between air and water. Only the wavecrests were visible above the ruin, heaving and smoking like dunes in a sandstorm *This is it*, I thought, *I'm going over!* as *Peregrino* rolled. It was all happening too fast. I was still clipped onto the quarterdeck for safety: the speed and the noise and the violence of the attack had left me numb. If we'd rolled then I would have gone down with the ship. But, miraculously, the roll stopped. *Peregrino* lay heeled over at an angle I'd never dreamt of before, let alone seen, but the engines rumbled and the screws bit and the sharp bow ploughed steadily on upstream. We were so far over that my shoulder scraped the superstructure's upright, but the boat wasn't going further.

Two minutes later the squall blew by, obliterating the leeward bank in its grey haze, and *Peregrino* popped gently upright again. The thunder of the departing gale was like a call from an old friend. Within ten minutes I was rumbling upriver between tree-clad slopes, safely screened from the worst of the weather. Four hours after that, protected by high embankments and higher buildings, I moored to a floating yacht pontoon in the very heart of Hamburg with no more difficulty than if I'd been cruising on a summer's day. Later, I rang the German meteorological office. They'd measured the strongest gust that day at 90 km/h, 49 knots, the lower end of force ten on the Beaufort scale. It had scared the life out of me, and that was in sheltered water. Force twelve, the full hurricane, *starts* at 64 knots.

I *don't* want to go to sea in a real storm.

Being in Hamburg was almost like being at home, and not just because there were hamburgers everywhere: Teutonically speaking, a *Hamburger* is either a round flat meat-and-onion patty from Hamburg or a resident of that city, just as a *Frankfurter* is a small nauseating sausage or person from Frankfurt and a *Berliner* is a doughnut or man from Berlin; hence the German affection for JFK's immortal line: '*Ich bin ein Berliner*.' I might have left Svein's Scandinavia behind me, but I'd come into the wild, marshy territories of the coastal Saxons, and where did all the Saxons go? Essex, Sussex, Middlesex and Wessex, and the only reason they didn't found Nossex was that they left that to the British. Whatever the influence of Forkbeard's followers, English culture started *here*.

With an Englishman, a Welshman and a Roman.

It all started in the fifth century, in the declining years of the Roman empire. In the winter of 406–407 a great federation of Germanic and south Scandinavian tribes stormed the Rhine frontier and ravaged the Roman province of Gaul. The general ruling Britain, Constantine, brought his armies across the Channel to deal with the invasion, stripping Britain of Roman troops. At once the Picts and Irish began attacking the Imperial territories. Soon Germanic pirates joined the raiders. Abandoned by the Romans, the Britons took up arms in their own defence. At this point historical sources vanish and legend takes over. After a generation of struggle, two rival war-leaders rose to command the British forces: Ambrosius, a Roman cavalry commander, and Vortigern, a British chieftain. They drove back the raiders and, in the manner of victorious generals the world over, promptly fell out over the spoils. In the ensuing power struggle Vortigern turned to the Saxons for help, hiring the brothers Hengest and Horsa and their following. They, seeing the weakness of the British defenders, turned on Vortigern. The relative sobriety of the *Anglo-Saxon Chronicle* gives way to legend and song as Ambrosius dies and the legend of Arthur is born . . .

The period that followed is the darkest of Dark Ages. From the departure of the legions and the breakup of Britain into small chieftaincies, some British, some Germanic, to the consolidation of the Anglo-Saxon kingdoms and the arrival of Christianity from Ireland and Rome two centuries later, only hints and legends survive. What seems certain is that, gradually, more and more bands of North Sea raiders made their way to a land already shaken by civil strife, pirate raids, and the financial disasters implicit in the disruption of Imperial trade, and proceeded to kill or enslave the inhabitants, establishing their own culture among the ruins. Roman Britain had functioned as one extremity of a vast international body. Its financial and military security had always depended on its continental connections. When those were severed, the society they had supported withered and died. The disruption of Roman power by the Germanic invaders of Gaul and Italy had already proved a mortal wound. The Saxon invaders struck the *coup de grâce*.

It took centuries to rebuild a strong state. Gradually the Germanic warriors supplanted the British tribes throughout the south and east. The warfare between the conquerors and the constant threat of a Celtic resurgence meant that only strong, efficient military leaders could survive. Those who did rapidly became kings. Kings need taxes, and taxes need stability: thus peace was imposed with an iron hand on the conquered territories. Coordinated government made it increasingly hard for the largely uncoordinated raiders from the North Sea fringe to prosecute successful attacks. Relative peace returned to the islands. At the very end of the sixth century Christianity began to penetrate the Anglo-Saxon kingdoms, bringing with it the literary and bureaucratic skills of the monastic missionaries. The kings capitalized on their organizational abilities, and by the end of the eighth century the kingdoms of England were as centralized and efficient as any in Europe.

Then the Vikings came.

Legend relates that the Saxons came to Britain as Vortigern's mercenaries. Historical economics argue that they moved westwards as their own population expanded and exhausted the land's ability to support them. Military considerations suggest that the initial migration was in part a flight from the Vandals and Sueves, who in their turn were fleeing from the marauding Huns, whose leader Attila is famed in France as the ultimate barbarian and in medieval Germany as the polished epitome of chivalry – for the same behaviour. This reveals a difference in values which explains about 90 per cent of subsequent European history . . .

However, having seen the Saxon homeland in the winter, I'd like to put forward another explanation: boredom. If I had to find one adjective to describe the banks of the Elbe, 'dull' is the one I'd go for; if I had to find two I'd add 'flat'. It's not just that the fields stretch out to the horizon in an unbroken line; they curve insidiously upwards, so that they seem *at one and the same time* to be very flat and entirely enclosing. If you stare at them for too long you end up feeling that the world has vanished and all that remains are the waterlogged furrows. Essex may not be the most strikingly dramatic area of Britain, but compared with the Saxon shore, it's paradise.

But then there's Hamburg. What's Hamburg famous for? You might well ask. Grimy industry, loads of shipping and a culinary tradition that the French would kill to avoid. What else? Beer and brothels. It's a major North Sea port forty miles from the sea on an uncomfortably tidal river barred with sandbanks. Ring any bells?

As far as geography and history are concerned, Hamburg and London might as well be twins.

There are differences. The main landmark on the Thames as I set off was the Millennium Dome. The Elbe equivalent is a long, low, round-backed structure housing *Buddy: the Musical*, which I nicknamed the Millennium Caterpillar. Downstream from Hamburg the river runs past the wooded heights of luxurious Altona, not quite an exact equivalent of Dagenham and the Isle of Dogs, but in revenge, the resuscitated glories of the London docklands entirely outclass the grim expanse of Hamburg's harbour area. But Hamburg remains one of the largest ports in the world. Its cranes and warehouses stretch for miles along the river's left bank – not scenic, but busy. And smelly. The main perfume of the Hamburg City Sport Harbour is burnt oil and diesel. Every time I smell a lorry's exhaust I think of winter in Hamburg.

I had a lot of time to examine the city's many-faceted splendours. As Christmas went by and the New Year turned, the weather celebrated with a display of pyrotechnics straight from the Caribbean – in hurricane season. The lightest breeze to hit the coast in the three weeks I spent there was a force seven, more than enough to make the Elbe estuary impassable for my small boat, and most of the time it was closer to storm force. I started every day by slipping and skating across icy jetties to the harbourmaster's office, where the master himself, a red-faced gentleman with a walrus moustache, greeted me with a happy 'Moing moing!', a weather report and a cup of coffee. The weather was never even remotely promising, so the coffee tended to take an hour or so while we swapped stories of life at sea and in harbour. After that he'd stump off to spread grit on the jetties, and I'd slide home to scrape the ice off the inside of my windows. My on-board heating system had, naturally, broken down in the first cold snap, so living aboard was more Siberian than sybaritic. I kept myself warm, and the boat functioning, by firing up the engines for an hour each morning and evening. Two three-hundred-horse power engines generate an awful lot of heat; I grew used to eating my evening meal sitting huddled between the two yellow-painted behemoths, in full thermals and woolly hat. At least the harbour provided electricity. Otherwise it would have been a long, dark winter.

But there were lights enough in Hamburg. The city was in full Christmas swing when I arrived, littered with small markets selling tourist trivia, mulled wine and pancakes with every filling under the sun (except, of course, lemon and sugar), and every market had its own portable jungle of fairy lights. The main shopping streets were ablaze with illuminations, from Christmas trees and candles to an immense animated Father Christmas climbing up and down the Town Hall tower, complete with sleigh and an appallingly mutilated soundtrack of 'Rudolf the Red-Nosed Reindeer'. In English. Two neighbouring department stores were broadcasting Christmas music into the streets – also in English – and I remember stopping dead in my tracks amid a horde of grumpy shoppers, listening to the pure tones of a boyish treble singing

'Silent Night'. Not 'Stille Nacht', you'll notice, but 'Silent Night'. Why the German broadcasters of a German carol should prefer the English translation is beyond me, but they did.

My first impression of the Hamburgers was that they were a) rich, b) well-dressed and c) miserable. In a one-hour tour of one Christmas market, mulled wine and all, I didn't see a single person smiling, let alone looking as if they were enjoying themselves. Come to that, I didn't see a single hamburger: everyone was eating pickled herring sandwiches, which might have explained a lot. Everywhere I went in the city, the faces confirmed my first impression. The shops were full of bad-tempered shoppers, usually in horrendous queues, the streets crammed with irritable parents lugging unfeasibly large shopping bags, and the shop doorways at night were crowded with sullen beggars. At least they had something to complain about. Night-time temperatures were usually well below zero, and their blankets and old newspapers were anything but adequate.

At least the streets were full of music. Brass music. Every brass player in Germany seemed to have headed up to Hamburg to busk for Christmas. In quick succession I saw three separate trumpeters, a French horn duet and a brass quintet who had travelled all the way from St Petersburg, who explained that they could make more money on the German streets than in concert halls at home. It was fascinating to listen to them. Their repertoire included much-requested hits like 'My Way' and the *Pink Panther* theme, but it was obvious from the way they played that they'd never heard the seminal performances of either piece. It was 'My Way' played by someone who'd never heard Sinatra: fifty years of political division, expressed in a single piece of music . . .

After four days – days of storms and ice and darkness, in

which the only friend I made was the harbourmaster –
I decided to check out the local bars and see if I couldn't
find someone at least vaguely happy. Germans reckon their
beer the best in the world, and Hamburg vaunts its brews
above all other cities, even Munich, so it seemed worth a try.
I'd just ordered a pint in a quiet bar not far from the waterfront
when the door banged open and a dozen young men burst
in, shaking the snow off their coats. A broad-shouldered individual with short dark hair, tattoos and chemical-warfare
aftershave elbowed me aside and said, 'Six pints of bitter,
please, boyo,' in an accent that could only have come from
one place.

'*Bitte?*' asked the barman, understandably confused.

'That's right, six pints of bitter,' came the reply, now speaking loudly and clearly in an impenetrable Welsh accent.

'*Bitte?*' he repeated, his voice now tinged with definite irri-
tation.

'Yes, bitter!' almost shouted. 'Are you taking the piss?'

I decided to intervene before Wales declared war on
Germany.

'*Er will sechs Biere,*' I explained to the barman. '*Kommt aus
Wales. Spricht kein Deutsch,*' and added to the son of Glyndwr,
'*Bitte* means "you what?" in German.'

He glared at me. 'You what?' Then light dawned. 'Hey, you
speak English!'

'That's right. The beers are on the way.'

'Tops! Hey, boys, he speaks English!'

They pressed in around me in a cloud of slicked-back hair
and cheap scent, friendly grins and crushing handshakes.
Within minutes I was seated amidst a small horde of small
Welsh warriors and one grinning officer, known as 'Top', trying to work out who was who through a hail of nicknames
and gossip.

'So you'd be army, then?' I asked. It seemed as good a place to start as any, but the officer gave me a funny look.

'That took a while, didn't it?'

'I'm slow,' I told him.

'We're Bravo Company of the Royal Welch Fusiliers,' he said, or something like that. The Royal Welch? I was delighted. I'd visited their headquarters at Caernarfon Castle as a child and spent a happy day scrambling round the battlements, but my chief memory had been of the regimental mascot, a stuffed goat with gilded horns.

'The ones with the goat?' I asked. Again he gave me a Look.

'We don't normally put it quite that way . . .'

'What are you doing in Hamburg? We haven't invaded, have we?'

'Getting pissed,' came the blunt response, and he buried his face in his beer.

'Hey, Ben! Know where we can find some cheap booze and girls?' one asked. Nothing if not direct.

As it happened, I did. There are some things in Hamburg you can't ignore. Every train in the city sported adverts for the legendary Reeperbahn, king (or possibly queen) of red-light districts, which made Flensburg's sinful one-sixteenth look like a dodgy back alley.

I told them so.

'Great! You going to take us there, then?'

I could see 'Top' grinning as I hesitated.

'Oh, come on, mate! You know you want to!'

'You'll be all right with us!' It seemed debatable.

'Come on!'

I looked round the ring of smiling faces, and wavered. 'Well . . . Maybe just for one . . .' As the Jómsvikings probably said at the funeral feast.

It was late afternoon. The legendary strip-bars were still

closed, their neon signs of anatomically impossible 'girls' (the German word) unlit. We adjourned to a café nearby, and the Gunners of Gwynedd promptly shoved three tables together, annexed some extra chairs, grabbed the waitress, demanded 'Thirteen beers, *Bitte*, love,' – quick learners – patted her affectionately and sent her on her way, flustered and angry. I was starting to feel apprehensive. This looked like an evening which would end up in the police station. Making a mental note to get out while I could, I settled back to watch the Cambrian cabaret.

I was sipping my beer with care. My playmates were not. Somewhere they'd picked up all the drinking games I'd tried to avoid as a student. Vodka followed beer, and tequila followed vodka, and I suspected that trouble would shortly follow the tequila. English conversation and Welsh accents filled the smoky air, the other customers were looking uneasy, and the unhappy waitress was developing a sidestep worthy of the Cardiff Millennium Stadium to avoid the 'innocent' hands. My companions were blithely happy. One lot were gossiping about who'd been doing what and who wanted to do what to which sergeant's wife, another were quizzing me about the fleshly delights of Hamburg. My street cred took a sharp dip when I confessed that all I knew about was beer and bread. It wasn't what they'd had in mind. The rest were exchanging extravagant boasts about what they intended to do for the rest of their leave. I couldn't get the sagas out of my head. Here were the Jómsvikings come to life.

When they clamoured for flaming sambucas, I decided it was time to leave. We'd been in there for an hour – two beers for me, a ship of the line's rum ration for them – and their hands were distinctly shaky. My instincts were right, but I was far too slow. The first tray arrived. The glasses went round. A ceremonial lighter did the deed. Blue flames licked around each beaker. One giggling fusilier spilled his Molotov cocktail all over the table. This is something best avoided on paper tablecloths. Flames cascaded across the table. With a wild yell another idiot flung *his* drink at the conflagration. It might have done some good if it hadn't been alight at the time. Burning splashes landed on the neighbouring tablecloth, which started to smoulder. Amidst oaths and scraping chairs and the clash of glasses we managed to smother the flames.

The waitress appeared, white and shaking.

'Get them out of here,' she told me, as the principal translator, 'before I call the police.'

'Time to go, lads,' I told them. 'Top' met my eyes, then nodded.

'Okay, lads, everyone out.'

Two left without paying their bills. 'Top' covered the damage and told me not to worry, he'd have it out of their hides later. The clan gathered on the pavement outside, laughing and reeling and eager for more. I made for the toilet and hid until they'd gone. Heaven only knows what happened to them that night. If the Jómsviking example was anything to go by – and they seemed dead set on following it – they probably ended up invading Norway.

Christmas passed and New Year approached with no sign of the weather improving, and suddenly the deserted harbour filled up. For ten days I'd been the only sport-boat owner in the place, sharing the harbour with two Dutch training vessels with skeleton maintenance crews and a single float-plane, but as New Year's Eve approached the icy berths became suddenly crowded. Hamburg harbour is renowned for its New Year fireworks – every office block and restaurant on the waterfront has its own display, and the competing exhibitions far outdo the municipal event in the city centre – and what better place to watch it from than the safety of your own quarterdeck? Well, in fact, there are many better places. 'Safety' is a relative term. Confucius, he say 'Man who send up firework better not be standing underneath it when it fall,' and the same applies to boat-owners sitting in the harbour below the firework launch-pads.

At last I found some happy Hamburgers. On the morning of 31 December a huge steel cruiser pulled into the berth next to mine; it was twice the length of *Peregrino*, half again as high, and its entire length was festooned with Christmas lights. I hopped onto the jetty to catch a bow-line as it grumbled into position; the deckhand, a smiling woman with an iron-grey pigtail, called a happy 'Moing!' and hurried astern to tie things off there. It broke the ice, as thirty-ton cruisers often do. They invited me aboard and poured me a beer. Their heating was working and they'd covered the immense spread of their windows with insulating bubble-wrap: after ten days on my personal iceberg it was paradise. The skipper, a round and smiling mariner in his fifties with a proper skipper's cap complete with gold braid, gave me a guided tour of his Transport of Delight, then turned me over to 'the Admiral' – his wife – while he got on with cooking lunch. The Admiral explained that they lived on board all year round, berthed in a little harbour just beyond the reach of the tide, working part-time and heading out to sea whenever they could. It seemed a fine life, and certainly made them happy and healthy. After lunch they came over to *Peregrino*, admired the cabin, deplored the lack of heat, vanished back aboard and reappeared with a huge and venerable paraffin heater which they insisted that I use for the rest of my stay. Then they invited me over for tea.

As so often happens, once I'd met one friendly person,

introductions snowballed. Captain and Admiral had been messing about in boats for years, and their ship, the *Barracuda*, was known in every harbour on the Elbe. As the afternoon went on and more and more brightly-lit boats wove their way between the breakwaters, we sat in the warmth of the bridge sipping mulled wine and talking cruising. All unknowing, I'd stumbled across the harbour's social centre. As other crews arrived they waved to my hosts, strolled across to the harbour office, paid their respects to the walrus-whiskered master and made straight for *Barracuda*. That afternoon I met a fisherman, two retired bankers, a computer programmer and a maker of stuffed toys. As night fell the harbourmaster came to visit and was greeted with full naval honours, in this case a two-litre bottle of rum from the island tax-haven of Heligoland. He gave the Admiral a kiss, wrung my hand, wished us all a Happy New Year and left us to our revelry.

The sun was still on the horizon when the fireworks began. The tide was out, the floating pontoons at their lowest, and high above our heads the walkway overlooking the harbour was black with onlookers slipping and sliding into position: there was an inch of ice and packed snow on the pavements and only a narrow causeway had been gritted. None of the official shows were due to start for hours, but Hamburgers are nothing if not independent, and the whole length of the harbour crackled and cracked with rockets and sparklers. It sounded like a civil war; perhaps my Welshmen were still at large? Across the water the Millennium Caterpillar was caped in lights, and amplified music drifted in and out of the smoky explosions. As night fell half the cranes in the harbour area started flashing with seasonal brilliance. One even had a Christmas tree perched on its end. Dressed in our finest outfits, we congregated aboard *Barracuda* for a huge dinner of ham, sausages and alcohol. 'No point hurrying,' said the Skipper, tilting his cap rakishly over one ear and pouring himself a brandy. 'Fireworks won't start until midnight.'

The crowds on the embankment grew and grew. Now people were scrambling up onto the Metro line above it, looking down on them; torches and sparklers glittered in the blackness. Detonations ran back and forth along the waterfront, like small-arms fire in films of Sarajevo. It made me nervous. I always get jumpy when people start letting off fireworks in the middle of crowds. A haze of steaming breath hung low over the throng: yet again, temperatures were well below zero. Further downriver a towering stack of lights appeared. Soon we heard the throb of massive engines, and a giant cruise ship nosed upstream, edging back and forth in the harbour mouth, waiting for the show.

Just after eleven o'clock the Skipper stood up, pulled a metal box from under his seat and snapped down the catches.

'Just to add to the noise,' he said.

Crackers?

He reached inside and pulled out a thirty-thousand-candle-power rocket-launched hand-held emergency flare, for use in offshore emergencies.

'Visitors first,' he said courteously, and handed it to me.

Yes. Definitely crackers.

Toy followed toy: signalling flares, orange smoke makers, inshore distress rockets, star-shells – all the tools of the distressed mariner. He caught my incredulous stare and grinned.

'Well, they go out of date next month, we might as well get our money's worth . . .'

The fireworks along the bank were reaching a climax. The bursts grew louder, more frantic, a drum-roll of explosions like an anti-aircraft barrage. And then the real displays started. Upstream and downstream golden sparks lanced into the sky and burst in shimmering cascades. The watching multitudes cheered. Two tower-blocks fired simultaneously, golden rain mingling with green bangers.

'Almost twelve! Come on!'

We poured out on deck, stood looking upwards as the heavens exploded. The entire waterfront blossomed with silver fountains; smoke and sparks drifted back over the town. Bangs and flashes rippled along the crowds, bounced back from the encircling buildings. Something black thudded down onto the jetty a few metres away: a spent rocket-case, rolling and reeking on the ice. Another one followed, further away. A third crashed into the water, making the volleying reflections dance. Midnight approached. The explosions were continuous, cascades and fountains of fire ringing the harbour. The cruise ship's working lights were flashing, on-off, on-off, on-off. The Admiral raised her rocket.

'Ready?'

The Skipper grappled with a magnum of champagne. It was midnight.

'Fire!'

The cork popped, and the quarterdeck erupted. I pointed my rocket upwind, slammed in the firing-pin, watched two red lights sear skywards as the toymaker fired simultaneously. Side by side the crimson stars flew, burst, drifted back downwind, blazing, smoking, sinking. The watchers on the banks cheered. The Admiral jumped onto the roof, a signalling beacon in either hand. The cruise ship sounded all its horns at once, rattling every window in the harbour. Orange smoke billowed to leewards, writhing between the lights.

'Cheers!'

A champagne glass was thrust into my hand. The Skipper and I toasted one another. The Admiral kissed us. The computer programmer and the fisherman danced round one another on the deck. More champagne frothed into my glass.

We stood in a circle on the quarterdeck, beaming and sipping, and a spent rocket-case whistled down out of nowhere, missed the Admiral by an inch, smacked down on deck in the middle of the circle and sat there smoking and hissing.

'Happy New Year,' said the Skipper drily into the sudden silence.

We finished our drinks inside.

15

FORKBEARD'S WAKE

'So Oláf gathered his ships and went raiding, first
about Frisia, and then in Saxony, and all over Flanders.
After that he sailed to England.'

Saga of Oláf Tryggvason

'And in this same year, before the month of August,
King Svein came with his fleet to Sandwich ... And
all submitted to him, and they gave him hostages ...
and all the nation regarded him as full king.'

Anglo-Saxon Chronicle, AD 1013

The year changed. The weather didn't.

Day after day the depressions came bowling in off the
Atlantic. Day after day the icy northwesters came piling onshore, filling the Elbe estuary with breakers. This was the mad
winter of 2000–2001: Britain endured endless floods; the wind
shifted from gale to storm and back, buffeting around the
compass; Holland and Belgium were swallowed by their rivers
and the east was buried in snow and ice. It was not a good
time to be boat bound. I spent most of my time sitting snug
in the little harbourmaster's office drinking coffee with the
Walrus, watching the grumpy shoppers of Hamburg battle
their grumpy way through the New Year sales, avoiding the

Welsh warriors, and wondering when the weather would break and let me get out to sea. I'd been in Hamburg for three weeks. Even Cuxhaven was starting to look attractive.

At the end of the first week in January I staggered over to the harbour office in my normal bleary-eyed fashion and was greeted by a grin that lifted the Walrus' moustaches so high they nearly poked his eyes out. 'Moing moing! Guess what!'

'What?'

'Weather forecast!'

He shoved a print-out into my hand. I blinked the morning haze out of my eyes.

'German Bight: NW 8 diminishing 7, veering and becoming S 6 by dawn.'

'Rock and roll!' It was the slenderest of chances. *If* the forecast was right, and *if* the wind shifted south, and *if* I managed to catch the falling tide coming out of Cuxhaven, then the day of the breakout had come. I'd spent so long staring at my charts, wishing for a weather-break, that I didn't even need to check them. From Cuxhaven my route would take me due north, then west, skirting the flank of the Scharhörn sandbanks: as long as the wind stayed in the south the reef would shelter me from the waves. From there I'd turn southwest, heading back towards the sheltering land and the mouth of the river Weser. That was the danger point. I'd be heading across the wind, and if for any reason the forecast was wrong and it picked up or swung west I'd find myself facing the full weight of the breakers, eight long miles from shore with the deadliest bank in the North Sea under my lee. It would be like the Brunsbüttel run all over again, a manic sea and no safe harbour in sight . . . But if I could make it! If I could claw my way across those eight miles and get close in to the shore then it wouldn't matter how strongly the wind blew. I could turn west, skirting the broken wall of the Frisian islands, run for Holland, run for home, and all I'd need would be one calm day to get me across the Channel to the Thames.

'When's high tide?' I asked the Walrus, who was standing there, grinning at me.

'Thirteen hundred.'

'Right. Excuse me, action stations.'

And I wrung his hand and plunged back aboard *Peregrino* to make ready for the sea.

I went through that ship like a devouring flame. I knew that what I was planning was reckless; I knew how evil the Elbe bay could be; I knew that no sensible yachtsman would go out in a winter force six without a very good excuse. But it was that or sit in Hamburg until the spring, and I wanted out. Down came the Christmas decorations, the books, the CDs, off their harbour shelves and into double-locked cupboards. Into the cabin went the saloon table and the skipper's chair, tied down in a secure corner to avoid any chance of their crashing about. Up came the floorboards, and I slid down into the engine-room and went over every bolt and connection on the motors, topped up the oil, checked the water, double-checked the filters, even rummaged around in the bilges to make sure that nothing was rattling around there. I hadn't done *that* since reaching Gothenburg, but if ever there was a time to propitiate the sea-gods, this was it.

One by one I switched on the electronics and made sure that everything was working: radio, navigation lights, radar, GPS, depth sounder, log and searchlight. The cabin, dim and grey in the matt winter light, shone brightly with screens and readouts as I switched on the engines and heard the immense coughing roar of starting drop back to the sustained growl of normal operation. Gases bubbled merrily out of my underwater exhaust pipes. As the motors warmed up I scoured the deck, coiling ropes, shutting lockers, re-positioning fenders, knocking the ice off the safety railings and even fetching a bucket of grit from the bunker on the jetty to strew across my frosted decks. When everything was ready I shut the systems down and walked into the city one last time to buy supplies, bread and cheese and packet soup and apples, everything for the healthy mariner. (Oh, and chocolate biscuits.) Just after one, as the falling tide began to whisper its way past the jetties, I said an emotional farewell to my Walrus – 'Safe journey and come back soon,' he said – and edged out onto the river.

Nothing of interest happened on the six-hour run down the Elbe. It's that kind of river. Nor did Cuxhaven shake off the image of its past and provide excitement, which did not astonish me. I tied up in the basin I'd left that stormy day three weeks ago – same dank, dripping walls, same grey-black mud smeared across the ladders – had a cup of soup and sat staring at the flying clouds as darkness fell. It had been a boring day, but my nerves were strung to a high pitch. I could hear the wind keening overhead, as strong and violent as ever. I could hear the dull rumble of the breakers in the estuary as the last of the ebb undercut the waves. When night came I went back out to the breakwater, looking northwards along the flashing line of marker buoys, green and red jewels strung along the neck of the Scharhörn reef. By the time the sun came up again I'd be out there . . . I shivered, pulled my jacket tighter around my neck and went back to roll myself in my sleeping-bag. It was a long time before I could get to sleep.

My alarm woke me at five, dragging me out of a pit of nightmares, all storms and waves and breaking water. I staggered into the cold cabin, my breath steaming in the faint orange glow of the streetlamps, pulled on full thermals and poured the first brew of the day from the thermos. A few sips brought consciousness, and I reached for the VHF and called the estuary radio station.

'Cuxhaven Elbe Traffic, this is *Peregrino*, over.'

'*Peregrino*, Cuxhaven, moing moing!'

'Moing moing, gentlemen' – *moing moing* is a great greeting to croak first thing in the morning – 'can you tell me the current weather off the Jade estuary, please?'

'One moment.' I waited in prickling impatience. '*Peregrino*, wind southerly six to seven, wave height one point five metres.'

Bingo. I could do that. 'Cuxhaven, thank you very much and have a good day.'

'*Peregrino*, safe passage. Cuxhaven out.'

I fired up the engines, switched on the electronics, and went out onto the quarterdeck. The harbour was silent. Streetlamps shone orange through the blackness. On the harbour bridge two red lights glowed like angry eyes. My steering lamps threw eerie reflections off the slick harbour walls. Away towards the sea the white beams of a lighthouse swept round, scythe-like. The wind was blustering by overhead. 'Time to go,' I muttered, and threw the dregs of my tea overboard. Three minutes later I rounded the corner into the outer harbour basin, and the lights were cut off behind me.

As soon as I left the harbour mouth the sea came alive. It was like stepping out of a stuffy house into a winter night. Great long waves were sweeping up from the south, rolling seawards on the black back of the tide. There were two hours of ebb left to run, two hours of current to carry me out past the Scharhörn, and then, I hoped, I'd catch the new tide and ride it towards the Frisian islands. If all went well ... As my bow came into the swell a wave lifted me sideways, broadside on at the harbour wall. I punched the throttles, popped forwards out of the danger zone, turned hard to port and saw the lights of a freighter dead ahead; a perfect head-on view for the first time in my life, the green and red lights almost touching. As I swung further to port out of his track, the lights shifted, just as the textbooks said, the red winking out of sight as the green swung towards me. He was turning to head upriver, *Richtung* Hamburg. I wondered if the Walrus would see him pass ... Then the next wave caught me and I felt *Peregrino* lift up and surf seawards, the walls of Cuxhaven twenty metres away. Concrete and rocks and breakers flashed by, and I was past and running for a green spark in the darkness. One flash every four seconds, counting under my breath, Starboard Marker 31 of the Elbe Approaches ... I was on my way.

My mind felt tense and brittle, which might have had something to do with the risk I was running and perhaps with the fact that it was five twenty in the morning and I never function properly before noon. The waves were running fast and high behind me, pushed by the full weight of the wind, and the further I got from shore the deeper and steeper they grew. For the first hour my full attention was on steering, spotting the channel buoys, holding the boat steady as the rollers threatened to push her towards the reef. I was intensely aware of the banks on my left, marked by a long line of white breakers luminous in the darkness, and of the gleam of my own wake and the sudden foam behind me as each new wave lifted up and kicked me forwards. The shore was long since out of sight, only the lighthouse winked in the surrounding night. Then, suddenly, it appeared again, and I realized that the light had been growing without my noticing, as the night faded from icy blackness to a damp grey dawn. The ebb had run out, the tide had turned, the waves were growing sharper and steeper. But here was the buoy. I swung westwards along the reef, and at once the waves lessened. Now the wind was on my cheek, and the sudden unexpected roar rattled my hood and blew down my neck. Over to the left in the gathering light I could see the long white ranks of breakers. God, that was a big sea. One-and-a-half-metre waves don't sound like much, but it's a different story when your bow's a metre above the water . . . But the reef was narrowing beside me, and the last buoy was ahead.

There! I swung around, feeling the stagger and crash as we hit the waves head-on, flinched as the wind rose to a new roar and fling a bucketful of spray into my face. Automatically my knees took the shock. Automatically I ducked as the next burst of spray broke over the bows. Foaming water spilled along the deck and gushed over the railings. My hands in their sodden gauntlets spun the wheel, and felt the rudder bite. *Peregrino* settled onto the new course. Close over the side the dull back of the reef lifted up from the waves. The whole world was grey and white; icy sea and icy sky. Spray had trickled down my neck and the wind bit through my clothes, but as I dashed the water from my glasses I felt a surge of triumph. Straight ahead and eight miles distant I'd caught a glimpse of the Jade lighthouse, a thin stick upon the waves. I didn't need GPS to find it. I didn't need to worry any more. The long waves came lurching towards me, grey-backed and savage, and each time *Peregrino* rose to meet them, shrugging off the impact in a burst of driven foam and plunging on down the back towards the next one. The wind shouted overhead, deep-toned and biting, chilling my face and making my ears ache, but I was heading back towards the shore, back towards shelter, and unless a new squall blew up I was going to make it.

An hour and a half later I turned to starboard into the sheltered water off the Frisian islands, pushed the throttles to full power and scudded westwards across the storm. Spray blasted in my wake, I was chilled to the bone and drenched with salt water; but I was out of the trap. The Elbe bay lay behind me. I fled past the long, low shapes of Wangerooge and Spiekeroog, past Langeoog and Baltrum and Norderney, angled southwest past Juist and Borkum with its countless wind generators, and set my head for home. Fifteen hundred years before, the longships of the Frisians and Saxons had crossed these grey seas to speed the ruin of Rome. Oláf Tryggvason sailed that way to begin his career of mayhem. Svein Forkbeard followed him to batter down Ethelred's kingdom. The pair had led me across three thousand miles of sea. Now I was following them home.

One week later, on Helena's birthday, I steamed into the Thames estuary past the Kentish Knock light and set my course for the Blackwater. The low sun shone out of a brilliant sky, the wind was a bare breath from the southeast, and the crisp January air bit icily into my lungs. The sea was a silver mirror as the lowlands of Essex rose out of the haze. It was all so familiar. It was barely eight months since I came that way with my motley crew on the very first crossing of all. The harbours were empty now, the hard stands behind them full of hibernating ships, and only a single Customs boat cruised the Harwich channel, ignoring me completely. Quietly I slipped up the Blackwater, tied up to a buoy, waited for the tide to rise. As it reached the flood I dropped the mooring and followed the river, followed the Viking path inland. The trees on Osea island were bare now, the reeds of Northey where Oláf had camped dead and brittle, but the lights of Heybridge shone warm and alive. I called the lock-keeper on the VHF, waited for the go-ahead, nudged into the lock and threw my ropes ashore. The gates ground shut behind me.

Water flooded the basin. I rode there, serene, watching the long sunshine sparkle in the frost-whitened grass. Ahead, the gates drew back. A solid sheet of ice spread over the water. I nosed into it with the creak and groan and snap of ice, sharp leaves folding and crumpling under my bow, swung into an empty berth, tied up, killed the engines, and looked up through the wintry air to the glowing lights of England.

There were three cars parked on the track above me.

All three were Volvos.

BIBLIOGRAPHY

Bibliography of texts referred to in the book or used for background information, and of passages too long to be included in the main text.

Translations mentioned here are recommended reading. With the exception of Francis Tschan's translation of Adam of Bremen, all translations in the book are my own.

Anglo-Saxon Chronicle – five manuscripts survive from various parts of the country. All are translated in a single volume by Dorothy Whitelock (Eyre and Spottiswoode, 1961)

Auckland – poem by Rudyard Kipling, one verse of 'The Song of the Cities', which itself forms part of his *A Song of the English*, in *Rudyard Kipling: the Complete Verse* (London, 1990)

Battle of Maldon, The – the sole original text was in British Library manuscript Cotton Otho A XII, which was destroyed in 1731. All modern texts are taken from the transcript of the manuscript made in 1724. A good translation is in *Anglo-Saxon Poetry*, S.A.J. Bradley (Everyman, 1982)

Beowulf – the original text exists only in British Library manuscript Cotton Vitellius A XV. The most recent and critically acclaimed translation is by Seamus Heaney (Faber and Faber, 1999)

Bible – in the Authorized (King James) version, St Paul's first letter to the Corinthians, 13, i–xiii reads, 'Though I speak with the tongues of men and of angels, and have not charity, I am become as sounding brass or a tinkling cymbal. And though I have the gift of prophecy, and understand all mysteries and all knowledge; and though I have all faith, so that I could remove mountains, and have no charity, I am nothing. And though I bestow all my goods to feed the poor, and give my body to be burned, and have no charity, it profiteth me nothing. Charity suffereth long, and is kind; charity envieth not; charity vaunteth not itself, is not puffed up, doth not behave itself unseemly, seeketh not her own, is not easily provoked, thinketh no evil, rejoiceth not in iniquity, but rejoiceth in the truth; beareth all things, believeth all things, hopeth all things, endureth all things. Charity never faileth: but whether there be prophecies, they shall fail; whether there be tongues, they shall cease; whether there be knowledge, it shall vanish away. For we know in part, and we prophesy in part. But when that which is perfect is come, then that which is in part shall be done away. When I was a child, I spake as a child, I understood as a child, I thought as a child; but when I became a man I put away childish things. For now we see through a glass, darkly, but then face to face; now I know in part, but then shall I know even as also I am known. And now abideth faith, hope, charity, these three; but the greatest of these is charity.'

Egil's Saga – a complete thirteenth-century manuscript survives in the Modruvallabók, in Copenhagen library. Two translations are by Hermann Pálsson and Paul Edwards

(Penguin, 1976), and in *The Complete Sagas of the Icelanders*, ed. Vidar Hreinsson (Reykjavík, 1997)

Grettir's Saga – a fifteenth-century manuscript survives in Copenhagen library. One good translation is *The Saga of Grettir the Strong*, in *The Complete Sagas of the Icelanders*, ed. Vidar Hreinsson (Reykjavík, 1997)

History of the Archbishops of Hamburg-Bremen, Adam of Bremen, trans. Francis J. Tschan (Columbia University Press, 1959)

Lord of the Rings, The, J.R.R. Tolkien, 1954. The closing paragraphs read, 'At last the three companions turned away, and never again looking back they rode slowly homewards; and they spoke no word to one another until they came back to the Shire, but each had great comfort in his friends on the long grey road.

'At last they rode over the downs and took the East Road, and then Merry and Pippin rode on to Buckland; and already they were singing again as they went. But Sam turned to Bywater, and so came back up the Hill, as day was ending once more. And he went on, and there was yellow light, and fire within; and the evening meal was ready, and he was expected. And Rose drew him in, and set him in his chair, and put little Elanor upon his lap.

'He drew a deep breath. "Well, I'm back," he said.'

Le Morte d'Arthur, Sir Thomas Malory, in *The Works of Sir Thomas Malory*, ed. Eugene Vinaver (Clarendon, 1990). The funeral oration for Sir Launcelot reads, '"Ah Launcelot!" he said, "thou were head of all Christian knights! And now I dare say," said sir Ector, "thou Sir Launcelot, there thou liest, that thou were never matched of earthly knight's hand. And thou were the curtest [courtliest] knight that ever bore shield! And thou were the truest friend to thy lover that ever bestrode horse, and thou were the truest lover, of a sinful man, that ever loved woman, and thou were the kindest man that ever struck with sword. And thou were the goodliest person that ever came among press of knights, and thou were the meekest man and the gentlest that ever ate in hall among ladies, and thou were the sternest knight to thy mortal foe that ever put spear in the rest."

'Then there was weeping and dolour out of measure.' (Vinaver, vol. 3, p. 1259)

Nautical Almanac (Macmillan Reed, 2001)

Nibelungenlied – numerous manuscripts survive, of which the oldest (early thirteenth century) is in St Gallen in Switzerland. The standard English translation is by A.T. Hatto (Penguin, 1965, 1969)

Njál's Saga – several manuscripts survive, mainly from the thirteenth century. Standard translations are by Magnus Magnusson and Hermann Pálsson (Penguin, 1960), and in *The Complete Sagas of the Icelanders*, ed. Vidar Hreinsson (Reykjavík, 1997)

Saga of Gunnlaug Serpent's-Tongue – two manuscripts survive, edited and translated in a single volume by P.G. Foote and R. Quirk (Thomas Nelson and Sons, 1957), and translated in *The Complete Sagas of the Icelanders*, ed. Vidar Hreinsson (Reykjavík, 1997)

Saga of the Jómsvikings – numerous manuscripts of this ripping yarn survive in Copenhagen and Stockholm. They have been edited and translated in a single volume by N.F. Blake (Thomas Nelson and Sons, 1962)

'Sea Fever', John Masefield, in *The Sea Poems of John Masefield* (Heinemann, 1978)

Seafarer, The – the original text survives only in the manuscript Exeter Book in Exeter Cathedral. It is translated in *Anglo-Saxon Poetry*, S.A.J. Bradley (Everyman, 1982)

A Seaman's Guide to the Rule of the Road (Morgan's Technical Books Ltd, 1985)

Third Collect for Evensong from the Anglican *Book of Common Prayer* – the prayer begins, 'Lighten our darkness, we beseech thee, O Lord, and by thy great mercy defend us from all perils and dangers of this night . . .'

The Thirteen Clocks and The Wonderful O, James Thurber (Puffin, 1983), p. 50. The description of the journey reads: The brambles and the thorns grew thick and thicker in a ticking thicket of bickering crickets. Farther along and stronger, bonged the gongs of a throng of frogs, green and vivid on their lily pads. From the sky came the crying of flies, and the pilgrims leaped over a bleating sheep creeping kneedeep in a sleepy stream, in which swift and slippery snakes slid and slithered silkily, whispering sinful secrets.'

Wanderer, The – as with *The Seafarer*, the original text only survives in the Exeter Book, and is translated in *Anglo-Saxon Poetry*, S.A.J. Bradley (Everyman, 1982)

Ynglinga Saga, Saga of Harald Fairhair, Saga of Oláf Tryggvason, Saint Oláf's Saga, Saga of Harald Sigurtharson, all in *Heimskringla*, Snorri Sturluson, c. 1230 – the original manuscript was burned in 1728. All modern editions are drawn from two seventeenth-century copies, and are translated as *Heimskringla: History of the Kings of Norway*, Lee M. Hollander (University of Texas Press, 1964)

Andersson, Ingvar, *A History of Sweden*, trans. Carolyn Hannay (Weidenfeld and Nicolson, 1956)

Binns, Alan, *Viking Voyagers* (Heinemann, 1980)

Holmes, George, ed., *The Oxford History of Medieval Europe* (Oxford University Press, 1988)

Keen, Maurice, *The Penguin History of Medieval Europe* (Penguin, 1968)

Lauring, Palle, *A History of the Kingdom of Denmark* (Høst og Søn, 1960, 1995)

Lawson, M.K., *Cnut: The Danes in England in the Early Eleventh Century* (Longman, 1993)

Magoun, F. Alexander, *The Frigate Constitution and Other Historic Ships* (New York, 1928)

Niles, John D. and Mark Amodio, eds, *Anglo-Scandinavian England: Norse–English Relations in the Period before the Conquest* (University Press of America, 1989)

271

Olsen, Olaf and Ole Crumlin-Pedersen, trans. Barbara Blue-stone, *Five Viking Ships from Roskilde Fjord* (Copenhagen National Museum, 1978)

Rumble, Alexander R., ed., *The Reign of Cnut: King of England, Denmark and Norway* (Fairleigh Dickinson University Press, 1994)

Scott, Franklin D., *Sweden: The Nation's History* (University of Minnesota Press, 1977)

Sjøvold, Thorleif, *The Viking Ships in Oslo* (Universitetets Old-saksamling, 1979)

Vebaek, C.L. and S. Thirslund, *The Viking Compass* (Vebaek and Thirslund, 1992)

Wood, Ian and G.A. Loud, *Church and Chronicle in the Middle Ages* (Hambledon Press, 1991)

INDEX

273